Introduction to Immigrant Detention in Poland. Theory and Methodology

STUDIES IN EUROPEAN INTEGRATION, STATE AND SOCIETY

Edited by Zdzisław Mach and Bożena Gierat-Bieroń

VOLUME 16

Dariusz Niedźwiedzki / Jacek Schmidt

Introduction to Immigrant Detention in Poland. Theory and Methodology

PETER LANG

Lausanne · Berlin · Bruxelles · Chennai · New York · Oxford

Bibliografische Information der Deutschen Nationalbibliothek
Die Deutsche Nationalbibliothek verzeichnet diese Publikation in der Deutschen Nationalbibliografie; detaillierte bibliografische Daten sind im Internet über http://dnb.d-nb.de.

Library of Congress Cataloging-in-Publication Data
A CIP catalog record for this book has been applied for at the Library of Congress.

This is an expanded and revised version from the original Polish paper: Niedźwiedzki Dariusz, Schmidt Jacek, (2020). Detencja cudzoziemców w Polsce. Perspektywa teoretyczno-metodologiczna. Kraków: ZW Nomos translated by Anna Moroz-Darska.

Translation and proofreading of this publication has been supported by a grant from the Faculty of International and Political Studies under the Strategic Programme Excellence Initiative at Jagiellonian University. This publication was financially supported by the Faculty of International and Political Studies of the Jagiellonian University in Kraków.

This publication has been peer reviewed by Sławomir Łodziński

ISSN 2193-2352
ISBN 978-3-631-90329-2 (Print)
E-ISBN 978-3-631-90757-3 (E-PDF)
E-ISBN 978-3-631-90758-0 (E-PUB)
DOI 10.3726/b21190

Published by Peter Lang GmbH, Berlin, Deutschland

info@peterlang.com - www.peterlang.com

Table of Contents

List of photographs

List of figures

List of documents

Introduction

In the spring of 2018, after almost a two-year long endeavour, our research team was unexpectedly granted permission by the Commander-in-Chief of the Border Guard of the Republic of Poland to carry out field studies in all the six guarded centres for foreigners (GCFs) in Poland. The research idea had been developed much earlier and we were awaiting an opportunity to implement it in the field, which tends to be inaccessible to external observers, including representatives of the academic world. It should be stressed that the permission did not include any expectations of the authority managing the institutions in question towards the researchers such as the right of access to source materials, making expert opinions, preparation of educational materials, etc.[1]

At the end of 2020, our book *Detencja cudzoziemców w Polsce. Perspektywa teoretyczno-metodologiczna* [*Detention of Foreigners in Poland. A Theoretical-methodological Perspective*] was published in Poland (Kraków: ZW Nomos). Because of the topicality of migration-related problems at the time and a considerable interest in detention practices involving foreigners in contemporary Europe, we decided to make our research available to the English-speaking reader. The current edition has been amended: we have extended it to include a substantial set of sample source materials providing a broader insight into the specific nature of the detention of foreigners in Poland and a large number of photographs we took during our study; we also clarified selected issues as suggested by our insightful reviewers, and finally we included references to source texts in the English language in place of their Polish translations.

The data provided in this book originate from the fieldwork carried out in the years 2018–2019. It was already after its completion and the preparation of our book that a long, still lasting migration crisis began on the Polish-Belarusian border in the summer of 2021 – it was triggered by the Belarusian authorities who intended to 'flood the EU with immigrants' brought from the Near East, pushing them into Poland through the so-called green border. This hybrid operation conducted by Belarusian intelligence forces significantly

---

1 The only arrangement was a declaration of the project leaders on the possibility to submit general descriptive information on the execution of the project and the expected scientific results by the end of 2019 as a part of a special symposium involving representatives of the Border Guard.as participants. The meeting did not take place in view of the lack of interest on the part of Border Guard authorities.

affected the functioning of the Polish guarded detention centres – their previous capacities were remarkably exceeded and their living standards deteriorated. Two additional, temporary guarded detention centres were also put up: one in Wędrzyn in the Lubuskie province and the other in Czerwony Bór in the Podlaskie province – both of them for men. In particular the former, organised from scratch for 700 foreigners in a military training area, failed to provide the basic standards required of guarded centres,[2] which led to periodical rebellions of the detainees. The temporary detention facilities were closed down in the summer of 2022, which coincided with the opening of a new centre, Lesznowola II, also built from scratch, which admitted families and offered space for 200 foreigners. The changes resulting from the measures of the Belarusian authorities also included a conversion of the profiles of the detention centres. For instance, at the beginning of the summer of 2021, the centre in Białystok was transformed from one for men into one for families, to return to being a centre for men in the summer of 2022.

This book, similarly to the previous one in the Polish language, has a theoretical-methodological character and seeks to familiarise the reader with our interdisciplinary, holistic and at many levels eclectic concept of the exploration of the detention of foreigners. Since the phenomenon has hardly yet been examined, and can even be qualified as *terra incognita* on the map of scientific knowledge in the Polish context, we have decided that it is our duty to exhaustively present our inspirations, philosophical worldview, research strategies and methods as well as all the details of the research procedure – following the idea of transparency described by John Van Maanen as a 'confessional tale' (Van Maanen 1988: 73–82, 91–100). Collecting all this information in a single place also seeks to satisfy a practical purpose of 'liberating' our subsequent publications from the burden of having to each time explain the joint idea behind the project, the adopted procedures, research techniques, etc.

The majority of research projects, in particular team ones, are executed owing to an internal finance promise acquired as a part of a competition procedure. In our case, because of the fact that the permission to perform our study was granted suddenly, and since there was a deadline for its performance, such a solution was not an option. Hence, we conducted our project and research works partially at our own cost and without any remuneration. It was already in the

2 See: 'Ośrodek dla cudzoziemców w Wędrzynie nie spełnia standardów ochrony ich praw. Wnioski po trzeciej wizytacji BRPO', https://bip.brpo.gov.pl/pl/content/rpo-wedrzyn-cudzoziemcy-osrodek-standardy [1.12.2022]

course of our fieldwork that we were provided supplementary financial support, which allowed us to pay for a professional transcription of about 300 hours of recordings of interviews, archive several hundred selected existing sources, selected study visits in the field and several workshops.[3]

The hardly comfortable state of things described above calls for some commentary. In the contemporary academic world, ranking lists documenting the effectiveness of the acquisition of sufficient funds for research projects from recognised organisations or other funders are among the most important elements of evaluation – and, what follows, the prestige of the researchers and their institution. The effectiveness also ennobles the very research topic as a testimony to its cognitive or social significance; in a way, it legitimises the research idea and its execution. In effect, what *de facto* is a result of the arguments provided as a part of the research project, which were to plead in favour of its realisation, begins to seem to be a result of the project rather than a reason behind its undertaking (Cheek 2018). In this context, our project and its delivery, at least until the publication of this book, and, subsequently, further works (presenting its results), remains 'invisible'[4] – it does not appear in reports

---

3 Programme of the Ministry of Science and Higher Education: Application for increasing the grant for the maintenance of research potential in view of special needs of the research entity, project no. 433369, amount: PLN 55, 650. Additionally, the cost related to the research was partially covered by the entities employing members of the research team.

4 Nevertheless, it is worth mentioning a number of our team members' actions undertaken so far so as to present the project during conferences, seminars and other events offering a chance to speak to the public. An *ad hoc* session entitled *Spaces of Detention: Formal, Organisational and Sociocultural Aspects* organised during the 7th National Conference of the Committee of Migration Studies of the Polish Academy of Sciences in Opole (20–21.08.2019), in the course of which all the project participants signalled their individual research ideas related to the project in question (texts of these speeches were not submitted for print) was an important form of presentation of our research initiative. The project was also presented during a number of conferences and guest lectures, including: two guest lectures by Maciej Stępka for members of the Amsterdam Centre for European Studies and the Amsterdam Centre for Migration Studies (Amsterdam, June 2019); IUAES 2019 Inter-Congress 'World Solidarities' (Poznań, 27–31.08.2019): Przemysław Tacik, *Legal Anthropology of Detention Centres Law as the Other's Gaze and a Hindrance to the Spiral of Micro-Power*; Maciej Stępka, *What kind of Europe does detention policy reveal? Discussing security and human (im) mobility in Poland*; Deutsch-Französische Hochschule / Université franco-allemande d'été / Sommerschule / Summer School Bayonne, Pays Basque, France (1–7.09.2019), *Cultural Institutions and the Migration Crisis in Europe*: Agnieszka Chwieduk, *Estime*

concerning the academic activity of its participants, it does not have its own website, it was not subjected to external review, and, finally, it was not evaluated by any ethical committee.[5]

For the reasons described above, we feel obliged to present arguments in favour of the significance of the project in question. Migration problematics is one of the central research and social areas in contemporary public discourse, and the so-called migration policies at the level of the European Union and each member state are its essential components. The reason behind this interest on the part of researchers and practitioners of social life is a recognition of people's spatial mobility as a key factor of the changing sociocultural reality marking today's world.

The shaping of the Polish migration policy in the years 1989–2016 has been thoroughly analysed and subjected to multilateral assessment (Łodziński and Szonert 2016, 2017). In October 2016, the government of the Republic of Poland took a formal decision to withdraw from this policy and invalidated the most important documents determining the directions of its development and monitoring.[6] In June 2019, assumptions of Poland's new migration policy,

---

dans une institution totalisante. Exemple des centres de retention administrative; 8th National Conference of the Committee of Migration Studies of the Polish Academy of Sciences (Wrocław, 10–11.09.2019): Jacek Schmidt, *Detention of Foreigners in Poland. Interdisciplinary Methodology of Examination of the Total Institution*; 17th National Sociological Congress (Wrocław, 11–14.09.2019): Dariusz Niedźwiedzki, *Intercultural Relations. An Analysis of the Phenomenon as Exemplified by the Guarded Centres for Foreigners in Poland*; 13th Pan-European Conference, EISA (Sofia, September 2019): Maciej Stępka, *Research 'under Surveillance' – Reflections from Ethnographic Research in Polish Migrant Detention Centres*; *Economic, Cultural and Social Dimensions of Migration* (Lublin, 24.01.2020): Dariusz Niedźwiedzki, *Stopped in Motion. Detention of Foreigners in Poland;* 4th Jagiellonian Security Conference (Kraków, 28–29.09.2022): Maciej Stępka, *Security and Invigilation Practices in Guarded Centres for Foreigners in Poland*; 3rd Jagiellonian Interdisciplinary Security Conference (Kraków, 28–29.09.2021): Maciej Stępka, *Polish Immigrant Detention Centres and Securitization of Migration*; 2nd Working Group Webinar on Immigration Detention Around the Globe, European Society of Criminology (15.04.2021): Maciej Stepka, Przemysław Tacik, *Unravelling Legal and Security Frameworks of the Polish Immigration Detention*; *Lipiec z Europejskim Programem w Zakresie Migracji* (Warsaw, 29.07.2020): Maciej Stępka, *Care and Security. The Logics of Securitization of Migration as Exemplified by Polish Guarded Centres for Foreigners*.

5 A separate fragment of the book (Section 1.5) shall be devoted to the complex ethical aspects of the project.

6 This is in particular about the document of the Department of Analyses and Migration Policy of the Ministry of the Interior and Administration (MSWiA) *Polityka migracyjna*

developed by the Migration Team (Department of Analyses and Migration Policy, Ministry of the Interior and Administration)[7] were disclosed. The document, which clearly highlights the risks related to migration and focuses on the issues of broadly-understood securitisation, discusses in many places the need to extend the competences of the Border Guard and increase the role of the detention of foreigners. Item 3 on the to-do list on p. 30 of the document in question postulates 'a development of the potential of the preventive measure in the form of the detention of the foreigner in a guarded centre or a custody for foreigners through a flexible management of the profiles of these centres and their extension'. In practice, this desideratum is already implemented, as documented by the investment plans of the particular centres we have managed to collect, as well as their modernisation in the situation when, during our project (summer 2019), the occupancy of these institutions did not usually exceed 65% of their capacity.[8] In July 2021, a draft resolution of the Council of Ministers of the Republic of Poland entitled *Migration Policy of Poland – Directions of Activity 2021–2022*, underlining the necessity to provide effective implementation of the return policy in relation to the foreigners illegally crossing the country's border, was published. In consequence, the time of the processing of cases related to the granting of international protection, in which decisions should be taken without delay, would be shortened, thus limiting the duration of the foreigners' detention. The adoption of the document has been postponed indefinitely due to the situation triggered by the mass illegal migration controlled by the Belarusian regime since August 2021[9].

In this light, the need for an in-depth inquiry into the detention of foreigners (a very specific and at the same time hardly accessible system of organisation)

Polski – stan obecny i postulowane działania [*Migration Policy of Poland – the Current State and the Postulated Actions*] (2019).

7 The document was subjected to a critical expert evaluation and instigated/ a protest of the Committee of Migration Studies, Polish Academy of Sciences (2019).

8 The data come from the internal documents of all the centres and apply to May 2019.

9 For more recent data on the specifics of changes in Poland's migration policy, see: Adamczyk Anita (2021). *(Nie)intencjonalna polityka migracyjna Polski*, Poznań: Uniwersytet im. Adama Mickiewicza w Poznaniu - Wydawnictwo Naukowe Wydziału Nauk Politycznych i Dziennikarstwa; Łodziński Sławomir, Marek Szonert (2023).

Polityka migracyjna „bez polityki". Antynomie tworzenia polityki migracyjnej w Polsce w okresie 2016-2022, „*CMR Working Papers*", Nr 130 (188), Ośrodek Badań nad Migracjami UW, Warszawa luty 2023.

seems to be an extraordinarily current challenge for research, the effects of which may prove useful also in the non-scientific context. The group of the potential beneficiaries may include all the social actors of the centres, representatives of the central bodies controlling the detention system, officials responsible for education and contact with foreigners, politicians and social activists, in particular representatives of non-governmental organisations dealing with the phenomenon of migration, and foreigners themselves (Chwieduk and Skórzyńska 2021).

In the case of the scientific milieu, an answer to the question of the potential readers of this book seems to be rather obvious. It is certainly addressed to everyone interested in research into different kinds of total institutions. It can also be useful for researchers doing work in the so-called difficult access areas. Finally, we hope that it shall be read by people connected with the methodology of the social sciences and humanities: ones creating their own concepts of research methodology or educating the subsequent generations of researchers.

The first five parts of the treatise, which make Chapter 1, introduce the reader to the topic – they provide information on the indispensable elements of the project description, and are a background for further methodological considerations. The opening part (Section 1.1) discusses the specificity of the detention of foreigners – its definition and legal determinants, purposes and course of admission to detention places, and finally the basic information on scientific and non-scientific sources concerning the phenomenon in question. The subsequent Section (1.2) presents our experience connected with our presence in the detention centres and familiarisation with the specific nature of the work of the officers of the Border Guard (heretofore referred to as BG), which preceded our research and which without any doubt motivated us to undertake it further, sensitised us to the problem, and initiated a discussion on its theoretical framework. In the subsequent Sections (1.3 and 1.4), the readers may acquaint themselves with the composition of the research team (the scientific profiles of its members are provided in an annex hereto), places in which the study was performed, its chronology, and the status obtained by the research team under the permission granted by the Commander-in-Chief of the BG. Finally, Section 1.5 is devoted to the ethical aspects of the execution of the project at all its stages – from the formulation of research problems to the publication of results.

The subsequent parts of the book are composed as a triad made up by elements of the theoretical/methodological reasoning, which we have called 'scenes'. Scene one (Chapter 2) contains a list of research problems and questions and presents the research teams' philosophical worldviews (research paradigms), which directed the planned study and resulted in the adoption of research strategies that were consistent with them, with relevant procedures and techniques of data acquisition and analysis which followed suit. This chapter contains a rich collection of documents illustrating different types of the acquired source materials. In scene two (Chapter 3) the readers may familiarise themselves with a set of notions, ideas and concepts, which inspired the research team as useful tools for a description and analysis of the phenomenon in question. Scene three (Chapter 4) bridges the entire content – it is a summary integrating ideas and concepts in the form of a theoretical/methodological scheme being a proposal of a heuristic and holistic examination of the phenomenon of detention.

It should be pointed out here that despite the fact that we are dealing with a book written by two authors, a lot of its contents result from the individual reflection of the research team members, which preceded the execution of the project, as well as joint arrangements adopted in the course of cyclical project workshops we held in Kraków and Poznań.

Acknowledgements

Our research would not have been possible without support from the high rank officers of the Border Guard, who understand that an optimisation of the functioning of the institution they co-manage should be executed on the basis of knowledge acquired by way of effective collaboration by and between the Academy and the Office. We owe special gratitude to our friend, Commander of the Chief BG Training Centre in Koszalin, Colonel Piotr Boćko, PhD who was to have been a member of our research team – for inspiring us to undertake research in the area of detention and for his continuous support in the form of consultations. We thank the Director of the Board for Foreigners of the BG Headquarters in Warsaw, Colonel Andrzej Jakubaszek, for his full understanding for our research initiative, convincing the Commander-in-Chief of the Border Guard to issue his permission for research in the guarded centres and, finally, his assistance in the organisation of our study visits via a liaison officer. We direct separate words of gratitude to the numerous group of BG officers and civil employees from the centres we visited – from the top authorities of their Units, facilities and centres, through medium management, to persons in regular positions. Without their friendliness, openness, hospitality, and consent to participate in our study, this project could not have been carried out.

1 The research project – 'behind the scene'

1.1. What does the detention of foreigners denote?[10]

In the legal vocabulary, the word 'detention' (Latin *detentio*) is tantamount to the enforced placement of an individual in a closed place covered by supervision, such as a custody suite, prison, psychiatric hospital, rehabilitation centre for children and youth, or camp or other centre for foreigners.[11] The history of detention practices in their different forms goes back to historical periods very distant in time, while their most spectacular contemporary forms included institutions established by the Nazis and communists (Bauman 1989; Applebaum 2003; Labanca and Ceccorulli 2014b: 81–108). It might seem that the traumatic experience of those times would result in the marginalisation of practices such as the limitation of the freedom of the individual being a migrant in the modern, democratic and liberal countries of the world of the West. However, during the three decades following the 1990s, we have been dealing with a very significant increase in the scale and scope of the application of detention in relation to foreigners (Wilsher 2014: ix; Silverman and Massa 2012: 677-678; Labanca and Ceccorulli 2014a: 3). Only in the years 2000-2012, the number of detention centres in all 28 states of the European Union and its 16 neighbouring countries increased from 324 to 473. In 2012 alone, detention covered 570,660 immigrants, with 252,785 of them subsequently subjected to return procedures or deportation (Migreurop 2014: 2). As results from data for 14 EU states for 2011, 2013, 2015 and 2017, the number of foreigners placed in detention centres stayed at the level of about 100,000 in each of these years (Majcher,

---

10 Polish relevant literature most often uses the term '*detencja cudzoziemców*' ('detention of foreigners').

11 This is inter alia for this reason that we shall refer many a time in this book to both theoretical settlements and the results of studies carried out in detention contexts other than migration, in which one may find many analogies and homologies. We found that the most inspiring texts from this category were works by Michel Foucault (1993), Erving Goffman (1961) and Giorgio Agamben (2008). Since the organisation of the detention of foreigners was largely inspired by regulations and practices in the prison system, while working on the conceptualisation of this project, we reached for works devoted to this segment of detention in the USA (e.g. Sykes 1958; Griffin 2001; Rock 2007), European countries (e.g. Crewe 2009; Moran, Gill and Conlon 2013; Ugelvik 2014), and Poland (e.g. Chomczyński 2013; Przybysz-Zaremba 2015).

Flynn, and Grange 2019: 3). Additionally, the time limit for keeping a foreigner in a centre in the EU was significantly extended and amounted to as many as 18 months in most states (Majcher, Flynn, and Grange 2019: 9). In consequence, the problematics of detention in EU member states became a significant issue discussed in documents of the Community institutions, as well as a subject of assessment by independent institutions and organisations.[12]

The relevant legal literature, EU and national legislation and other documents provide many definitions of the detention of foreigners, marked by a different scope and level of detail (e.g. Sieniow 2016: 15–16). We believe that the gist of the detention of foreigners is well expressed in the following definition by Stephanie Silverman and Evelyne Massa (2012: 679): *…we define immigration detention as the holding of foreign nationals, or non-citizens, for the purposes of realising immigration-related goals. This definition is characterised by three central elements: first, detention represents a deprivation of liberty; second, it takes place in a designated facility in the custody of an immigration official; and third, it is being carried out in the service of an immigration-related goal.*

The issues related to the detention of foreigners should be analysed in several legal contexts. The first one is international documents exposing the right of each individual to personal freedom and providing protection against its arbitrary deprivation. This is the case of the UN Universal Declaration of Human Rights (1948), the International Covenant on Civil and Political Rights (1966), the UN Geneva Convention (1951), as well as the detailed recommendations of the UN High Commissioner for Refugees and the UN High Commissioner for Human Rights, which have been adopted already in our own century. We may locate the Convention for the Protection of Human Rights and Fundamental Freedoms (1950, with later amendments) in the same space. The second context

---

12 See for example European Asylum Support Office (2019). *Judicial analysis. Detention of applicants for international protection in the context of the Common European Asylum System.* https://euaa.europa.eu/sites/default/files/Detention-JA-EN-PDF.pdf [1.12.2022]; European Law Institute (2020). *Detention of Asylum Seekers and Irregular Migrants and the Rule of Law: Checklists and European Standards.* https://www.europeanlawinstitute.eu/fileadmin/user_upload/p_eli/Publications/Detention_and_the_Rule_of_Law.pdf [1.12.2022]; Arbogast, Lydie (ed.) (2016). *Migrant detention in the European Union: a thriving business*, Migreurop.; European Council on Refugees and Exiles (2021). *Reception, detention and restriction of movement at EU external borders.* https://ecre.org/wp-content/uploads/2021/07/ECRE-Heinrich-Boll-StiftungReception-Detention-and-Restriction-of-Movement-at-EU-External-Borders-July-2021.pdf [1.12.2022]

is provided by the European Charter of Fundamental Rights (2012), and four detention-related directives: the Return Directive (2008, recast in 2018), the Reception Directive (2003, recast in 2013), the procedural Directive (2005, recast in 2013) and the Qualification Directive (2011, recast in 2013), as well as the Dublin III Regulation (2014). Legislation generated on the grounds of the Polish law provides the third context and includes the Polish Constitution (1997), the Act on granting protection to foreigners within the territory of the Republic of Poland (2003, recast in 2015), the Aliens Act (2013) and a number of regulations which were the consequence of the above and determine the procedural practice of detention in Poland. These documents and relations between them are discussed in rich relevant literature (Dąbrowski 2011; Chlebny 2011; Borraccetti 2014; Sieniow 2016).

The Polish law is aligned with the EU law and the international law, but just like in other states of the European Union, practices related to its implementation are based on local interpretations and take into account the specificity of the local institution administering the detention, the categories of individuals placed in the centres, etc. Decisions on the placement of foreigners in the guarded detention centre (or custody) are taken by the court of law competent for the place of stay of the immigrant at the request of the Border Guard. This procedure aims primarily at securing a return procedure (Sieniow 2016: 43–62). Under relevant legislation, detention may be applied in relation to foreigners for the purposes of the determination or verification of their identity, the prevention of abuse in proceedings in cases concerning the granting of international protection, the prevention of threats to security, health, life or property of other people, the protection of national defence or the state's security or the protection of the public safety and order.[13] In practice, the above means that both individuals who illegally crossed the border and immigrants seeking various forms of international protection are placed in the guarded centres.

13 The Act on Foreigners (2020: Art. 398a) quotes four grounds under which foreigners can be placed in guarded centres.

Photo 1. The building of the GCF in Biała Podlaska (photo by Dariusz Niedźwiedzki)

Since 2008, the institution managing the detention of foreigners in the current administrative structure is the Polish Border Guard (Ottavy 2014: 139; Rafalik 2012: 52). Supervision over the guarded centres and custody facilities for foreigners is performed by the Board for Foreigners in the BG Headquarters. These centres function in different local organisational structures of the BG. In the case of the centres in Biała Podlaska and Lesznowola, they are located within the structures of the BG facilities existing in these locations. The other four centres for foreigners function directly as a part of BG Units, in consequence of which their heads are simultaneously heads of the Departments. The centre in Białystok is located in the Podlaski BG Unit, the centre in Kętrzyn in the Warmińsko-Mazurski BG Unit, the centre in Przemyśl in the Bieszczadzki BG Unit, and the centre in Krosno Odrzańskie in the Nadodrzański BG Unit. Additionally, the particular centres have different profiles: for men (Krosno Odrzańskie, Lesznowola, Białystok), for families (Biała Podlaska), for families, women and unattended minors (Kętrzyn), for men and women (Przemyśl). The centres are able to provide space for a total of 573 foreigners: 130 in Biała Podlaska, 122 in Białystok, 120 in Kętrzyn, 103 in Przemyśl, 50 in Lesznowola, and 48 in

Krosno Odrzańskie.[14] In Poland, an average of 1,200 people are detained each year (Global Detention Project 2019: 21).[15] In comparison with other European countries, Poland stands out with its detention of a large number of families with children (ibidem: 12–14).[16] The largest number of foreigners placed in the guarded centres are consistently the citizens of Russia, Ukraine and Vietnam.[17]

---

14 The data come from the internal documentation of all the centres and concern May 2019.

15 In 2014, there were 1,322 detainees, in 2015 – 1,051, in 2016 – 1,201, and in 2017 – 1,290. As results from our working calculations on the basis of internal documents obtained from all the guarded centres, the situation did not change significantly in 2018 or 2019.

16 For instance, there were 347 children in 2014 (including 18 unaccompanied minors aged 15–18), and 292 in 2016.

17 It is worth underlining a great ethnic and religious mosaic of foreigners detained in the guarded centres. For example, as at 12.04.2019, the GCF in Białystok had 81 foreigners. Their ethnic identity covered the following countries: Vietnam (15 individuals), India (5), Georgia (3), Bangladesh (1), Kenya (2), Russia (6), Iran (3), Ukraine (1), Nepal (1), Pakistan (4), Afghanistan (21), Tajikistan (3), Turkey (5), Algeria (2), Syria (1), Somalia (4), Tunisia (1), unidentified/other (2).

Photo 2. The building of the GCF in Białystok (photo by Dariusz Niedźwiedzki)

The detention sector (we are talking about the guarded centres) has about 700 full-time jobs, but in practice some of them are vacant.[18] Jobs in the security teams/sections, operating on a shift basis, constitute a decisive majority. Apart from BG officers and civil employees, work for the benefit of the guarded centres is performed by external subjects (catering, healthcare, educational facilities, clergy, cleaning firms).

18 In some locations, the number of vacancies reaches as much as 20 % (data from internal documents of the centres for May 2019).

Photo 3. The building of the GCF in Kętrzyn (photo by Dariusz Niedźwiedzki)

Although detention is a relatively small part of the complex process of the management of international migration (Castles and Miller 1993), it raises a lot of controversy in the legal environment and a firm opposition from defenders of human rights, being sometimes also a spectacular topic for the mass media when 'crisis' situations emerge.[19] It is accepted by politicians as an indispensable tool for the execution of a sovereign state's security policy. At the same time, as a topic being specifically 'embarrassing' for the authorities, it is veiled in an aura of secrecy, hermetic and inaccessible to an external observer. We have much more information concerning the open centres for foreigners in Poland, which in some scope can be useful for detention studies (e.g. as much as it concerns the attitudes of the staff to immigrants and forms of communication with them, as well as relations between groups of immigrants). The most significant works in this scope include those edited by Halina Grzymała-Moszczyńska and Ewa Nowicka (1998), Maciej Ząbek and Sławomir Łodziński (2008) and Marta Kochanowska (2008).[20]

19 Such situations include the detainees' hunger strikes and other forms of their protest, as well as incidental escapes from the centres - such events normally attract the mass media's attention.

20 A review of relevant literature can be found in: Kluszczyńska 2017.

Photo 4. The building of the GCF in Krosno Odrzańskie (photo by Angelika Poniatowska)

Reports from monitoring conducted by non-governmental organisations are an interesting direct source of knowledge on the functioning of the Polish detention centres for foreigners.[21] What deserves special attention here are the materials collected in 2012 and 2013 as a part of a collaboration between the Helsinki Foundation for Human Rights and Association for Legal Intervention[22]

21 The most energetic non-governmental entities in the area of the detention of foreigners include: the Association for Legal Intervention, the Halina Nieć Legal Aid Center, the Helsinki Foundation for Human Rights and the Rule of Law Institute Foundation. Independent state authorities (the Polish Ombudsman, the Ombudsperson for Children), international institutions (the UN High Commissioner for Refugees) and charities (Caritas) are also involved in actions for the benefit of foreigners covered by detention.

22 The Association for Legal Intervention carried out such monitoring also in 2010 as a part of collaboration with the International Humanitarian Initiative Foundation; financing: Open Society Foundations, project Watch 24; see Cegiełka, Chrzanowska, Klaus and Wencel (2011).

(Klaus and Rusiłowicz 2012; Białas and Klaus 2014). They concern all the centres and cover a broad package of issues which are also of interest to us.[23] Reports from visits of the National Preventive Mechanism for torture prevention,[24] which took place in the years 2016–2018,[25] are yet another important source of this kind.

Photo 5. The building of the GCF in Lesznowola (photo by Dariusz Niedźwiedzki)

Source materials on the detention of foreigners in Poland also include two voices of individuals detained in such centres. We are referring here above all to a book by Ekaterina Lemondżawa (2017), a Georgian journalist detained in a guarded centre

23 The following issues were included in the broad range of interests of the authors of the monitoring: appearance, technical condition and furnishing of the facilities, the order of the day, offers to do with the spending of one's free time, food, shopping orders, clothing of the officers, their linguistic competences, attitude to the foreigners, access to information and legal, medical and psychological assistance, contact with the outside world, the issue of the placement of children, and the used security measures.

24 As of 2008, the tasks of the National Preventive Mechanism for torture prevention are coordinated by the Polish Ombudsman.

25 Seven such reports from visits carried out in all the guarded centres for foreigners can be found on the website of the Polish Ombudsman: https://www.rpo.gov.pl/.

for more than two months and a participant of a hunger strike in Lesznowola. The second source is also authored by a journalist - a reporter working for TVP, Endy Gęsina-Torres, who as a part of a journalistic provocation aimed at documenting the appalling situation of foreigners in guarded centres for foreigners was detained in the facility in Białystok and stayed there for three weeks.[26]

Photo 6. The building of the GCF in Przemyśl (photo by Dariusz Niedźwiedzki)

The few empirical studies carried out on the grounds of Polish detention centres concern detailed issues loosely connected with the very guarded centres, but concerning a selected group of their detainees (e.g. Buchowska 2016).[27] The

26 A Polish court of law sentenced the journalist to a fine of PLN 2,000 for forging documents and providing false explanations to the court, which resulted in his detention in the centre. The decision was appealed against to the European Court of Human Rights in Strasburg, which decided that the penalty was justified and consistent with the standards of freedom of expression (Sobczak 2018).

27 This is about studies in the area of human trafficking, as a part of which foreigners who were victims of such practices were interviewed. During our stays in the detention centres, we had contact with several employees who applied for permission to perform empirical studies in the form of surveys and interviews with the staff and detainees

problematics of detention also appears in analyses by lawyers (e.g. Sieniow 2016; Jankowska 2017).

For obvious reasons, the greatest involvement in the scientific consideration of the phenomenon of detention and its practical functioning in Europe[28] is recorded on the part of lawyers, political scientists, representatives of the security studies and sociologists.[29] Their research interests are often directed at controlling state legal norms regulating detention-related issues, including their interpretation and subsequent use by the administration with all the consequences for foreigners (Cornelisse 2010; Ryan and Mitsilegas 2010; Jansen, Celikates and de Bloois 2015; De Bruycker 2015; Nethery and Silverman 2015; Guia, Koulish and Mitsilegas 2016; Ugelvik 2016; Flynn and Flynn 2017; Majcher, Flynn and Grange 2019).[30] From our point of view, very valuable material collected during an almost two-year long ethnographic research in all the six detention centres in Great Britain is presented in a monograph by Mary Bosworth (2014).

Relevant literature often provides that despite functioning as a part of the same rules and legal standards, every detention centre is different to the others, that they are closed microworlds (e.g. Labanca and Ceccorulli 2014a: 9–10). This applies to both the differences at the international level and in the context of a single country. Our findings fully confirm this state of things and will be the subject of our special attention in the subsequent chapters of this book.

1.2. Our first steps in the field

Our experience connected with collaboration with the Polish Border Guard dates back to 2013. It was at that time that some members of our research team began to perform a three-year long research and development project financed by the National Centre for Science and Research (NCBiR), as a part of which

for the purposes of their doctoral dissertations in the area of linguistics, sociology and the management sciences.

28 Detention of foreigners in non-European immigration countries (such as Australia and USA) and in Asian and African states is carried out on the basis of different legislation and detention-related 'traditions'. Hence, their descriptions proved to be of little use in the context of our study.

29 We purposefully did not mention sociocultural anthropologists here, since their interest in the migration aspect in question has so far been relatively small.

30 As a part of the project, we intend to present elaboration on the state of research on the detention of foreigners in the European context.

the Border Guard played the role of the administrator.[31] The project's tasks included the development of an extensive educational programme in the area of intercultural identification and communication addressed to BG employees together with an IT tool for its use. This work required constant consultations with the milieu of the future users of the project. On this occasion, we managed to recognise to some extent the 'climate' of the institution – its style of work (in particular at the level of management), the specificity of interpersonal relations in this highly hierarchised structure, as well as the legal and organisational conditions and the routines largely determining the daily functioning of the BG. Obviously, we were aware that the picture of the institution we acquired while performing this project was very fragmentary. This was because it was largely carried out in the office and was not related to any fieldwork at the BG itself, which would have enabled a deeper insight into the principles of the functioning of this institution and its staff's motives and rules.

Another important experience connected with the familiarisation with the functioning of the Border Guard is related to the agreements signed by and between our universities (Jagiellonian University and Adam Mickiewicz University) and two BG Units managing guarded centres for foreigners (Biała Podlaska and Krosno Odrzańskie). Owing to the above, some members of the research team were able to participate in a series of a dozen or so several-day long study visits to these institutions in the years 2014–2019. They inter alia consisted in conducting educational workshops during which we tested our own training projects, performed – together with students – voluntary work in the area of the organisation of free time for the foreigners detained in the centres, and could acquaint ourselves with the specificity of the staff's work at many levels of the hierarchy of the institution.[32] These visits were not related to research – at the time, we did not have a permission to perform it – and were

31 Research and development project *Sociocultural Identification of Foreigners* financed by NCBIR No. 0018/R/ID2/2013/03. Research entity: UAM – MEDCORE consortium. Principal investigator and head of the consortium's steering committee: dr hab. Jacek Schmidt, prof. of UAM [Adam Mickiewicz University]. Project execution period: 21.05.2013–20.05.2016. See e.g. Schmidt and Niedźwiedzki (eds), 2016a, 2016b; *Studia Migracyjne. Przegląd Polonijny*, 2017, No. 2 – the issue devoted to the discussion of the project in question.

32 As a part of this collaboration, our team members visited centres for foreigners for a total of about 45 days. During this time, they conducted 25 training units for officers, and almost 70 students completed their internships combined with voluntary activity.

reduced to the performance of hardly systematised observations and informal conversations with all the social actors of the institutions we visited.

The conversations concerned the functioning of the guarded centres, but were all carried out mostly with the staff employed within the BG. Obviously, they were focused on the officers' relations with the detained foreigners, but they also covered issues to do with the legal-formal conditions and the practical functioning of the centres as institutions. The information we managed to acquire during meetings with foreigners concerned their experience which caused them to freeze their motion and interrupted their migration aimed at a West European country, rather than the functioning of the system of detention. The non-systematic observations allowed us to acquire limited data concerning above all the interactions between the various actors present in the detentive space. It was then that we came up with the idea to perform a comprehensive and systematic research into the phenomenon of the detention of foreigners in Poland and discussed the concept of the future study in the place in which it was to be performed, searching for an answer to the Popperian questions of 'what', 'how' and 'what for'. It was also at this time that we decided that our research should be focused above all on the officers and civil employees of the BG employed in the centres rather than on the detained foreigners. The latter are, naturally, a very important link in the functioning of detention. The guarded centres were established for them. The staff's mode of work is determined by the temporal dynamics of their stay. Certain actions are undertaken in connection with an admission of foreigners to the centre, while others concern the course of the procedure leading to a decision obliging the individual to leave Poland or the acquisition of some form of international protection. Some other ones are related to the process of the foreigners leaving the centre. The way the staff act is also determined by the number of detainees, which is subject to frequent and dynamic changes. Nevertheless, BG staff adopt the legally enforced regulations and create formal regulations as well as practices and routines determining the daily functioning of the centres. In consequence, the understanding of detention calls above all for becoming acquainted with and explaining the multi-aspect determinants of the way of activity of the BG officers and civil employees involved in the detention, and, to a lesser degree, the detained foreigners, who are an important, but greatly changeable category of social actors.

We consider these two types of experience, familiarising us with the specificity of the BG and the guarded centres for foreigners, of key significance for the shaping of our preliminary picture of this institution. Of course, they were supplemented with information of a scientific and media-related nature concerning the role and participation of the BG in the process of the execution of the external and internal dimension of the migration policy in Poland. Moreover, this picture was also made up of theoretical knowledge concerning issues to do with the structure and functioning of the institution. In this case, we classified the BG as the total institution – one which, inter alia, limits privacy and physical intimacy as well as contact with the external social space to the minimum and is marked by an extremely far-reaching planning of actions and omnipotence of authority.

In this place, it should be stressed that at the beginning of the project, one of the members of the research team possessed knowledge of a different nature, resulting from her long-term work in the Guarded Centre for Foreigners in Biała Podlaska – she is currently employed in the position of a manager of the Educational Team and a psychologist. Nevertheless, the knowledge resulting from her direct experience was of no significant importance for the creation of the research project, since the said civil employee of the BG joined the team at the stage of the commencement of the fieldwork. Her presence, knowledge and professional experience turned out to be important in the context of the transformation of the team members' idea of the guarded centres as the research progressed.

The initial image of the BG and in particular guarded centres for foreigners, constructed on the basis of the above-mentioned sources of knowledge, can be described with the help of many features we attributed to it.

First, it is an institution with its own organisational culture. The key dimension of this organisational culture is totality understood in the categories of Erving Goffman's concept (1961). What is therefore of great significance for the functioning of this institution is a system of relations between – to use Goffman's nomenclature – the staff and the detainees, i.e. the superiors/people who manage and the subordinates/people who are managed. We preliminarily assumed that the former group is composed of the BG officers and civil employees, and the latter – of the foreigners detained in the centre. The gist of this relation is based on the domination of the staff and the subordination of the detainees.

Secondly, what is most important for the functioning of this institution is the role of the legal acts and internal regulations in the form of different kinds of rules and regulations. An analysis of these documents constitutes a basis for the understanding of the principles of operation of the institution and behaviour of the people who remain within it. We also expected that the reality of this total institution would be legally and administratively overregulated, and that the emerging internal discrepancies would be interpreted and practiced in a variety of ways in the particular detention centres.

Thirdly, the human being, the individual, is a secondary element in relation to the reality of the rules, norms and standards of operation resulting from these regulations. People are important within it from the point of view of the functions and roles they play rather than their personality (an idealised scheme of the functioning of the total institution). In consequence, we shall deal with a limited field of informal actions.

Fourthly, the BG and in particular the guarded centres for foreigners provide a limited field of creative actions. Under the concept of Margaret Archer (1995), we are dealing here with a subordination of agents to structural requirements. Human subjectivity, which transforms the structure of the society and systematically transforms itself, is in this case shaped and transformed by structural requirements. At the same time, we assumed that the subjective agency would be fully correlated with one's position on the specific level of the hierarchy of authority in the institution.

Finally, fifthly, we preliminarily assumed that in general, all the six centres for foreigners would be similar to each other in the aspect of their organisation and principles of functioning. Differences between them would apply to secondary dimensions of the comprehensive view and relate in particular to the specificity resulting from the profiling of the centres: their division into ones for men, and ones for families and women.

Photo 7. A recreational sports yard in the GCF in Krosno Odrzańskie (photo by Angelika Poniatowska)

The above-mentioned experience (which we today qualify using the fashionable – in anthropology – term 'preliminary domestication of an alien cultural landscape'), and the creation of a preliminary vision of the institution under study played an important role during our research. Owing to this domestication, our team members found it easier to avoid the shock or trauma which are normally experienced by people who appear for the first time in isolated total institutions. Nevertheless, because of the sense of staying in a closed space – one marked by attributes such as security passages, the need for passes, bars, wires, detailed rules and regulations and the related procedures or constant supervision, we had to resort to relaxation techniques after a day-long visit to the guarded centre. Apart from these cognitively individualised needs determined by personality, we normally had a daily team discussion, often lasting for several hours, during which every member shared their experience of the working day. Such actions made it possible to limit the negative psychological consequences of staying for many hours in an environment radically different than the daily experience of academics.

Photo 8. A recreational complex in the GCF in Białystok – 2019 (photo by Dariusz Niedźwiedzki)

The said preliminary picture of the institution became a framework of reference to the knowledge acquired during the study itself. Venturing into the field, we were aware that the empirical reality always takes the researcher who prepared the project in the privacy of their study by surprise – and all the more so in the case of a largely exploratory project. Indeed, it soon turned out that this primary vision had to be essentially reconstructed. Along with the subsequent field experience, the change went in several directions. First, the increase in the knowledge and experience was accompanied by a growing awareness of the diversity of the reality under research: not only in terms of the architectural space, but also the regulations concerning different aspects of functioning of the institution.

Photo 9. A recreational sports complex in Biała Podlaska (photo by Dariusz Niedźwiedzki)

Secondly, our visits to the subsequent centres made us notice a huge significance of the material diversity of the space of the individual GCFs for the functioning of the institution and the behaviour of the people who stay there. A different organisation of the foreigners' meal attendance, related to the different spatial solutions concerning the kitchen and the dining room, can serve as an excellent example here.

Photo 10. A kids' playground in the GCF in Przemyśl (photo by Dariusz Niedźwiedzki)

Thirdly, we soon changed our way of thinking about the centre in terms of the interpersonal relations characteristic for the classical concept of the functioning of the total institution. Hence, a need emerged to identify the specific features of the totalisation of the detentive reality. In particular, our awareness of a very complex structure of relations within the group of the staff and between the staff and the detainees was growing. This was because we noticed a significant role of the personality of the actors, which was particularly important in the case of the broadly understood management, as well as the role of a secondary adaptation to the institution. At the same time, we came to a conclusion that within this total institution there are agents modifying the structural conditions that limit them.[33]

33 This situation can be well exemplified by the creation of the patron–client system (Section 3.3.4) as a part of which the possession of a patron occupying a high position in the hierarchy of authority allows the client to have more agency than that resulting from their formal position in the structure of the institution.

Photo 11. A recreational sports complex in the GCF in Kętrzyn (photo by Dariusz Niedźwiedzki)

Fourthly, the fieldwork in the subsequent centres was accompanied by a change of our perception of the institution's organisational, but above all, cultural and social structure, its richness and diversity between the individual GCFs.[34]

34 This diversity applies for instance to the organisation and conducting of the foreigners' going outside the buildings and their use of the available sports and recreational infrastructure.

Photo 12. A recreational sports complex in the GCF in Lesznowola (photo by Dariusz Niedźwiedzki)

Fifthly, the above-mentioned reconstructions of the initial picture of the institution made us aware of the necessity to broaden the theoretical framework of the reality under study, starting with paradigmatic assumptions, through a search for additional inspirations in various theories and concepts, to modification of the tools. It was already our first fieldwork experience which made us limit our study in relation to foreigners. Sticking to the observation of their reality (e.g. the course of their interactions with the BG staff), we only interacted verbally with them when they initiated such interactions. Our earlier doubts as to their agency in the area of the organisation of the social space of the centres, resulting from the adoption of specific assumptions concerning the organisational culture of these institutions, were strengthened by our observation in the field. As it turned out, the foreigners usually create an extremely unstable, changing group of social actors, whose impact on the creation of the reality in the detention centres is thus very limited.

1.3. The research team

The composition of the research team was determined by several factors. First, the planned broad substantive scope of the study called for an inter- and multidisciplinary approach. The second significant premise behind the composition of the team was the fact that the research in six guarded centres for foreigners, situated in very different parts of Poland, was connected with the necessity of long travels to distant locations. The third one was the limitation of the period for doing the fieldwork to ten months. The fourth one was the fact that the project leaders originated from the academic centres in Kraków and Poznań. The fifth factor was our awareness that the undertaken project is largely exploratory, which is related to particular challenges connected with the preparation of fieldwork methodology. The final, sixth important factor was assuring the BG of the strictly scientific nature (in the understanding of the basic research) of the project and a certain transparency of actions undertaken in the field.

In consequence of these conditions, the project leaders appointed a team composed of individuals who had previously cooperated with each other and represented different disciplines.[35] The number of its members was to allow the possibility of conducting fieldwork at the stage of the research proper in two subteams. Additionally, the project leaders decided to invite BG employees onto the research team.

As a result, the team included members living in Kraków, Poznań and Biała Podlaska.[36] This territorial dislocation was related to specific communication-related challenges connected with the organisation of the teamwork. This resulted in the necessity to conduct intense communication concerning both the scientific and the organisational aspects of the research project's execution via email, telephone and internet communicators. It also necessitated the organisation of seminar-like meetings, during which the researchers took key decisions concerning issues related to the design and execution of fieldwork as well as the collation of the existing and the first-hand data in direct interactive contact.

---

35 For more information on the particular individuals, see the *Annex*: *Notes on the authors and other members of the research team*.

36 In the initial stage of the study, team members included BG Colonel Piotr Boćko, PhD, residing in Kołobrzeg and working in the BG Central Training Centre in Koszalin. He participated in the preparation of the concept of the study, but in view of an absence of permission from his superiors, he could not participate in the fieldwork.

The execution of the fieldwork project by a team constructed in this way carries along with it many challenges at each stage of the study; coping with them successfully is one of the significant conditions of the acquisition of satisfying empirical material. The negotiation of a joint scope of the research problem – one taking into account the individual interests of the team members – turned out to be the fist challenge.[37] Its importance results from the fact of the translation of the commonly determined research problem into techniques and tools, the construction of questions to be asked during interviews, the rules of conducting observation and guidelines concerning the stock-taking of space, and the collection of existing data in the form of documents.

Another serious challenge was the organisation of communication between the team members who were territorially distanced from each other, practically at each level of the research process. First, it applied to the design of the fieldwork. In practice, during this initial stage of the study, communication between the researchers was focused on the negotiation of a package of theoretical-methodological positions, research attitudes, methods, tools and procedures of acquisition of empirical data and systems of recording the empirical material, in particular in the form of the adoption of specific templates of various types of observation notes,[38] that would be accepted by everyone. Secondly, of special significance was the maintenance of communication between the researchers during fieldwork in the detention centres, allowing the maintenance of the uniformity of research attitudes during the acquisition of the empirical material and the use of research methods, tools and procedures in a way guaranteeing the acquisition of source data satisfying all the team members. Of huge importance was the maintenance of communication relations concerning information exchange, sharing experience related to the execution of empirical research allowing to develop community knowledge covering the characteristics of the area under study, and being accessible to all the team members. Thirdly, mutual communication was of huge importance during the ordering of the collected empirical data. It was to provide all the researchers with a relatively equal access to the empirical material by adopting uniform ways of the introduction of comments to the interviews and the drawing up of the final versions of various types of observation notes, the adoption of a uniform system of archiving the existing data, the collected documents and the obtained photographic material, as well as the selection of a joint system of the processing of qualitative empirical

37 For more information on this topic, see Section 2.1.

38 For more information on the tools of data collection, see Section 2.4.3 and the *Annex*.

data. Fourthly, a communication-related challenge also concerned the stage of analysis of the acquired data. This applied in particular to the determination of the categories of coding taking into account the substantive interests of all the researchers, as well as consultation in the area of the emerging doubts in the scope of the interpretation of comments in the interview transcripts as well as the interpretation of different types of observation notes.

As already pointed out, the research team was composed of representatives of different disciplines. These included social and cultural anthropology, ethnology, security sciences, political science, law, psychology and sociology. This state of things resulted in a theoretical and methodological diversity of the researchers and their routines pertaining to the research performance. Moreover, team members differed in terms of their experience in the execution of fieldwork as well as their methodological knowledge. This differentiation resulted in, first, a broad diversity of interests in the area of the research problematics, and, secondly, significant differences in the scope of preparation for the performance of the fieldwork. These two factors enforced the necessity to conduct cyclical workshop meetings of the entire team, which, in view of the territorial dislocation of its members, posed a considerable challenge. It was connected with the mode of financing of the research, including the necessity to use finance acquired from the researchers' home institutions during stage one. Additionally, the research was conducted simultaneously with the team members' due academic, didactic and organisational work in their universities; in the case of one researcher, it was along with her duties related to her employment with the BG. Because of the above, team consultations were also carried out on the occasion of events resulting from the team members' other activities, such as their participation in conferences, symposiums, and meetings of various scientific bodies.

Obviously, the interdisciplinarity of the team resulted in a number of consequences. The identification of team members with different disciplines led to challenges related to the maintenance of theoretical and methodological consistency, and above all consistency of the research procedure regardless of the team members' different routines and habits resulting from their individual disciplines.[39] It is noteworthy that owing to the fact that BG officers/civil employees also became team members along with scholars, the study became intersectoral. They were invited into the research for several reasons. First, we were guided by a desire to be able to enter the hardly accessible field in a more efficient way owing to their assistance. The already mentioned pressure of the

39 For more information on practical ways of coping with the problem of the maintenance of consistency of the research procedure, see Chapter 2.

time during which we were to carry out our fieldwork was of significance here. Secondly, we had previously cooperated with the chosen individuals and trusted them, which was a necessary factor for this project. Thirdly, one of them is a professional psychologist, and the other one not only a civil BG employee, but also a holder of an academic position in a 'civil' university. The above guaranteed an initial professional preparation for the research.

The composition of the team had not only specific internal consequences related to its functioning, but also external ones, pertaining to the execution of the fieldwork: in particular ones connected with contacts and relations between the researchers and the subjects. The most important internal consequences of such a composition of the research group included the necessity to conduct research at all its stages using discourse understandable to all the team members. Moreover, the intersectorality called for negotiating research attitudes, and, as a result taking into account the constructivist attitude, activism and pragmatism, and the creation of a platform for cooperation as a part of these different research positions. In turn, the most important external consequences of such a composition included the subjects' problem with the identification of the team as a research team, its perception as a committee, control group, etc.,[40] as well as the subjects' different perceptions of individual team members.

1.4. Sites, time, and conditions of the research

Our research was performed in all the six guarded centres for foreigners in Poland. They are located (see Fig. 1) in Biała Podlaska (Nadbużański BG Unit), Białystok (Podlaski BG Unit), Kętrzyn (Warmińsko-Mazurski BG Unit), Krosno Odrzańskie (Nadodrzański BG Unit), Lesznowola (Nadwiślański BG Unit) and Przemyśl (Bieszczadzki BG Unit).

40 While doing the fieldwork and collecting documents, we came upon minutes of briefings of the centre managers with the employees providing evidence that our team was presented as a committee authorised to conduct controls.

Fig. 1. Border Guard Regional Units and guarded centres for foreigners (own elaboration).

The time designated for the performance of our research was determined by the BG Commander-in-Chief's written permission and was not to exceed one year. In connection with the above, our team developed a schedule, under which the study was commenced in September 2018 and finalised in June 2019. We divided the research into proper and complementary sections. The proper research was carried out in the form of ten-day long stationary visits of a subteam composed of three researchers in each centre – between September 2018 and April 2019. The complementary research in the form of three-day long visits took place in May and June 2019. It was agreed that every team member should participate in the proper research covering three locations, and subsequently in the complementary research in a further three locations. This meant that each researcher stayed in the field and conducted research for 39 days. In terms of the person-day as a unit of measure used in reporting, this is tantamount to 234 person-days used for the study. Workshops – working consultation meetings of the entire project team, carried out during the intervals between the subsequent study visits – were an integral part of the study. During the workshops, the researchers exchanged reflections from their study visits, commented on the effectiveness of research tools, etc.[41]

The permission to perform research covered the following:

1. unconstrained observation of the space of the centre between 8:00 a.m. and 8:00 p.m., including the possibility to use the recorded space monitoring;
2. collection of iconographic documentation (photographing) and copies of photographs concerning the history of the centre and its relevant adaptations;
3. documentation of the physical space of the centre, including iconographic documentation – respecting the principle of the protection of the images of individuals (staff and detainees);
4. collection of documentation (taking photographs or acquiring their copies) regulating all the aspects of the use of the space and the staff's work, including regulations, and rules and regulations in this scope;
5. conducting interviews with the management concerning the space of the centre, its use and the interpersonal relations taking place within it;
6. conducing individual and group interviews concerning the topics specified in item 5 with the staff of the centre;
7. conducting interviews concerning the topics specified in item 5 with the detainees.

Initially, the scope of rights granted to the researchers greatly surprised the authorities of the centres and their subordinate teams of employees, for whom – with the exception of audits by representatives of non-governmental organisations (such as the Helsinki Foundation for Human Rights) – such study visits were entirely uncommon. In connection with the this, there were even some suspicions that the declared purpose of our visit was inconsistent with the actual one and that the researchers were an undercover group of auditors from the BG Headquarters whose task was to evaluate the operation of the institution. Fortunately, these fears were soon alleviated, and the atmosphere of research – understood as the staff's attitude to our research needs – can be assessed as very kind, sometimes even friendly. Indicators of this state of things included openness and frankness not encounter a single case of a refusal to provide us with any documents. Apart from this, although the study was conducted in six

41 Workshops covering all the team members took place in Poznań (29.11-01.12.2018) and in Kraków (24-25.01.2019).

locations, it turned out that the detailed information about the course of our study and the research team was informally provided to fellow officers in other guarded centres.

In the context of fieldwork, terms such as 'difficult access area', 'difficult research conditions', or 'difficult access groups' are often encountered. There are many reasons why ethnographers use them. First, they may apply to physical and sociocultural environments, which for a variety of reasons have undergone long-term, broadly understood disorganisation due to political, economic and ecological changes (Turnbull 1972). Secondly, they may result from sudden, temporary changes consisting in a disturbance of a social, ethnic or other situation and stemming from migration flows, military conflicts or humanitarian crises (jakieś źródło !). Thirdly, they are sometimes used in reference to exclusive groups and institutions – such as many subcultures, the so-called deviant groups or organisations classified as totalizing ones. (Kamiński 1990). It is worth stressing that research in this sort of field poses significant ethical challenges to the researchers (Miszewski 2007).

Simultaneously, these terms appear in the researchers' descriptions referring to their psychophysical states, feelings and emotions emerging in the field during their contact with the environment under study. In most cases, this applies to the uncertainty, sometimes even anxiety the ethnographer feels as a result of, for instance, occupying a marginalised position among the subjects and, in consequence, feeling stress with all its disadaptative physical and mental symptoms (Hammersley and Atkinson 1995: 86–94). Moreover, the feeling of stress can result from a discomfort related to the conditions of the fieldwork (low living standards, exposure to potential hazards of various kinds, etc.), and finally the researcher's ambivalent feelings to research participants (and the other way round) resulting from a broadly understood 'culture clash', different systems of values, lifestyle-related and moral norms and standards, and, finally, the researcher's alienation from the reality under study (Malinowski 1989).

All the above-specified determinants/circumstances of research pose special challenges related to the access to the area as such, the selection of the optimum or simply the possible place of access to the social situations requiring exploration, and finally the adjustment/modification of the research tool kit to fit the specific nature of the place and the social environment (Angrosino 2007: 30–33; Flick 2007a: 58–59).

If we put together the above conclusions and the context of our study, it is easy to identify the features of the place, group(s) and institutions, which qualify them for the categories of 'difficult' and 'marked by difficult access'. Firstly, we undertook research in a fully controlled totalizing environment, in which, regardless of having obtained a permission to be present, we nevertheless were subjected to constant control by a 'double surveillance' (cameras and direct visual supervision). Secondly, our movement around the detention centre was difficult due to our lack of access to codes and cards enabling movement from one segment to another – hence, we had to each time ask officers for support in this scope. Thirdly, the sight of bars, barbed wire, security passages, cameras and uniformed officers made the detention space difficult not only to make 'familiar', but even to accept. This state of things persisted, as confirmed by entries in our journals and protocols from our daily briefings, throughout the duration of our research. Fourthly, the very sight of the foreigners under detention, in particular the children, raised frustration and objection against the legal-administrative system sanctioning this state of things, and affected our view of the organisational culture under study. Fifthly and finally, our presence in the guarded centre to some extent disturbed the normal course of work of the officers, who were obliged by their superiors to assist us (searching for documents and making them available, providing explanations, participating in the study and subjecting themselves obligatorily to our participant and extrospective observation). Moreover, they did not understand our presence or status – they associated it with an audit rather than a study. We found the staff's mistrust towards the researchers a considerable challenge and an additional task requiring arrangements, which could not always be accomplished successfully

1.5. Ethical issues

Ethical values, standards of reliability and good practices are a constructive element of the world of the people of science understood in the categories of a social circle having competences in the subject area. In consequence, ethical values are significant elements shaping models of thought and conduct valid for all the people belonging to this circle (Goćkowski 1999: 70). We have no doubts that their use highlights the ethical and social responsibility of scientists.

During the last few decades, inter alia as a result of the change of research paradigms (e.g. Kaniowska 2010; Lincoln, Lynham and Guba 2018), the interest in the ethical aspects of conducting research on the grounds of the social sciences and humanities has grown considerably. It has been manifested inter alia in an increased institutional control of the ethicality of the undertaken topics, forms of performance of empirical research and dissemination of its results, accompanied by the endeavours of their codification. It should be underlined that this phenomenon, primarily recorded in the USA and Great Britain, covered Poland only to a limited scope.[42]

Today, every author of a methodological textbook devoted to the execution of fieldwork, regardless of the area of reflection, feels obliged to include a chapter or at least a smaller *passus* devoted to ethics (Hammersley and Atkinson 1995: 209-229; Silverman 2014: 139-162; Banks 2007: 85-92; Angrosino 2007: 63-64, 85–89; Flick 2007a: 68-76; Kvale 2007: 23-31; Barbour 2007: 92-101; Flick 2007b: 124-129; Gibbs 2007: 90-104; Creswell 2009: 92–97). The same applies to the majority of authors of fieldwork monographs and reports (e.g. Chwieduk and Schmidt 2012: 46, 52; 2015; Chwieduk 2015: 163–179).

At the same time, qualitative researchers are aware that ethical issues cannot be limited to any universal set of rules or standards, which can be applied in just any empirical context. Ethics constitutes an integral element of research practice, and ethical dilemmas and doubts emerge at every stage of the empirical procedure – from the formulation of the topic to publicising its effects. Reflections on the morality and ethics as an immanent element of both individual and team research need to be constantly controlled, and in many cases revised and optimised.

Our research project was connected with special challenges of an ethical nature, since we had to face a very difficult area – centralised, closed, hierarchical institutions placing particular emphasis on domination, subordination and control as a fundamental communication rule. This is reflected not only in the relations between the staff and the foreigners, but also in the subgroups into which their team of employees is divided. The relatively high status of the researchers resulting from their rights granted under a decision of the top authorities of the Border Guard overlapped with the above.

42 The text by A. Seweryn (2010: 33-51) discusses two most important anthropological codes developed towards the end of the previous century: *Ethical Guidelines for Good Research Practice* (Association of Social Anthropologists of the UK and the Commonwealth 1999) and *Code of Ethics of the American Anthropological Association* (1998). J. Creswell (2009: 92-93) refers to analogical codes developed by psychologists, sociologists, pedagogues, etc. There are also codes developed for interdisciplinary research fields, taking into account the welfare of the particular category of the research participants, such as *Code of Ethics: Critical Reflections on Research Ethics in Situations of Forced Migration* (2018). International Association for the Study of Forced Migration ‹IASFM› . G. S. Canella and Y. S. Lincoln (2018: 172-194) indicate many negative phenomena to do with an increased supervision over qualitative research, leading to bureaucratisation, the exclusion of novelty paradigms, epistemology and cognitive perspectives, as well as preserving the modernist model of doing science.

This situation was not without its impact on one of the basic ethical requirements burdening the researchers, i.e. the obligation to obtain an informed consent to participate in the study (e.g. Hammersley and Atkinson 1995: 210-212; Creswell 2009: 94; Chuk and Latusek-Jurczak 2012: 26–31). The management of every centre learnt about the approaching visit of the research team from the coordinator for centres for foreigners working within the structures of the Foreigners Department, BG Headquarters. Further details regarding the team's arrival and stay were agreed between the project leader and the manager of a given centre by phone. As a result, the employees, informed about the planned research by their management, felt to some extent obliged to actively support the researchers in their work.[43] As a result, apart from incidental cases, we did not encounter refusals to talk, although on many instances we felt that some of our interlocutors from the group of the staff were under stress when in contact with us, and perceived talking to us as a specific test of 'rightmindedness'. In a couple of cases, our interlocutors expressed a concern that providing us with information may have negative consequences for them.[44] To neutralise this state of affairs, when commencing the so-called problem-specific interviews with the staff, we each time provided a package of information on the solely academic purpose of our visit and research topics. We also guaranteed a complete anonymisation[45] of their statements. Each interviewee was asked to express their consent for the interview to be recorded on a dictation machine and was assured that the recorded material would be removed immediately after being transcribed.[46] Despite these measures, we were aware that the situation was far from meeting the postulated model of obtaining an informed consent – nevertheless, the only alternative would be to discontinue research in this environment. In the case of group interviews, the situation was slightly different – and we shall discuss the

43 As indicated above, it resulted from the internal documents we managed to acquire that in some cases we were presented as controllers conducting monitoring of the quality of the centre's work.

44 In one of the interviews, the interviewee expressed the following belief: 'If I am transferred to the border, I shall know that this is because of this interview'.

45 As a part of this guarantee, the subjects were also informed that their statements shall not be connected with the institution (centre) in which they were recorded in any materials published in future.

46 Refusals were very rare, and sometimes our interlocutors asked us to switch off the dictating machine when they wanted to talk about the topics they considered confidential – concerning their private issues or relations with other employees.

issues of the solving of ethical problems connected with the application of this research technique further on in this book (Section 2.4).

As for the daily informal conversations with the detainees, which were not based on focused research guidelines, the situation was much easier, as they were not perceived as research and were not recorded. In principle, such contacts with the detainees were not initiated by the researchers. The conversations normally had the form of friendly chats in places such as recreational grounds or smoking rooms. We provided in-depth answers to the foreigners' questions concerning the purpose of our presence and our profession. Such conversations were never initiated by the researchers, they were not based on focused research guidelines or intentionally recorded on a Dictaphone. However, they were sometimes recorded when we were simultaneously making observations and recording them on a dictating machine. These conversations usually had the form of friendly chats, and they were initiated and, in the vast majority of cases, also 'directed' by the foreigners. Nevertheless, the foreigners seemed to still have some doubts as to the real purpose of our stay in the centre. The above was manifested in their attempts to start conversations with us and ask us for intervention or aid in solving the various problems they were facing whilst being kept in the detention centre.

Many methodological discussions undertake the issue of the non-ethical nature of research conducted using covert non-participant (extrospective) observation – hence, its choice calls for some explanation in the context of the specific nature of the place in which the study was conducted. In the conditions of the institution under study, a constant monitoring[47] of the majority of its space, usually equipped with several dozen cameras (with the exception of residential rooms, bathrooms and toilets) is a rudimentary activity of the guard services, who have a set of monitors in their spaces. The situation is similar in the case of some spaces of the guard service, which are equipped in one-way mirrors allowing to see the corridors or computer rooms. Foreigners are fully aware of this state of affairs and are used to it. An analogical situation takes place when direct, but fully open non-participant observation is conducted in such places as an open yard for sports and recreational activities. In connection with the above, we decided that our work connected with the use of the research technique under discussion in this specifically organised institutional space is not burdened with symptoms of immoral activity. In turn, the participant observations we carried

47 Camera recordings are archived and stored for some time – usually a couple of weeks.

out in public places were not connected with an abuse of the right to privacy of the observed people, a false presentation of the purpose of the study or the construction of the so-called false identity to be granted access to the observed situation (Angrosino 2007: 61–63).

The obligatory or postulated principles pertaining to relations between the research team and research participants are yet another important element of the reflection in question. Strategies of the research team in this scope were guided towards the gradual passage from official, highly formalised relations to informal communication free from actions in the 'official' mode. This shortening of the distance between the groups lay inter alia in the creation of the so-called 'good atmosphere' – using jokes, providing detailed information about ourselves, having friendly chats over coffee, etc. In some cases, we soon started to switch to first name terms, simultaneously making sure that such a form of familiarity was not perceived as favouring selected individuals. We underlined and maintained a subjective attitude to our interlocutors, marked by considerable understanding of their responsible work, which they in many cases performed in difficult conditions, etc. In our opinion, this strategy proved effective.

Additionally, we tried not to disturb the daily, routine actions of the staff by making our presence felt or by formulating requests disturbing their work.[48] However, despite the above description, we did not deal solely with an idyllic situation. In some institutions, the researchers encountered various conflicts among the staff on different grounds (such as mobbing, competing for positions, inability to cooperate), as well as unacceptable relations between the staff and the detainees (such as xenophobia and prejudices). In all these situations, we avoided positioning ourselves in the role of an advocate of any of the parties or becoming involved in solving these local problems. Above all, we were guided by the Weberian principle of value-free research. In our opinion, this protected us against excessively emotional reactions to the reality encountered in the detention centres, thus allowing us to obtain access to the data which pictured the functioning of the GCF as an institution with a specific organisational culture in an objectified way.

We should also mention several ethical principles concerning cooperation within the research team, which were formulated already at the stage of its

48 The authorities of each centre delegated an officer to cooperate with us. The individual was responsible for the collection and copying of the ordered documentation.

organisation. The first one provided that each researcher, regardless of the profile of their own interests pursued as a part of the topic, would participate in the same or very similar degree in all stages of the research procedure, taking into account in particular the package of tasks related to the fieldwork. The second principle was a guarantee of a comprehensive 'co-ownership' of all the acquired source materials and a constant access to them (for more information in this scope, see Section 2.4.4), based on jointly accepted rules of their protection, and subsequently the possible scope of their use as a part of the individual's work on publications. The third consistently applied principle concerned the style of our work, involving the organisation of cyclical meetings in the form of workshops – in turn in Poznań and Kraków. They were related to all the issues connected with the current project activities, including dilemmas of an ethical nature. When writing these words, being participants of many other team projects over the last several decades, we may conclude with considerable satisfaction that the comfort of work with this particular team was exceptionally high.

It was very important for us to prevent the potential harmfulness of the study for its subjects by way of the revealing of their identity. Hence, we focused on data protection procedures as a part of the archiving works. Apart from the researchers, only an experienced and trusted transcriber, with whom we had already worked on previous projects, had access to them. After being transcribed, the recordings were deleted. All the materials from the study were coded in compliance with the template developed by the team. Nevertheless, the discussion concerning the publicising of results in published materials and during conference speeches continues to be conducted by members of the research team. This discussion, which takes into account the profile of the potential recipients and the potential consequences for all the parties, will always include numerous moral/ethical aspects (Silverman 2014: 402–414).

Describing the above activities, we do not attempt to convince the reader that we are under an illusory belief as to the role of ethical reflection as an effective remedy for an entirely successful optimisation of relations with research subjects. These relations were a sort of a game in which we were some of the social actors whose goals, the resulting tasks and the applied means often did not correspond with the ideas and expectations of the other party and were sometimes incomprehensible to them. A model of research which does not raise any ethical concerns, in which the researcher takes the role of a fully empathic, friendly and transparent partner of the research participant (Fine 2010: 87–95), is in practice impossible. This state of things was well documented and at the same time we were made aware of it during our daily briefings in the field, during which our sociocultural burden and its components such as professional stereotypes, individual emotions and levels of intensity of the so-called sensitisation emerged.

Further on in this book we will refer to the above threads and discuss them in more detail together with the overriding issues pertaining to the ethical aspect of our research goals and the posed research questions.

2 Research project: 'scene one'

2.1. The anticipated problems and research questions

Every qualitative study, including one with an exploratory profile, preferring analytic induction, must feature a package of 'anticipated problems', which constitutes a specific nucleus of a particular scientific endeavour. The very choice of the topic of the study, being a natural consequence of the particular motivations to undertake research, is included in the package. When developing a conspectus of the project, which we submitted to the institution managing detention to acquire their permission to perform our study, we included in it a set of information which might be described as the problems in questions. The first piece of this information was the title that we used: *The Organisation of Space in Polish Detention Centres For Foreigners*. Concentration on space understood both in the physical and the proxemic perspective as a distinct key for the interpretation of processes related to the self-organisation of its authors, the existing interactions and the individual behaviours, was connected with our experience described in Chapter 1. The trauma of staying in detention spaces (the isolation and its attributes: wire, bars and security passages), norms and standards ruling the use of places, their limitation, the specifics of non-places (the so-called transitory spaces), a clear division into sociopetal and sociofugal places – all these attributes of the institution shocking us already at the initial sight had a decisive impact on the selection of the profile and content of the research questions (mainly additional details, but also the final form). They can be put together in the form of several thematic blocks.

A. A block of questions concerning the formal/legal conditions affecting the specificity of the organisation of the physical and social space of the detention institution:
   1. What are the most important formal/legal conditions of the organisation of the physical and social space of detention in Poland?
   2. Are there any differences in the formal-legal conditions of the organisation of space in the particular detention centres in Poland (and if so, what are they)?
   3. Questions related to the above: In what way does a specificity of the profile of the detention centre (for men, women or families) influence the organisation of its physical and social space?

4. To what extent do the formal-legal conditions of the organisation of the physical and social space of detention centres in Poland differ in comparison to the ones adopted in other selected European countries and what are the consequences of this?

B. A block of questions concerning the 'interpretation' of the social space of detention centres by all the actors functioning within it:
   1. In what way is the organisation of the social space of the detention centre interpreted by the BG uniformed employees and what are the differences in this scope related to their positions?
   2. In what way is the organisation of the social space of the detention centre interpreted by the BG civil employees?
   3. In what way is the organisation of the social space of the detention centre interpreted by foreigners and what are the differences in this scope related to their heterogenic cultural baggage?

C. A block of questions concerning the behaviours of all the actors functioning within the detention space, manifested both in intra- and intergroup relations:
   1. To what extent does the organisation of the social space of the detention centres determine the behaviours of each of the actor groups?
   2. In what way do the particular groups of actors try to transform the physical and social space of the detention centres?
   3. In what way do routines and habitual actions in the particular detention centres affect the organisation of the social space?

D. A block of questions focusing on the consequences of the particular group of actors' attitudes – in the cognitive, behavioural and emotional dimensions – for relations between them, and their constructed self-images:
   1. In what way does the organisation of the social space and attempts at its transformation affect the distance between the above-mentioned groups of actors?
   2. In what way does the organisation of the social space and attempts at its transformation affect the distance between culturally different foreigners?
   3. In what way does the organisation of the social space of detention centres disturb the social identity of the foreigners?

E. A block of questions concerning more general issues related to the functioning of the detention facilities:

   1. To what extent does the physical space influence the diversity of the organisation of the social space of detention centres?

2. In what way does the organisation of the social space of detention centres influence the attainment of its goals?

The presented catalogue calls for a broader commentary. First, the above questions were not subjected to a 'facelift' for the purposes of this text – we are quoting them in their original wording so as to faithfully illustrate our course of the conceptualisation of the project. Secondly, these questions – being a starting point for making them much more precise – are marked by a relatively high level of generality. They were solely guidelines for research. Their precisation lay in the indication of the optimum sources for giving answers to each of the questions and tools allowing to acquire these sources. Thirdly, at the subsequent stages of the conceptualisation, the provided list of questions was made more detailed or complemented with subsequent questions that we found in our research *credo* (a package of detailed research interests prepared by each member of the research team). Fourthly, some of the questions posed were not answered in a way that would satisfy us, which resulted from a lack of sources or an impossibility to acquire them within the time framework we had for our research (A–4; D–2; D–3). Finally, fifthly, we may say with satisfaction that the materials we acquired fully correspond to the information-related needs voiced in the above questions, and in some elements extend beyond the formed expectations, constituting added value.

Answers to the above questions allowed us also to gain information enabling the satisfaction of the diverse individual interests of our research team members. These interests can be presented in the form of six thematic blocks.

Block I – securitisation-related aspects of the functioning of detention centres in Poland: analysis of security practices (securitization practices), manners of the 'management' of foreigners as a security issue (Mountz et al. 2013). Our interests were focused inter alia on: the daily security practices and routines (tasks, roles, tactics, strategies) connected with interactions between officers and migrants/detainees, forms of the use of discretionary powers towards foreigners by officers, perception of security in the context of detention – the officers' definitions of security, hazards and tools designed for their minimising (e.g. monitoring, control of the Internet, searches), indicators used when labelling people staying in the detention space (the particular categories of foreigners, but also all the so-called guests) the appropriate categories of hazards/risks.[49]

49 The research team member interested in this problematics was Maciej Stępka. His research perspective fits the trend in research started by the so-called Paris school of security studies, focusing on administrative practices, daily routines, technology

Block II – the functioning of the organisational culture of the detention of foreigners in the perspective of different 'economies of morality' generated by the migration policies of European states (Fassin 2005: 366), but also the specificity of the local environment. In the conditions of total institutions, two aspects of economies of morality seem to be particularly significant: attitudes of gratitude and attitudes of control. They manifest themselves in routine practices (both at the verbal and non-verbal level) resulting from a codified scheme of the operation of detention, but also spontaneous, contextual reactions. Economies of morality should be considered taking into account the role of institutions supporting the detention centres, such as healthcare and non-governmental organisations. The perspective under description mainly aims at an analysis of the scope of subjectivity of all the social actors participating in the daily life of the total institution.[50]

Block III – the legal aspects of the functioning of the detention system. The customary questions of sociology of law, concentrating on two layers of the impact of law (socio-psychological and behavioural) are only a starting point for the construction of a more complex methodological research paradigm. In connection with the above, it should be complemented with three additional approaches. The first one, legal pluralism (Vanderlinden 1986; Griffiths 1986; Quane 2013), allows to grasp the heterogeneity and complexity of the legal order present in detention centres. Pluralism turns attention to the role this order constructs for the social actors forced to resolve conflicts of norms and interpret complex cases on the basis of their own intellectual capital or prompts

---

and spaces connected with the implementation of security policies and programmes and making them effective(Bigo, Bonditti and Olsson 2013; Waever 2004). It should be pointed out that in this critical approach, the term 'security' is an empty signifier, which is only saturated with meanings and definitions through the practices of officers (Huysmans 1998, 2011; Laclau and Mouffe 1985). In this case, in consistence inter alia with the theory of Michael Lipski's street-level bureaucracy (Lipsky 2010), security officers act as public (e.g. migration and asylum-related) policy translators, interpreting the policies while performing their daily duties (Cote-Boucher, Infantino and Salter 2014). In this way, through their practices, they construct specific phenomena and objects (e.g. migrants and migration) as a security problem, strengthening or weakening the dominating security discourses related to these objects and phenomena (Balzacq i in. 2010). In this approach, security practitioners securitize, i.e. construct security, with the help of their practices, routines and administrative rights.

50 The research team member interested in this problematics was Agnieszka Chwieduk.

offered by other elements of the organisational culture. The second approach is based on the paradigm of law as an autopoietic system (Luhmann 2007; Teubner 1991–1992). It allows to grasp the constantly renewed border between the law and the space beyond it, which is marked out across all acts of communication in the organisational culture of the detention centres. Additionally, it shows in what way the same social actors change their attitude to their actions or their description depending on whether they consider that they use the law or not. The third approach is a paradigm of law as a tool of control of the micro-authority. As a part of this approach, the law is perceived as a 'foreign body' in the centre's organisational culture. It is something largely externally enforced and controlled by external institutions, which strive to control commonplace or spontaneous practices of exercising micro-authority over the foreigners. For the social actors, the law in this vision is related to a vision of constant control, the possibility of crossing the often incomprehensible norms, due to which external institutions may draw consequences from them.[51]

Block IV – psychological aspects of the functioning of the detention centres in Poland. The most important research thread was the exploration of the relation between the organisation of the detention space and the emotional condition of the detainees and the staff (officers and civil employees) within it. The package of detailed issues included questions concerning defining the places and artefacts within them which seem to be particularly stress-provoking and disturb people's mental and emotional welfare; the potential possibilities for changing (optimizing) the space from the point of view of the needs and expectations of all its users, without interfering with the formal-legal tasks executed by detention centres; the impact of the presence of external subjects on the reduction of the sense of detention coercion; the organisation of space and ways of coping with broadly understood difficult situations. This area of interest was directed not only at a diagnosis, but also the search for practical solutions, which would be beneficial for all the social actors functioning in the detention space.[52]

Block V – the impact of the organisation of the detention space on the processes of interpersonal communication, the development of bonds and the construction of identity. This relation is analysed from the perspective of three issues. The first one concentrates on forms of adaptation to the social space of the centres of all the social actors staying within it (detainees and the staff; both these groups are considerably diverse internally), and, more specifically: ways

51 The research team member interested in this problematics was Przemysław Tacik.

52 The research team member interested in this problematics was Angelika Poniatowska.

of creating and protecting territories within this space being the subjects of demands of the social actors (in terms of Goffman's theory: personal space, the stall, the use space, the turn, the sheath, possessional territory, information preserve, conversation reservoir),[53] and the forms of 'domestication' of the closed centre used by its various actors applying different interactive techniques, which should also be identified. The second issue is related to forms of socialisation constructed by social actors in detention centres, and more specifically: kinds of bonds developed between the culturally and socially diverse social actors and the foundations (norms and values), on the basis of which these bonds are created, the ways of the development and maintenance of intergroup cultural and social distances, and finally, characteristics of the system of verbal and non-verbal communication between the diverse groups of the social actors. The third issue is connected with processes of the reconstruction of the identity of social actors, and more specifically: identity-related consequences of staff members' staying and temporarily living in a total institution and in the 'normal' reality', with the identity-related consequences of the foreigners' long-term stay in isolation, in the conditions of the total institution.[54]

Block VI – Identification of the features typical of the organisational culture of detention as a form of organisation. The various styles of operation of the staff being in a constant, daily contact with the foreigners (social guardians and sentry guards) lay in the centre of interests of the organisational ethnography. These actions are a resultant of the understanding of the mission of the institution, the degree of acceptance of regulations and standards ruling the performance of work, and the stay of foreigners in the guarded centres, the attitudes adopted in relation to cultural diversity and the situation of multiculturality, the level of sensitivity and empathy, etc. Owing to the recognition of these determinants it was possible to appropriately interpret the symbolism of style-generating behaviours and reaching the world of norms and values of culture.[55]

Block VII – methodological issues. For the majority of the research team members, study visits to detention centres were an opportunity to reflect on research procedures and techniques in the conditions of the total institution. The list of topics was very broad, covering issues related to the execution of different types of observations, triangulation in the dimensions of the source, the theory and the researcher, and the execution of a collective (multiple) holistic case study.

---

53 Theoretical proposals of E. Gofman (1971).

54 The research team member interested in this problematics was Dariusz Niedźwiedzki.

55 The research team member interested in this problematics was Jacek Schmidt.

The presented individual research intentions, independently of their small modifications along with the progress of the project, aptly illustrate not only the diverse interests of the research team members, but also the inter- and multidisciplinary nature of the work.

2.2. Research paradigms

The determination of a single philosophical approach in relation to the exploration of the social space in the guarded centres for foreigners proved to be a considerable challenge. We did not have any doubts that the adoption of the constructivist paradigm should be a starting point in the scope of the worldview-related assumptions. The issue is complex – contemporarily, constructivism – in view of its presence in many disciplines and subdisciplines of science (such as the sociology of knowledge, cultural and social anthropology, philosophy of culture, communication studies, literary criticism, developmental psychology and pedagogy) – consists of many diverse scientific positions and theories, adopting in effect different forms and becoming social, radical, epistemological, systemic or historical constructivism.

For us, the basic reference point in our research approach was epistemological (methodological) constructivism, the foundations of which were established by Peter L. Berger and Thomas Luckman (1966), and further developed as a part of the sociology of knowledge, which underlines the construction of subjective meanings in interactive processes as a result of the impact of social and cultural norms (Flick 2007a: 12). In effect, we adopted methodological situationism, which assumes that the actions of the social actor are entangled in different cultural and social determinants (Knorr-Cetina 1981). In this context, not only our subjects create the surrounding reality, but also we, researchers, construct the scientific reflection determined by local factors - in this case, the characteristic features of the guarded centres for foreigners. The context as a part of which people interact with each other, and in consequence the spaces of relations, in which the human habitus clash as systems of guidelines for the actions of any social subjects, gained key importance in our research (Bourdieu and Wacquant 2001:114). This is so because the individuals, although they construct the reality, do not do it freely and autonomously - they are always limited by the framework of social functioning. As agents, while acting, they encounter various structural limitations, and these sometimes modify the human agency, while in other moments, the individuals become the object of shaping, reconstruction by the acting agential subjects.

In the cognitive perspective, constructivists generally express their belief that objects existing in the world do not exist independently of the cognizing subject. They are not so much discovered as constructed by the individual as a part of the process of cognition. Their conceptualization has an instrumentally useful nature, allowing a control of the world and, in consequence, effective action within it (Sikora 2007: 21). We basically agree that constructivism as a cognitive position functions in three dimensions having a different scope. In the narrowest sense, it is a position from the area of the philosophy of science and methodology of scientific knowledge. In a broader understanding, it refers to the theory of cognition and scientific knowledge, but also common beliefs. In its broadest sense, it is tantamount to a philosophical position relating to the sociocultural reality as such (Zybertowicz 2001).

We agreed that there are important arguments in favour of the selection of the constructivist paradigm. We were aware that our research was unique (even pioneering), and difficult for structural, organisational and emotional reasons. These difficulties concerned both the researchers and the subjects, including the BG officers and civil employees, who had interpretative problems related to the research team. What raised a surprise was the very fact that we were granted a permission to conduct research and free access to both the space of the closed centre and the institution's documents. There were also doubts as to the purely scientific nature of our study – suspicions that the research team is simultaneously a form of a committee controlling the operation of the GCF, and, in consequence, various fears concerning the effect of its work. We also expected – which was actually confirmed in reality – that the foreigners staying in the centres would perceive the researchers as people who could help them leave the GCF. In consequence, they would approach the scientific nature of our work with some disbelief. Both the staff employed in the centres and the detained foreigners gave our team socially- and culturally-conditioned meaning. In connection with the above, we were conscious that in order to acquire an unquestionable position of researchers, we would have to inculcate it in the actors present in the detention space through our interactions.

This study posed a great challenge to the research team. Firstly, due to the above-mentioned perception of our work, we were aware of the necessity to consistently maintain our scientific narrative connected with our stay in the guarded centres. Secondly, we were conscious of the fact that our stay in closed centres, moving around space constrained by security passages and bars would also affect us – in particular in the emotional layer. Finally, thirdly, we were aware that regardless of our openness and frankness in the research procedure, we might encounter attitudes of negation, puzzlement or rejection in view of the above-mentioned possibility of different interpretations of the goals of our visit to the total institution.

The adoption of the constructivist paradigm turned out to be a specific necessity. This was not only because of the belief that the world is created by people who act, using their agency. We were also conscious that its construction would be subject to change under the impact of our presence, as the research was planned to last for 10 months, and that we should/would examine the particular guarded centres one by one – as already mentioned, between September 2018 and April 2019 for the research proper, and between April and June 2019 for the complementary research. We assumed that not only our perception of the centres would change over time – we were also convinced that the authorities and employees of the centres under study should have some knowledge resulting from our visits to the previous places, leading to the emergence of the phenomenon of 'preparation' of the management and other employees of the centres to our research, which would need to be taken into account as social constructions in our exploratory actions.

In effect, we adopted several basic assumptions of constructivism (Crotty 1998). First, that we need to take into account the beliefs of the participants of the research situation. This applies both to the subjects – BG officers and civil employees in the first place – and the foreigners staying in the centres. We had no intention to conduct interviews with the latter, but their role in the construction of the reality was so important that we subjected them to observation in the context of the construction of relations with the staff. Moreover, we assumed, which turned out to be correct in the courses of the research practice, that they would be creators of the reality, turning directly or indirectly (through BG officers/civil employees) to us as participants of the cultural and social space in which they found themselves.

Secondly, we attempted to formulate broad and general questions, which would allow one to construct meanings in a way typical for the interaction with other participants of the research situation. We were aware that depending on the research situation and our interlocutor's individual traits and positions in the structure of the institution, the set of particular questions and the area of the discussed research problems would have to be diversified. This was accompanied by a belief that a complementary research approach connected with the execution of the interview – the observation of behaviours of other participants of the research situation, in particular BG officers and civil employees – is very important in this context.

Thirdly, we assumed that we had to focus on the interactions between the officers/employees of the BG and their relations with the foreigners as well as us as researchers. This resulted from the belief that the views, attitudes and behaviours of the participants of the research situation are subjectively constructed as a part of the interactions with the other, above-mentioned categories of people participating in that research.

Fourthly, as results from the previous assumptions, a significant element of our research was our interest in the contexts in which the subjects under study live and work, so as to be able to identify and explain the spatial, temporal and in particular cultural determinants of their attitudes and behaviours. We have no doubts that this is the case because all meanings are constructed by people in contact with the social and cultural outside world.

The fifth element important for us was a reconstruction of the process of the socialisation of our subjects related to their employment with the BG, and in particular with the guarded centre for foreigners. This was because we were convinced that their attitudes and behaviours are constructed on the basis of their cultural competences acquired as a part of socialisation. These meanings constructed by the subjects always have a social nature and even if they are subjective, they use the categories, notions and meanings which have social value.

The adoption of the constructivist paradigm was a starting point for the preparation of research methods and techniques. Nevertheless, our approach was soon verified by the clash with the empirical reality. It can always surprise researchers regardless of the degree of theoretical and methodological preparation of fieldwork. Hence, we have no doubts that also the activist paradigm appeared in our research.

We know that this paradigm basically lies in personal involvement and co-participation in the studied environment. It also has an emancipatory dimension in relation to cognition as the basic purpose of research, as it contributes to the rejection of irrational and unjust structures in the society. It also has a practical and co-participatory dimension consisting in the inclusion of the subjects, who become active collaborators of the researcher (Kemmis and Wilkinson 1998). In other words, it attempts to combine research work with broadly understood actions of a political nature. This location of the researcher in the circle of actors of non-institutionalised policy was typical for representatives of the so-called Frankfurt school, above all Herbert Marcuse and Jürgen Habermas. The activist paradigm is also connected with the so-called critical sociology (Mucha 1986), aimed not only at the exploration of the social reality, but also a search for practical solutions to the social problems emerging in it.

We would like to stress that we had no intention to take on the therapeutic role of the social activist towards the phenomena of injustice or discrimination identified in the reality under study and created by the discourse of power, the ideology of domination or discriminatory mechanisms appearing in daily practices. In the cases of our team as a whole, this activist attitude was an effect of the specificity of conducting research in a closed space, where we were 'losing' our fight for the maintenance of the research distance in a situation when this space allowed us limited possibilities of distancing ourselves to the subjects. Referring to the reality of the fieldwork, the GCF in Przemyśl is an excellent example here, since due to its specific layout, weather conditions and the generated routine procedure, we were 'condemned' to staying in the educational section during every break in our research works. This was tantamount to conversations with the employees of this section, during which, without any doubt, our involvement and co-participation in the environment under study appeared.

The activist paradigm appeared in our study also because of the fact that two people employed with the BG (one of them during the fieldwork) participated in the preparation of the study. Firstly, this team member had to cope with the situation of a clash between the daily practice of work in the BG and participation in research. Secondly, without any doubt, our scientific briefings before and during the fieldwork affected her perception of the daily reality of the work in the BG.

During the research itself, an additional dimension of the involvement characteristic for an activist attitude was the fact that in the environment of the guarded centres we encountered people who in our opinion were unjustly marginalised or deprived of specific rights. This mostly applied to children placed in the centres together with their parents. For instance, in the GCF in Przemyśl, one of the researchers did, on a board, a jigsaw puzzle with an image of a racecar with the child.

As a result, we were dealing with elements of personal involvement in both the research and the reality under analysis (from the point of view of the research proper, with some thought of an introduction of changes in practice). This was accompanied by emancipatory thinking, which was to 'free' the reality under study from irrational and unjust structural limitations. To some extent, this was related to empowerment, i.e. an indication of possibilities for the subjects' liberation from the structural limitations of the institution in which they functioned.

Finally, as confirmed during the execution of the research, we adopted a practical and cooperative attitude, which was tantamount to introducing research subjects into collaboration. Apart from the research situations, with several individuals participating in them, we had informal meetings outside the space of the guarded centres. The membership of a BG employee in our team was an important reason behind the subjects' cooperation with our team. One of the effects of this state of things was a different treatment of the team in which representatives of science worked along with a person employed with the institution. Owing to the above, in particular people who knew this member of our research team felt to some extent obliged to undertake a broader cooperation with us.

We are also convinced that the pragmatic paradigm, representatives of which refer to works by William James, George H. Mead and James M. Peirce, also emerged in practice in our research approach. Contemporarily, its supporters include Richard Rorty (1990), Paul Patton (2002) and David L. Morgan (2007). Why was this so? It seems that the most important reason was the fact that we were dealing with exploratory research. Independently of our knowledge, competences and research experience, the world of the GCFs turned out to be a definitely new world. What is more, it was one constructed in a different way in the particular centres – something we did not initially expect from the total institution. In consequence, the will to explore coupled with the surprise with the empirical reality must lead every researcher, who wants to explore and understand the reality under study, to a pragmatic paradigmatic attitude. This resulted in the research procedure consistent with the methodological logic of the grounded theory.

We believe that our study was well-grounded in the basic characteristics of the pragmatic worldview, which can be described after John W. Creswell (2009: 28). Above all, it is worth pointing out that pragmatism was not connected with any specific philosophical system concerning the nature of the reality. It took the position that all research is conducted in specific historical, cultural and political contexts, which in the case of the particular guarded centres became an important aspect of our fieldwork. Moreover, it basically assumed a unity between the reality in the mind and its creation in the observed world.

In the pragmatic vision, the world does not constitute a unity, and in consequence qualitative and quantitative research techniques are mixed. In the case of the performance of our research, this turned out to be a necessity. The sociocultural reality of the detention centres turned out to be pluralistic, a reality in which the participants, being 'reflective' social actors, can undertake agential actions stepping beyond structural determinants and modify them through a different definition of the situation.

Research consistent with the pragmatic paradigm is marked by a liberty of selection of research methods, techniques and procedures, and above all their modification in compliance with the rule of 'open method in time'. We are certain that this is exactly what we did during our research in the particular centres. Such behaviours were above all motivated by the will to maximise the effectiveness of the research activities at a given moment. This is because we were aware that firstly, we were performing unique research, and secondly, that it could not be repeated if we failed to obtain satisfying material in the form of empirical data.

2.3. Research strategies

2.3.1. Qualitative approach

Labels such as 'field of qualitative studies' or 'qualitative studies' hide a broad range of very different, sometimes exclusive approaches and related methodological practices. Hence, many researchers calling themselves qualitative ones feel obliged to familiarise the readers with their own perspective of the execution of their research idea. Let us begin with an indication of several features of the adopted approach that are obvious to us. The first one is the acquisition of information in the natural - ordinary, daily context of functioning of the social actors through the keeping of face-to-face contact with them for a prolonged time. The second one lies in the perception of the research process as a project 'under construction', subject to a constant revision in the source, methodological and theoretical dimensions. The third feature, closely related to the second one, is the attachment to thinking – inductive analysis followed by the integration of the experience and theory (theory-creating role of the field).[56] The fourth feature consists in the use of an extensive package of source materials and techniques of their acquisition, as well as methods of their analysis. The fifth feature concerns the idea of the interpretation of images, meanings and contexts, which assumes polyphonism, dialogicity with the participation of all the research 'parties', and subsequently the recipients of the effects of project works (e.g. Hammersley and Atkinson 1995; Silverman 2014; Angrosino 2007; Creswell 2009).

The meeting of these declarations is to lead to the acquisition of a holistic perspective illustrating the complexity of the phenomena under study by referring to many ways of their perception and interpretation – an attempt at

---

56 Martyn Hammersley and Paul Atkinson use the metaphor of the funnel: "Ethnographic research should have a characteristic 'funnel' structure, being progressively focused over its course. Over time, the research problem needs to be developed, and may need to be transformed; and eventually its scope must be clarified and delimited, and its internal structure explored. In this sense, it is frequently well into the process of inquiry that one discovers what the research is really about; and not uncommonly it turns out to be about something rather different from the initial foreshadowed problems" (Hammerley and Atkinson 1995: 160).

their explanation, a platform of understanding. Authors of a compendium of knowledge on qualitative studies (Denzin and Lincoln 2018: 41-44) indicate eight historical stages in the more than one hundred years old development of the field and practice of qualitative studies. In our research project, we reached for elements developed as a part of the majority of these stages, while simultaneously trying to remain faithful to the paradigms discussed in Section 2.2. Because of this circumstance, as well as for other reasons, which we are going to present in more detail while discussing research strategies further on, we consider the project eclectic. These actions dovetail the metaphor of a bricoleur – a creator of patchworks, a picture editor – in all its methodological, interpretative, theoretical, and political references, as indicated by Norman K. Denzin and Yvonne S. Lincoln (2018: 45-46). The above characteristics are best matched by ethnography as a highly flexible approach, permeating all the social sciences, successfully applied in different forms on the grounds of separate theoretical orientations (symbolic interactionism, ethnomethodology, feminism, critical theory, cultural studies, postmodernism, etc.).

A long-term research experience of a half of the research team, including project coordinators, related to the application of ethnography in its various variants, was yet another natural premise behind the selection of this research method as the leading one (e.g. Chwieduk 2019; Niedźwiedzki 2010; Schmidt 2009). Another argument in favour of this choice was that ethnography is a method used in all the fields of the social sciences represented by the members of the project team and, hence, present in their project practices (e.g. Stępka 2018). Apart from the above, which seems to be particularly significant, when selecting ethnography, we were guided by the principle of responsibility (Flick 2007a: 4–5). We had been hearing about its usefulness for some time as a part of methodological discourses connected with specialist research niches. We are talking here about studies into management, organisational culture, total institutions, and their proxemic and kinesic aspects (e.g. Kostera 2013, 2011; Sułkowski and Sikorski 2014).

2.3.2. Interdisciplinarity – transdisciplinarity – multidisciplinarity

The majority of authors of collective works devoted to the issue of interdisciplinarity indicate a popularity of this conceptual category, and at the same time its usefulness and significance in contemporary scientific considerations (e.g. Frodeman, Klein and Mitcham 2010; Repko 2012; Kurczewska and Lejzerowicz 2014). Simultaneously, one may often hear during disputes devoted to interdisciplinarity that it is an intellectual fashion, a project remaining in the imaginary (utopia) and postulatory sphere, an idea threatening the disciplinarity of sciences as a knowledge generation tradition that has been grounded for centuries. One thing is sure – we are dealing with a certain vagueness of the meaning of the term under discussion, related inter alia to its use in the contexts of different disciplines and disciplinary partnerships, and in the colloquial vocabulary Hence, it is necessary to familiarise the reader with a longer list of reasons for which we defined our project as interdisciplinary and with the adopted scope of understanding of the notion in question.

An obvious but yet insufficient premise to begin to call our study interdisciplinary was the constitution of a team of researchers interested in the exploration of the phenomenon of the detention of foreigners, who represented several disciplines. What is important in this context is that the above was not limited to the joint development of the programme of interdisciplinarity: defining and justifying links between the particular disciplines by way of the creation of a joint conceptual apparatus and packages of not incompatible theoretical approaches and methodological assumptions, i.e. the vertical structure of interdisciplinarity (the term is borrowed from prof. Jagna Brudzińska). What was equally important was the generation of the so-called situation of interdisciplinarity (Kurczewska 2014: 276). It is manifested in the creation of a social space as a part of which regular, even intensive cooperation takes place at every stage of the procedure, on the basis of principles and standards accepted on the grounds of each of the disciplines represented in the research project. In this way, the postulate of a horizontal structure of interdisciplinarity is satisfied (Brudzińska 2014: 252–253).

The decision to create an interdisciplinary project was based on the complexity of the very area of research, which fits the migration studies – as a standard, they are described as a sphere of interdisciplinary inquiry.[57] Many problems and issues giving rise to tasks, the execution of which steps beyond the competences of a single scientific discipline, emerge as a part of this research field. We are dealing with such a situation in the case of a description and analysis of the detention of foreigners, which actually enforces a collaboration of an anthropologist, sociologist, lawyer and psychologist.

57 It was not accidental that the idea of interdisciplinarity became apparent on the grounds of classical area studies (such as different fields of Oriental studies), and, subsequently, complex research areas such as communication, urbanization or mobility as a tendency to combine research efforts of different sciences (Calhoun and Rhoten 2010).

Our research concerned a problem we considered, for a variety of reasons, necessary to be explored in a relatively short time and the broadest light possible in view of its potential socio-practical significance (Calhoun and Rhoten 2010: 114–115). In connection with the above, we considered the project in question as urgent (Posern-Zieliński 1987: 34–36), calling in particular for an interdisciplinary approach, and a holistic explanation based on a collaboration of different sciences.

In the project under description, the leading role was assumed, for a variety of reasons, by sociocultural anthropology.[58] First, 50 % of the research team members were anthropologists. Secondly, this science is marked by the openness of its vision of practising science, including an inclination (as mentioned on so many occasions) to skirt the edges of other disciplines, accepting the state of 'blurred genres' (Geertz 1983: 19–35) as both a condition and a direction of development of the contemporary social sciences. The third premise is the positively verified usefulness of the conceptual apparatus of anthropology and its methodology in studies into institutions and their organisation pursued by representatives of the management sciences (e.g. Hatch 2013; Sułkowski and Sikorski 2014; Kostera 2013). Finally, we need to mention the increasing anthropologisation of science and its discourses in the social sciences, which plays a significant role in interdisciplinary studies, activity conducted as a part of subdisciplines, breaking the educational autarchy,[59] etc. (Pomieciński and Sikora 2009; Schmidt 2014: 327–334; Kurczewska 2014: 277–280).

The project in question fits the metaphorical idea of interdisciplinarity referred to as bridge-building. In no place did we postulate the idea of restructuring, which would lead to the creation of hybrids reconfiguring the disciplines being part of the consilience system (Klein 2010: 21). We perceive interdisciplinarity understood as carefully considered eclecticism – a both holistic and coherent approach to the complex sociocultural phenomena – as an optimum activity allowing to acquire a polyphonic point of view, while at the same time a means of the transfer and merger of segments of disciplinary knowledge.

All conceptualisations testifying to backing up the execution of the idea of interdisciplinarity understood in this way, which shall be discussed

58 We use this term consciously in order to highlight a departure from the traditional division of anthropology into cultural and social, which remains contradictory to contemporary trends in practising this science.

59 The idea of academic interdisciplinary education using the Delphi method was discussed by Allan F. Repko (2006).

further on in this book, will be above all declarative. The extent to which we have been consistent and whether our project proved to be integrated in the interdisciplinary context, and whether the acquired knowledge took on an interdisciplinary nature (reached 'bonding' strength); (Walczak 2016: 121-125) will only be assessed by the reader of the research team's subsequent, resultant publications.

The second term specified in the eponymous triad of this section, i.e. transdisciplinarity, raises fewer doubts than the interdisciplinarity and is perceived as a more promising project, although it is understood and interpreted in a variety of ways (Moran 2010: 14). Some researchers perceive transdisciplinarity as a radical form of an interdisciplinary project, an attempt at a subordinate integration of knowledge through a synthesis of theory and methodology from several disciplines (Klein 2010). In turn, Besarab Nicolescu (2006) indicates that the very prefix *trans-* means that transdisciplinarity is located beyond, between and across disciplines, which results in the constitution of an entirely new research field abolishing boundaries between disciplines, and, in consequence, unifying the acquired knowledge. This specific transcendence of scientific disciplines is based on a package of methodological axioms: ontological, logical and epistemological (Nicolescu 2006; Kita 2012: 22–25).

The very narrow understanding of transdisciplinarity which we adopted applies only to the situation when the methodology of one discipline, understood both in the descriptive and normative sense, is used for studies as a part of another. This strategy results, inter alia, in the development of subdisciplines and specialisations as a part of which research involving representatives of different sciences is performed. This issue was particularly important to us in connection with the implementation of the ethnographic method, selected analyses of discourses, conceptual models (real and metaphorical) between anthropology and sociology on the one hand, and management, security, and law sciences on the other.[60]

Some of the project's research questions and tasks posed were related to team members' individualised interests and were provided with more autonomy. We qualified these sectors of our research activity as multidisciplinary as they consisted in independent observation by the particular researchers who maintained the identity and set of instruments of their own disciplines.

---

60 It is difficult to agree with a supposition (Koczanowicz 2014: 267) that this form of borrowing is 'robbery'.

2.3.3. The idea of triangulation

Uve Flick (2007b) points to the primary role of triangulation as a measure leading to a systematic, but also systemic increase in the quality of qualitative studies in modern, reflexive studies of this type. This activity is very important for the researchers themselves, who are naturally interested in the effectiveness of the implemented research concepts, procedures and techniques, and, in consequence, the evaluation of the reliability of the generated results, for the institutions financing the project, for publishing houses and editorial boards disseminating the research results, and, last but not least, for the readers. In each case this is about sketching a full picture of the research project, which is to be a form of its 'credentials', the 'researcher's hallmark', which can be produced to document the legitimacy of the acquired data and its relevance for the proposed explanations (Malinowski 2005: 46–48). Triangulation leads to the development of a broader interpretative model allowing the researchers to fulfil their obvious desires, such as more realistic analyses of social life and its cultural rules (Schmidt 2009: 18).

During the five decades which passed since Denzin's (1978) postulate of the implementation of a multi-aspect triangulation procedure together with its consistent conceptualisation, its methodological perspective became a rudimentary element of procedure in most qualitative studies.[61] Its usefulness lies in its effective accomplishment of several purposes. The first one consists in seeking to reflect aspects of the explored reality from many angles – in particular, conducting comparative analyses of the obtained knowledge resources originating from different stages of the research procedure, generated with the help of different tools, from various points of view adopted by the researcher. The second one is an in-depth assessment of methodological and theoretical accuracy as well as the reliability of results (Hammersley and Atkinson 1995: 183–185; Silverman 2018: 384–398).

---

61 A review of the 20th-century history of anthropological, sociological and psychological research, documents many projects whose authors implemented the idea of triangulation without using the actual term at selected levels (sources and methods) indicated in N.K. Denzin's concept. For instance, U. Flick (2007b: 38–39) refers to studies by such classics as G. Bateson, M. Mead, W. Thomas and F. Znaniecki. Reaching deeper into the history of qualitative studies, one may indicate many earlier examples of triangulation (e.g. Goring 1913, after: Klineberg 1940: 350–351, 526–527). In turn, theoretical and methodological reflections postulating triangulation-related activities appeared in psychological texts published in the 1940s and '50s – however, they focused on the issue of validation (Hornowska et al. 2012: 74–75).

Let us recall that Denzin (1978: 294–302) distinguished four types of triangulation: sources, researchers, theories, and methods.[62] Our research procedure at the level of the triangulation of sources (using several different source data – see Fig. 2) was related to several needs. One of them could be described as the task of collection and, subsequently, comparison – the confrontation of sources to determine the extent of the consistency and discrepancy of their contents. Another good example is the issue of the organisation of the daily life of the detainees. A framework of information reference was provided by the existing sources: documents determining the order of the day, the use of the particular spaces, the codified requirements concerning the foreigners' behaviour, etc. We confronted information contained in the sources with observational data acquired in the course of round-the-clock study visits. The third, complementary source of knowledge on the topic in question, was information acquired from the staff. In this way it was possible to define the relation between the 'theory' (legislative and administrative regulations) and practices applied in the institution under study. The examination of documents entitled 'A detailed scope of rights and duties' concerning each position, which often contained different content in relation to the particular position, was an analogical triangulation activity. In this case, the data was compared to the source information generated from the observation of practices, as well as conversations with officers and their superiors. A comparison of the architectural plans of the centres and inventory documentation containing descriptions of the particular elements of space and the scope of their use with what we encountered on the spot and subjected to an 'as is' description, was yet another example of this type of source triangulation. It is worth stressing here that the activities in question should not be reduced to a control of the accuracy and reliability of the particular sources, which is only one of the elements of the triangulation procedure under discussion.

62 In his later works, Denzin (e.g. Denzin and Lincoln 2018) modified and provided more details to his concept, partially due to it being criticised (see Flick 2007b: 45–48), and partially in connection with new perspectives and forms of performance of qualitative studies he was a propagator of (e.g. Denzin 1997).

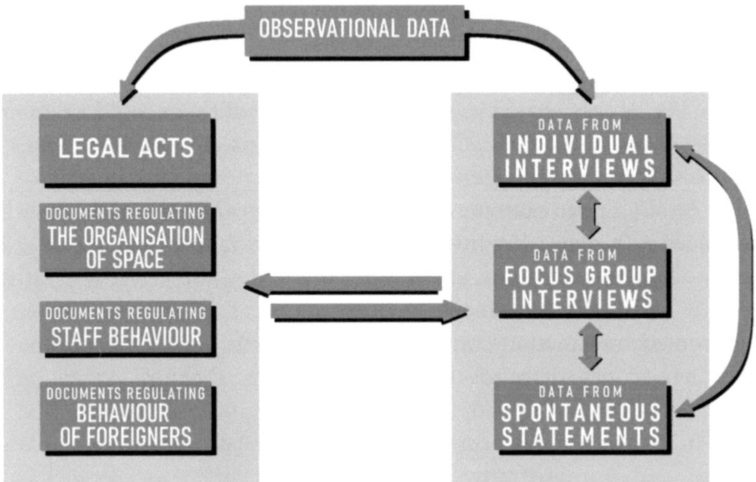

Fig. 2. Triangulation of data sources – confrontation of regulations and declarations with practices (own elaboration)

The second need related to the application of source triangulation was the achievement of the effect of the broadening of the perspective of the inquiry into the phenomena in question. This was by no means about searching for and finding identical results, but rather about similar or mutually complementing data as well as the so-called deviations. Each of the potential sources of data has its strong and weak points, specifics allowing an unveiling of the reality to a limited extent. Further on in this work (Section 2.4.1) we shall include a broader description of the acquired source resources and relations between them.

In turn, the postulate of the triangulation of researchers (see Fig.3) can be classified among the greatest challenges in the practice of qualitative fieldwork. Many of the so-called research situations exclude the possibility of a simultaneous participation of two or more researchers in the observation procedure or conversation with a research subject. There are many reasons behind this – they include the oppressiveness of the situation felt by the interlocutor or the observed person in connection with the presence of several researchers, the artificiality of such situation resulting in an unwanted formalisation of contact, and in consequence a distortion of the recorded results, and, finally, a lack of the possibility to conduct a simultaneous interview/observation in view of the specificity of the place, category of the interlocutors or confidentiality of the discussed topics. In the case of our team research project, there were particularly favourable conditions for the implementation of the procedure in question, which resulted from the specific nature of the total institution: its organisation of space, permanent electronic monitoring, communication-related rules and standards of social interaction. Owing to this, it was possible to carry out simultaneous participant and non-participant observation, as well as conversations with selected categories of social actors (foreigners, management of the centres, and middle managers). As a result, we managed to generate many observation notes concerning the same research situation authored by different researchers, and introduce to the transcription of conversations autonomous comments of the persons who conducted them, including for instance individual interpretations of statements and the accompanying non-verbal behaviours. Independently of this, during the daily briefings of the team, we shared our current experience, discussed its interpretation, and made notes – protocols of consistency and discrepancy. Without any doubt, the effectiveness of the triangulation of researchers was also facilitated by the already mentioned organisation of the team's work consisting in proportional participation in all the research activities in the centres.

Fig. 3. Triangulation of researchers (own elaboration)

Triangulation of theory is tantamount to putting together various theoretical points of view of the phenomenon under study in order to assess their strength and usefulness. In the classical approach by Denzin (1978: 297-300), this type of triangulation is inter alia to protect research projects against an unjustified attachment to assumptions adopted at the stage of the initial conceptualisation, ignoring alternative interpretations and explanations, and giving up attempts at developing one's own, eclectic theoretical concept based on a collage of theories exposing the usefulness of different source resources and methods. In the case of the collective and interdisciplinary exploratory project under discussion, which took into account a broad range of the researchers' interests and questions posed, and, in consequence, perspectives and ways of explanation, these issues took on a special meaning. The activity of developing a coherent model based on a broad package of theoretical inspirations and related notions and typologies was connected with an in-depth reflection at the theoretical level of triangulation. The results of these considerations are presented in chapter 8, and here we would like to accentuate a permanent nature of these measures, which results from the adoption of the concept of the integrity of experience and theory, in particular the 'theory-creating role of the field' (Malinowski 2005).

Another postulate, the triangulation of methods (methodology), refers both to ways of the acquisition of materials (such as through observation, conversation, focus, projective techniques), and methods of their analysis (e.g. through the comparative method, documentary method, discourse analysis, bricolage). Denzin (1978) indicates two subtypes of this level of triangulation: within-method triangulation, and between-method triangulation.

In turn, Flick (2007b: 48–53, 55-74) points out that the implementation of the idea of triangulation in its comprehensive form calls for supplementing Denzin's classification with one more element, i.e. the consistent triangulation of perspectives. This level of reflection should appear at the earliest stage of the project work, and is connected with the adopted paradigm (or paradigms) and the specificity of the applied qualitative approach and the posed research questions. This is *de facto* about theoretical foundations indicating specific ways and excluding other approaches to the phenomena, thus profiling triangulation measures at the level of sources and methods. What is an important element of the consistent triangulation of perspectives in the case of team research projects is the triangulation of research themes followed by the generation of knowledge and the discussion of the results – which we wrote about a moment ago in the context of the collaboration of researchers. The use of the ethnographic method is naturally connected with a flexible triangulation of perspectives, and in view of the domination of the area over methodology, it is a permanent activity, which cannot be located as a part of a single stage of the research procedure (e.g. Flick 2007b: 77–90).

Further on, we shall refer on numerous occasions to all the threads signalled in this subchapter. It is worth underlining here that our triangulation-related activities reflect above all a desire for an 'in-depth understanding' – a term borrowed from Denzin (2012) – of the phenomenon under study, and a construction of a multidimensional and simultaneous (by no means sequential!) picture of a section of social life that would document inter alia the diversity of results generated by way of the application of different sources, methods and theories. In connection with the above, we do not perceive the effect of an inconsistency or non-confirmation of results as a shortcoming of the triangulation strategy, since we reject the theses of naive realism, which assumes the possibility of the existence of procedures that will guide the researcher to a faithful reflection of the reality (Kempny 1994: 129–132). Because of the above, the issue of validation as a triangulation task seems to be of little importance, sometimes leading to as much as misunderstandings concerning the role of triangulation in a qualitative study. Finally, it is worth pointing out that all the actions related to the application of triangulation were connected with considerable methodological rigorism at all stages of the research procedure, starting with the stage of its planning by the team. Positive consequences included an increase in the level of reflectiveness, as well as criticism in relation to the acquired sources, used methods and generated results.

2.3.4. Autoethnography and reflectiveness

The beginnings of autoethnographic reflection can be traced to the 1970s and '80s and are related to different turns in the social sciences (such as 'blurred genres' or 'crisis of representation'), which are connected with interpretative, reflective, postmodern anthropology and sociology.[63] Today, the practising of autoethnography has entered, in a variety of ways (scopes), the canon of research practices as the very act of auto-narration, a form of recording this act (autoethnographic writing), a technique of the acquisition of source data, research strategy, and, finally, a model of practising science (Kacperczyk 2012: 32–74).

Researcher's self-analysis in terms of examining their origin, temperament, biographical experience, ethnicity, class, and gender may unveil the impact of these factors on the disturbance of the overview of the reality under study and

63 For instance, (Kuligowski 2001; Lubaś 2003).

explain the motivations behind the selection of the topic of research and the methodology used (e.g. Geertz 1988). Pierre Bourdieu (2001: 32–35, 45–52, 2008, 2009: 62–74) complements the above self-analysis with reflection on a specific deformation of the overview of the reality related to the functioning in the microcosm of the academic world (the figure of *Homo academicus* and its field), leading inter alia to a reduction of the practical logic to theoretical logic. What follows is inter alia a postulate of the constant control of the research practice.

When commencing the conceptualisation and, subsequently, execution of the project, we were fully aware of our role in the research process and we concluded that the researcher as a research tool should become an object of analysis to the same extent as the people and phenomena existing in the field of the researchers' interests. Rather than undertake unproductive activities to eliminate their impact on the subjects and the process of data acquisition and interpretation, we endeavoured to focus on a determination of the essence of this impact (Hammersley and Atkinson 1995: 16–17). However, due to organisational limitations (in particular ones related to time), our considerations concerning autoethnography emerged only on the sidelines, in the context of discussing the principles of keeping research journals. At the time, we did not develop any rules or standards profiling autoethnographic records and neither did we define the scope or form of their use in analytical works or the preparation of future texts. The topic returned only when we started to perform the research, during our daily meetings. It was then, when we were sharing our impressions from the conducted observations and the experienced interactions, that their different interpretations appeared along with the accompanying emotions, which may be connected with every researcher's individual sensitivity, educational profile and biographical experience (including the duration of on-site internships in camps for foreigners). As a part of such consultations, we drew up the so-called sensitisation notes. This mode of work can be classified as acts of auto-narration and an element of the research strategy.

It is now difficult to assess to what extent these autoethnographic reflections will be expressed in writing,[64] i.e. in the post-project written texts of the particular authors. It is even harder to anticipate to what degree they will refer to the postulates of evocative or analytical autoethnography (e.g. Ellis and Bohner

---

64 The very 'visibility' of the researcher in the text, manifested inter alia in the used personal form, and the highlighting of the active presence of the researcher's Self in the text belong currently to rudimentary elements of the writing style of researchers representing all theoretical orientations.

2003; Denzin 2014; Anderson 2006). A number of research threads (such as economies of morality, spatial traumas) and our guiding idea of the dialogicity of the parties in research and the related negotiation of meanings suggest that the types of materials under study will be taken into account in our elaborations.

2.3.5. Case study

The phenomenon of our interest, i.e. the detention of foreigners in Poland, is complex. At the same time, it is very special to the point of being unique, which makes it easier to delineate its boundaries, and, in consequence, select for the case study an optimum research strategy. Let us confront our vision of the approach in question with Robert Stake's typology of case studies, which we find closest to us from the point of view of the goals/tasks we set for ourselves during the conceptualisation of the project, and then modified in the field. Stake (1994: 237–238) distinguished three types of them: intrinsic case studies, instrumental case studies, and collective case studies.[65]

The approach used is fully fit to be called an intrinsic (significant) case study, since it was a case (system of the detention of foreigners in Poland) itself which was the cause of our cognitive interests. This declaration does not mean that this approach has fully excluded an attempt at an exploration and understanding of a broader phenomenon – the functioning of total institutions, a specific, not necessarily typical form of which is represented by our case. In this context, the described strategy dovetails the instrumental case study. Robert Stake (1994) himself points out that it is very difficult to draw a clear border between the intrinsic and the instrumental approach in research practice and that it is easier to distinguish a sphere of mixed approaches.

The described project is a collective (multiple) case study.[66] The decision to carry out this type of study was accompanied by our full awareness of the related

---

65 Robert Yin (2014) proposed a different classification, which included the following studies: exploratory – mainly descriptive, preliminary for later research; explanatory – analysis of causes and effects of phenomena using competitive or complementary theories; descriptive – with a theoretical model preceding the experience. Other authors propose their own division of case studies fitting the specificity of a given case (e.g. biographical cases in a German school), adopted methodological assumptions (in particular the control of reliability) or research traditions developed on the grounds of the practiced disciplines (history, pedagogy, sociology, etc.). It is also worth indicating an interesting proposal by Bent Flyvbjerg (2006), based on the criterion of the study's usefulness in terms of its informative content.

66 We may dispute with Robert Stake as to whether a collective study is related to an instrumental approach, whether it is an expression of scant interest in a given case.

challenges: the requirement to obtain an extensive set of source materials, the very high discipline of team work (rigid calendar of study visits and workshop work), high cost-intensiveness, and, finally, the above-standard coordination of analytical works and the collegiality of work on the elaboration of the outcomes of the project. The temptation activated by an unexpected, one-off permission to perform this study in the form of a comprehensive and complementary exploration of 'cases comprising a case' was so great that the team took the decision in question unanimously. Some methodologists (Miles and Huberman 1994: 208) indicate different threats related to the application of this procedure and propose that for instance separate reports from the particular cases be drawn up beforehand in order to make sure that their contexts correspond with one another, and that they can thus be legitimately integrated in the joint analysis. We shall refer to this issue later on.

Although our case study was sequential, the short time intervals between our visits in the subsequent centres, resulting from the content of the permission for research issued by the institution managing the detention of foreigners in Poland, made the due preparations for the subsequent visits more difficult. Hence, it was impossible to edit (e.g. transcribe interviews, prepare observation notes on the basis of the researchers' journals) and thus read the complete set of source materials obtained in one location before starting research in another. However, because of the experience acquired in the course of each study visit – both individual, usually recorded in the researcher's journal, and being a result of group discussions in the field and cyclical project workshops – our study was consistently modified and broadened. These changes concerned the increased need for the existing sources (Section 2.4.1), a construction of subsequent research tools (Section 2.4.3), the creation of coding guidelines and a profile of analysis (Section 2.4.4), and, following all these, the construction of theoretical and methodological models (Section 4.1). Entering the stage of complementary research in all the centres into the schedule of our study visits proved to be a very good decision, as it allowed for the acquisition of the missing existing and first-hand data and in this way to accumulate fully comparable material for all the explored constituent cases.

As a part of the research project in question, we explored all the six cases composing the system of the detention of foreigners in Poland. The issue of selection as a part of the collective case study (time, people, contexts) is presented in Section 2.4.2. In this place, it is worth making a reference to Robert Yin's (2014: 57–62) reflection on the logic of replication in collective case studies. Basing on an analogy to multiple experiments, he writes about literal replication (selection predicting similar results) and theoretical replication (selection predicting different results due to reasons assumed by the researcher). Launching the project in question, we were aware of the internal differentiation of the cases, resulting from their profiles (for men, for families, mixed), the number of staff and the detained foreigners, their different positioning in the organisational structure of the particular units of the Border Guard, and the infrastructure, in particular the architecture of the facilities as an element of the organisation of space. Our fieldwork practice showed that the number of the factors differing the particular centres from one another was much greater and that the differences were related inter alia to the location of the centres in regions marked by the specific labour market[67] and the management style at the level of the high and middle management.[68] Reflections on this topic were discussed and recorded by the research team in the course of every study and at its conclusion in the form of notes containing the most important threads from the relevant findings.

Our collective study fits the holistic type. A resignation from distinguishing subunits of analysis[69] as is the case in the immersive type, was a conscious methodological choice resulting from the need to approach the isolated space and its organisational culture in a global manner (Yin 2014: 49–50, 53–56, 61–63). All case studies are directed towards a comprehensive analysis of the context-related conditions (physical, social, cultural, political, ethical, aesthetic, etc.) as a part of which they function. In the situation of our collective case study we are dealing with six internal contexts, a reconstruction of which is an indispensable condition for a collective analysis based on a comparison. The final effect, i.e. a comprehensive reconstruction of the picture of the institution of the detention of foreigners in Poland, should take into account both the localness of contexts and their universal dimension, and illustrate the detailed, the unique features in both the internal dimension, and in reference to the world which is external to the organisational culture under study.

A case study protocol is a rudimentary element of the research procedure for case studies – in particular collective ones (Yin 2014: 84–86). It has an

---

67 This factor turned out to be significant for example for the stability/instability of employment, commuting to work, mode of work, and the staff's expectations.

68 We are talking about a different understanding of the mission of the institution, the level of involvement and creativity, and interpretation of the legislation.

69 As a part of the case in question, these potential immersed units of analysis could include the particular sections or teams (e.g. the educational section/team, the sentry guard), whose tasks are performed in the easily distinguishable, isolated places and spaces of the guarded centre for foreigners.

internal nature, is to contribute to increasing the research reliability, cover the issues related to both research procedures and research techniques, include a description of the potential evaluation, and provide guidelines for the final report, and general characteristics of the study. In our case, the role of such a protocol was played by the research outline.

The so-called local reports were subsequent significant documents we drew up during our research. We began working on them directly following the completion of our study visit (the research proper) in each centre. A template of the report was prepared as a result of collective team work before the commencement of the fieldwork. Writing reports was connected with several tasks. The inventory-related works, ordering, coding and digitising of the source resources, was the first one. Task two was related to the need to record all possible conditions connected with the execution of the study, which could affect the quality (reliability) of the acquired data, sensitisation of the researchers and their reflectiveness. Thirdly, the content of the reports was to include descriptions and preliminary microanalyses facilitating future comparisons and analyses of detention as a system. A template of a local report is presented below.

Local report – template

Introductory remarks:

1. The local report shall not cover elements that are common to the entire system of detention – elements of the so-called organisational macrostrategy (external legal framework, mission, goals and plans of the authority managing the detention system).
2. The local report is an internal document of the project team – it cannot be made available to third parties due to the confidentiality of the data it contains.
3. In consistence with project arrangements, no local report can be used for the drawing up of any text devoted to a discussion of only the detention centre for foreigners it concerns, since this could violate the anonymity of information sources. The local report is a material on the basis of which diagnoses/analyses of the phenomenon of the detention in Poland *en bloc* will be drawn up.

I Introduction

1. Place and time of research, research team – authors of the project.
2. Research conditions:

(a) attitude of the authorities of the centre (both at the high and the middle level) to the fact of the performance of research and the very presence of researchers in the centre;
(b) attitude of the centre's staff to the fact of the performance of research and the very presence of researchers in the centre;
(c) the impact of the structure of the institution on the way in which the research is conducted (both limitations and positive elements);
(d) availability of research participants;
(e) reactions of foreigners to the presence of the researchers;
(f) the locus of the researchers and the locus of the research;
(g) organisation of research work (including arrangement activities and styles of work).

3. Source resources – lists of coded sources (existing sources).
4. Comments on the research tools (any drawbacks in the context of the research performance, modifications, proposed changes).
5. The source resources collected during research (lists of problem and supplementary interviews, lists of iconographic data, lists of report notes, incl. observation notes, etc.; lists of existing sources).

II Organisational microstrategy

Local goals and plans resulting from the profile of the facility and the style of management of the authorities, but also the possessed resources – goals of 'owners', goals of 'administrators', goals of 'staff' - reflection of the 'mission'.

III Organisational structure

Describe and analyse at three levels: from the perspective of the whole (including: the centre vs the unit), the individual parts of the whole, and the relations between these parts. In every single case we should examine relations of different types:

(a) define tasks of a given entity (such as a section) as a part of the centre;
(b) define hierarchy, i.e. authority and its scope of competence, the formal side of the relations of the superiors–subordinates, and staff–detainees;
(c) define the scope and forms of cooperation between parts of the structure, including the communication flow.

Therefore, attention should be focused on such features of the structure as specialisation/division of work, work standardisation (routine and repetitiveness), coordination of actions, centralisation of management combined with configuration of the structure.

IV Resources 1 (people)

- headcount (staff and detainees) with indication of places of work, positions, etc.
- the staff's careers and employment stability.

V Resources 2 (places and physical space)

- (physical space: the entire facility in the context of its surroundings; layout of the interiors with an indication of their functions; limitation of space/availability of space to the particular categories of its users).

VI Resources 3 (furnishings – results of inventory)
VII Resources 4 (safety measures)
VIII Resources 5 (finances of the institution and their distribution; goods and services for the detainees and their obligations in relation to the institution)
IX Interactions in the staff group

(a) interactions along the line: top authorities of the centre – middle level authorities;
(b) interactions along the line: top authorities – employees;
(c) interactions along the line: middle level authorities – employees;
(d) interactions in the space of a given section;
(e) intersectional interactions.

X Interactions between staff and detainees

(a) interactions along the line: top authorities of the centre – detainees;
(b) interactions along the line: middle level authorities – detainees;
(c) interactions along the line: employees of the particular sections – detainees.

XI Interactions in the group of detainees

Commentary regarding the block devoted to interactions (It. IX–XI):

- what needs to be taken into account as a part of descriptions and preliminary interpretations of interactions of all types is both the narratives of employees with the included rationalisations/valorisations and results of the researchers' observations – each time with a reference to sources; both these sources should be confronted with each other with a focus on diagnosing their consistencies/discrepancies (as well as grasping the stereotypes of viewpoints of the described relations);

- communication-related habitual practices should be exposed (daily 'rituals', etiquette, which may reflect professional, but also other interpersonal relations).

XII Use and perception of the physical space and its artefacts

(a) authorities;
(b) employees;
(c) detainees.

XIII Use and perception of space in the social aspect

(a) authorities;
(b) employees;
(c) detainees.

XIV Conclusions

Annexes:

- research tools,
- transcriptions of interviews,
- report notes,
- existing sources.

In practice, in the course of our project, it turned out that the drawing up of the above document in a complete version for each of the locations was very laborious, multi-stage, and related to activities distributed/planned for, on average, six months. In connection with the above, the emphasis of these works was placed on strictly descriptive content and inventory-related activities, with analytical measures shifting to the far background.

2.4. Research methods

2.4.1. Source databases

The project materials will be presented using a traditional division into the existing and first-hand sources. The existing sources can be divided into 14 categories.

Category 1 – legislation. This type of sources is extremely significant as it constitutes a specific framework of reference to the macrostrategies of the detention system (the mission of the organisational culture and tools for its execution), but also local microstrategies (the interpretation of the law - its execution in practice).

Even before the commencement of our work on the project, we had an extensive and ordered database of all the legislation governing the broadly understood status of foreigners in Poland, as well as the functioning of subjects responsible for the so-called migration management.[70] It comprises Polish, international,[71] and EU legislation. Legally non-binding acts are also of significance here. In the case of Polish legislation, along with statutory regulations, we also decided to collect all the implementing acts to the particular acts. The set under description contains both the text of legislative acts, and their complete collective lists divided into the following categories:

- international legislative acts concerning foreigners;
- European Union legislative acts concerning foreigners;
- Polish legislation: legislative acts concerning national and ethnic minorities;
- Polish legislation: legislative acts concerning foreigners based on legal acts concerning everyone;
- Polish legislation: list of legislative acts concerning foreigners and relevant implementing acts;
- documents without binding legal force, but significant in migration policy. Since the database in question was updated as at 20 May 2016, we took efforts to complement it, already at the stage of project-related works, with the legislation which appeared in the subsequent three years (21.05.2016–20.05.2019). In the course of these endeavours, it turned out that many detailed legal documents related to regulations in the area of the detention of foreigners in Poland were not taken into account in the previous searches. This resulted from the fact that we were not aware of their existence because of their absence in register journals and on the websites of institutions governing the detention. We encountered them no sooner than whilst studying this type of documentation during our fieldwork in the BG centres.

70 Research project of the consortium UAM–MEDCORE – see footnote 30.

71 Relevant international agreements were complemented with government declarations on their ratification and binding force.

Doc. 1. Organisational and order-related rules and regulations governing the stay of foreigners in guarded centres and custody suites for foreigners (source: attachment to the regulation of the Minister of Internal Affairs of 24 April 2015 – Dz. U. of 30 April 2015)

Attachment to the regulation of the minister of internal affairs of 24 April 2015 on guarded centres and custody suites for foreigners (*Dz. U.* of 30 April 2015)

Organisational and order-related rules and regulations governing the stay of foreigners in guarded centres and custody suites for foreigners

Art. 1. Rooms for foreigners, residential cells and other spaces, in which foreigners stay, shall be controlled on an ad hoc basis by the manager of the guarded centre for foreigners, hereinafter referred to as the 'guarded centre', an officer responsible for the functioning of the custody suite for foreigners, hereinafter referred to as the 'custody suite' or other persons designated by them.

Art. 2. The Manager of the guarded centre or an officer responsible for the functioning of the custody suite may organise meetings with foreigners, in particular related to the conditions of their stay in the centre or custody suite.

Art. 3. For reasons of security and order, the headcount of foreigners staying in the guarded centre shall be checked.

Art. 4.

1. Foreigners brought to the guarded centre or custody suite shall be admitted at all hours. From 16:00 to 8:00 the foreigners brought to the centre shall be admitted after previous relevant notification of the manager of the guarded centre or an officer responsible for the functioning of the custody suite.
2. Foreigners shall be admitted to the guarded centre or custody suite on the basis of an order of admission and a decision on the placement of the foreigner in the guarded centre or an order to remand the foreigner in custody, issued by the district court.
3. The officer admitting the foreigner to the guarded centre or custody suite shall check their identity and provide him/her with information in writing, in a language understandable to him/her, on his/her rights and duties, regulations governing the stay in the guarded centre or custody suite and the fact that the guarded centre or custody suite is equipped with devices for the observation and recording of visual imaging, operating round the clock, if such a system has been installed.

Art. 5.

1. The foreigner shall be provided with bed linen and personal care products.
2. The foreigner shall be provided with clothes, underwear and shoes if their own clothing is unfit for use or inappropriate for the particular season or for reasons of security or health considerations.
3. The foreigner shall confirm the reception of the objects referred to in Items 1 and 2 with their legible signature in the card of objects issued to the foreigner.
4. In the case of the foreigner's refusal to place his/her signature or impossibility to do so, the officer shall, in the presence of another officer, make a note in the card referred to in It. 3, specifying reasons behind the absence of the foreigner's signature, place his/her own legitimate signature under the note

and indicate the presence of another officer during this activity, as confirmed by that officer's legitimate signature.

Art. 6.

1. The objects placed in deposit shall be specified on the deposit slip together with their specific features.
2. Valuables shall be understood in particular as:
   1. cash;
   2. bank payment cards, savings books, premium tokens, certificates of deposit, capital certificates, bills of exchange, cheques, letters of guarantee, shares, bonds, equities and other securities issued by national and international banks;
   3. jewellery, in particular rings, including wedding rings, neck chains, brooches, bracelets, earrings;
   4. electronic devices;
3. Objects which may pose a danger to the order or security in the guarded centre or custody suite include in particular:
   1. objects with sharp edges or ends (such as razors, razor blades, metal cutting tools);
   2. substances which may pose a threat to human life or health;
   3. alcohol;
   4. matches and lighters;
   5. objects the dimensions or amount of which would disturb the prescribed order or safety of the stay in the guarded centre and custody suite.

Art. 7.

1. The foreigner shall confirm the placement of the objects in deposit with his/her legible signature on the card of the settlement of deposit.
2. In the case of the foreigner's refusal to place his/her signature or impossibility to do so, the officer shall, in the presence of another officer, make a note on the deposit slip, specifying reasons behind the absence of the foreigner's signature, place his/her own legitimate signature under the note and indicate the presence of another officer during this activity, as confirmed by that officer's legitimate signature.
3. Responsibility for non-deposited objects shall lie with the foreigner.

Art. 8.

1. Cash placed by the foreigner in the deposit shall be recorded on the card of settlement of the foreigner's cash.
2. In the case of the foreigner's refusal to confirm the presented balance of their cash, the officer shall draw up a relevant note to be presented to the manager of the guarded centre or the officer responsible for the functioning of the custody suite.
3. If the foreigner reports inconsistency of the presented balance referred to in It. 2, the manager of the guarded centre or the officer responsible for the functioning of the custody suite shall determine the reason behind the inconsistency and inform the foreigner about the result of the determination.

Art. 9. If the foreigner wishes to use any objects placed in the deposit, their issue and admission shall be each time recorded on the card of the settlement of deposited objects.

Art. 10. The foreigner shall confirm that he/she has been issued objects from the deposit with his/her own signature.

Art. 11.

1. The following shall be taken into account when placing the foreigner in a room for foreigners or in a residential cell:
   1. the area of the room for foreigners or the residential cell cannot be smaller than:
      (a) 3 m2 – per man,
      (b) 4 m2 – per woman or a minor;
   2. the need to secure order and safety in the guarded centre or custody suite;
   3. medical, psychological and rehabilitation-related recommendations;
   4. the foreigner's age;
   5. the need to maintain family bonds;
   6. cultural and religious factors as well as the need to create a friendly atmosphere among the foreigners;
   7. the necessity to prevent aggression, self-aggression and crime during the foreigner's stay in the guarded centre or custody suite.
2. In cases justified by security or order maintenance reasons, the manager of the guarded centre or the officer responsible for the functioning of the custody suite may at any time relocate the foreigner to another room or residential cell.

Art. 12.

1. When determining the order of the day in the guarded centre or the custody suite, the manager of the guarded centre or the officer responsible for the functioning of the custody suite shall take into consideration the necessity to maintain safety, discipline and order as well as to provide the appropriate living, sanitary and health conditions.
2. The order of the day shall in particular specify:
   1. mealtimes;
   2. times and manner of the checking of the headcount of foreigners staying on the premises of the guarded centre;
   3. times for organised cultural, educational and sports activities;
   4. times of admissions of the foreigners to the medical staff;
   5. times and place of walks in the custody suite;
   6. days, times and place of admission of the foreigners by the manager of the guarded centre or the officer responsible for the functioning of the custody;
   7. days, times and ways of submission of applications, complaints and requests;
   8. days, times, place and order of visits;
   9. days, times and place of activities and meetings of a religious nature;
   10. frequency and days of purchases of foodstuffs, tobacco products and other objects allowed to be consumed and used in the guarded centre or custody suite;
   11. way of collecting and handing-in of parcels;

12. place of direct contact with Polish state authorities, diplomatic representations or consular post of another country, as well as non-governmental organisations or international organisations dealing with the provision of assistance, including legal assistance, to foreigners.

3. The text of the order of the day shall be placed in a visible place on all residential floors of the guarded centre and custody suite in the Polish, English and Russian languages. The text of the order of the day may also be translated into another language understandable to the foreigners who stay on the premises.
4. The manager of the guarded centre or the officer responsible for the functioning of the custody suite shall designate a space for smoking tobacco products, which shall be equipped with a lighter or matches.

Art. 13. The manager of the guarded centre or the officer responsible for the functioning of the custody suite may organise cultural, educational or sports activities in the guarded centre or custody suite with institutions, organisations, associations and other entities or individuals.

Art. 14.

1. Foreigners shall be issued their official or registered correspondence after entering date and confirmation of receipt in the register kept in the guarded centre or custody suite with a legible signature containing first name and surname and recording the fact in the register.
2. In the case of a refusal to confirm, a relevant note shall be made on the official letter or on the confirmation of receipt.

Art. 15. In the case of the foreigner's refusal to collect non-official correspondence, it shall be sent back to the sender.

Art. 16.

1. Envelopes with official correspondence sent by the foreigner shall be marked with the date and address of the guarded centre or custody suite and expedited without delay.
2. The foreigner shall be provided with a confirmation in writing of his/her official correspondence having been sent.

Art. 17. Foreigners' applications, complaints and requests shall be received by the manager of the guarded centre or the officer responsible for the functioning of the custody and other persons authorised by them also during direct contact with the foreigners.

Art. 18. The cost of the dispatch of correspondence, with the exception of official correspondence, shall be born by the foreigner, and if he/she does not have funds for the purpose, the correspondence shall be sent at the cost of the entity responsible for the functioning of the guarded centre or custody suite.

Art. 19. Parcels delivered to the foreigners to the guarded centre or custody suite shall be controlled – also with the help of the appropriate technical means and devices.

Art. 20. Objects delivered in parcels, which for reasons of safety and order must not be kept in the guarded centre or custody suite, shall be returned to the sender or placed in the foreigner's deposit.

Art. 21.

1. Visits shall not last longer than 90 minutes.

2. In justified cases, in particular ones resulting from psychological recommendations, the manager of the guarded centre or the officer responsible for the functioning of the custody suite may allow the visit to be prolonged or grant the foreigner more than one visit on the same day.
3. Apart from the foreigner, the maximum of two adult individuals may participate in visits. The number of minors having the required permission to participate in a visit shall not be limited; minors under the age of 15 may only participate in visits under the care of adult individuals having a permission to participate in a visit.

Art. 22. If it is discovered during a visit that the foreigner or a visitor display inappropriate behaviour threatening the safety or internal order of the guarded centre or custody suite, the visit may be discontinued.

Art. 23. The manager of the guarded centre or the officer responsible for the functioning of the custody suite may derogate from the manner of the organisation of visits in the scope allowing the foreigner to maintain and consolidate emotional bonds with their family and other close individuals as well as provide permanent care to their children.

Art. 24. Foreigners shall have the right to have their hair cut at least once every two months.

Art. 25. Foreigners shall undergo medical check-ups at least once every three months, directly before being released, and, as much as possible, when it is necessary to transport them.

Art. 26.

1. Medicines shall be issued to foreigners by the medical staff.
2. In exceptional situations, in the absence of medical staff, medicines prescribed by the doctor or prepared by the medical staff may be issued by the provost.

Art. 27. If further stay of the foreigner in the guarded centre or custody suite may pose a threat to their health or life, the foreigner shall be referred to a hospital or a medical facility providing inpatient, 24-hour medical services, in consultation with the doctor, by the manager of the guarded centre or the officer responsible for the functioning of the custody suite.

Art. 28. The treatment of the foreigner at their own cost, by the doctor selected by them, shall require a permission of the manager of the guarded centre or the officer responsible for the functioning of the custody suite.

Art. 29. In the case of foreigners with special needs, the manager of the guarded centre or the officer responsible for the functioning of the custody suite may, at the request of or having consulted the doctor, determine a different manner of handling the provision of the appropriate conditions of stay to the foreigners.

Category 2 - documents concerning the space of the GCF (see Fig. 4-6): architectural plans and other iconographic sources made available by the GCFs, including videos and photographs as well as the already implemented, currently conducted and planned modernisation projects in this scope (including budget-related data - sources and outlays).

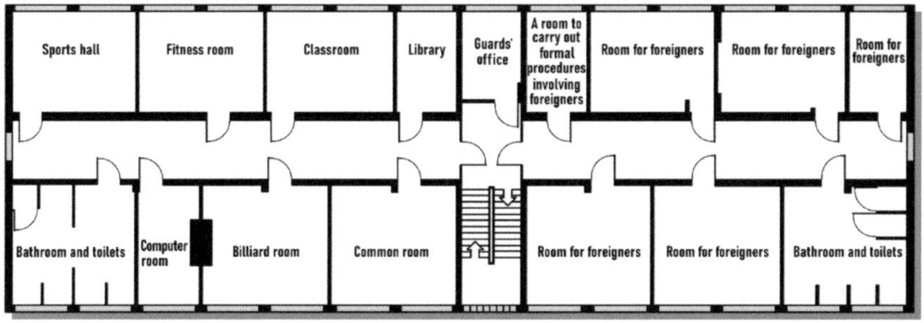

Fig. 4. Sample internal layout of the guarded centre for foreigners – level 1 (own elaboration on the basis of materials made available by the Border Guard)

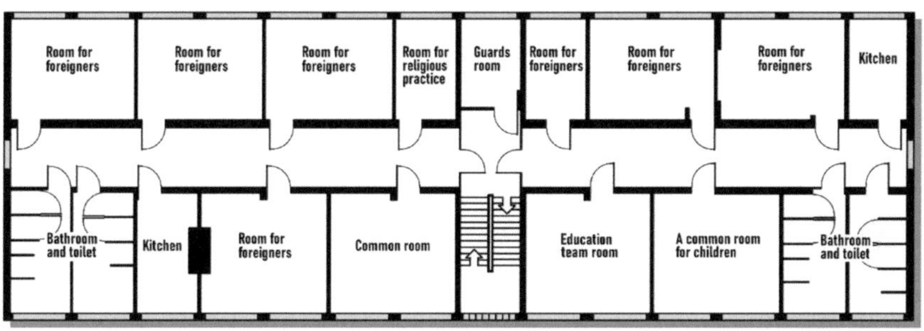

Fig. 5. Sample internal layout of the guarded centre for foreigners – level 3 (own elaboration on the basis of materials made available by the Border Guard)

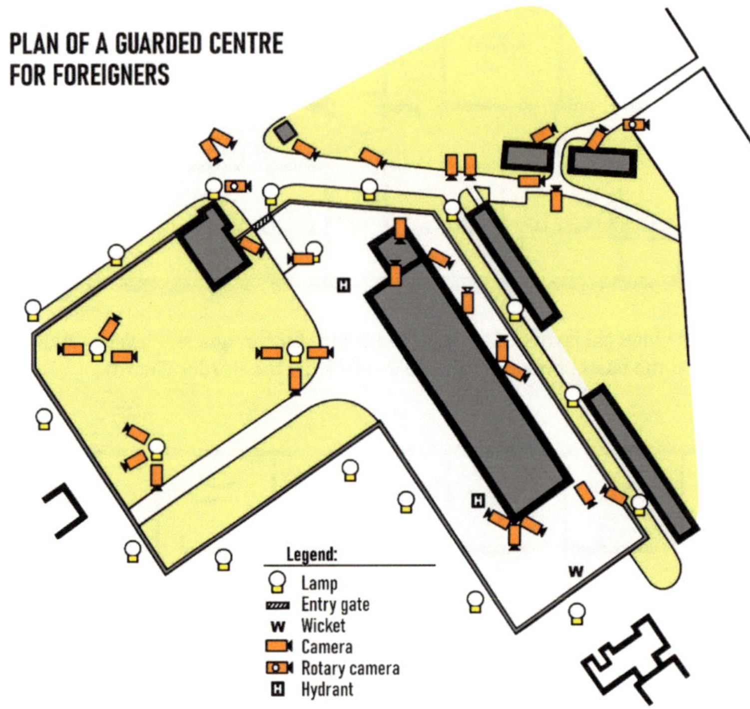

Fig. 6. Sample plan of external space of the guarded centre (own elaboration on the basis of materials made available by the Border Guard)

C a t e g o r y 3 – documents concerning the organisation of the use of spaces and places (such as rules and regulations of the GCF, orders of the day, rules and regulations concerning the use of the particular spaces and places).

Doc. 2. Order of the day in the guarded centre (source: materials made available by the Border Guard)

[a rectangular stamp with the following content:] Head of the [illegible] Department [illegible] Approved 14 Feb. 2019
[an illegible signature]

Order of the day

I. Mealtimes

1. Weekdays
   breakfast: **8:30 a.m. – 9:30 a.m.**

lunch: **12:30 p.m. – 1:30 p.m.**
supper: **5:00 p.m. – 6:00 p.m.**

2. Sundays and holidays:

breakfast: **8:30 a.m. – 9:30 a.m.**
lunch: **12:30 p.m. – 1:30 p.m.**
supper: **5:00 p.m. – 6:00 p.m.**

II. Headcounts – times and manner
The headcount of the detainees is checked in the mornings and in the evenings when the detainees stay in their rooms and when they head for meals.

III. Times for organised cultural, educational and sports activities

1. Cultural and educational activities are organised by officers and civil employees of the Educational Section.
2. Detailed dates and types of the activities are announced to the detainees on a weekly basis. When determining the dates and types of these activities, the detainees' suggestions and requests are taken into account.

IV. Organisation of own activities by the detainees

1. During their own activities, the detainees may use the common room, the computer room, the library, the recreational sports yard and the games field.
2. The library is open Monday-Saturday during the times of work of the Educational Section, i.e. from **08.00 a.m. until 8:00 p.m.** (books can be borrowed for up to 14 days).
3. The detainees may use the common room and watch TV at all times provided they do not disturb the internal order.
4. Computer rooms can be used from **7:15 a.m. until 10:00 p.m.**, in consistence with the schedule determined by the manager of the guarded centre.

V. Walks in the custody suite*
Individuals admitted to the custody suite may have a maximum 2-hour walk from **2:00 p.m. until 4 p.m.**, unless something else is recommended by the doctor.

VI. Principles of admitting foreigners by the manager of the guarded centre

I. The manager of the guarded centre or a person authorised by him/her admits detainees on **Tuesdays and Fridays** between **1:00 p.m. and 2:00 p.m.**, and in emergencies on an *ad hoc* basis, reporting the fact beforehand to the officers on duty.
2. Meetings are arranged in room no. **115**.

* applies to the custody suites for foreigners in the Guarded Centres for Foreigners in Przemyśl and Białystok.

VII. Principles of the submission of applications, complaints and requests.

1. Detainees have the right to submit applications, complaints and requests at all times, through boxes for correspondence.

2. Boxes for correspondence are opened at least twice a day from Monday to Saturday between **8:00 a.m. and 7:00 p.m.**
3. Applications, complaints and requests may also be submitted during direct meetings with the management of the guarded centre.

VIII. Principles of visits

1. Visits take place in the visiting room on a daily basis between **9:30 a.m. and 12.15 p.m.** and between **1:30 a.m. and 4:45 p.m.** and last no longer than 90 minutes.
2. In justified cases, the manager of the guarded centre or the designated officer may allow the visit to be prolonged or grant the detainee a permission for more than one visit on the same day.
3. The maximum of two adults may participate in visits. The number of minors is not limited – however, individuals of less than 15 years of age may participate only under the care of adults having the permission to participate.
4. Visits take place under the supervision of an officer on duty using TV monitoring, without voice recording.
5. In justified cases, the officer may be present in the room in which the visit takes place.
6. The individuals who obtained a permission to participate in a visit and their luggage are subject to control in terms of the presence of dangerous objects and objects which are not allowed in the centre.
7. The visit may be discontinued in the case of inappropriate behaviour of the detainee or any of the guests posing a threat to the security or internal order of the centre.
8. Foodstuffs must not be provided to the detainees during visits.
9. The manager of the guarded centre may make exceptions to the organisation of visits in the scope allowing the detainee to maintain and consolidate their bonds with their family or close individuals and perform permanent care over their child.

IX. Principles of religious activities and meetings

1. Detainees may practice their religion and use religious services in the room for religious practices at any time provided they do not disturb the internal order of the guarded centre.
2. Detainees may also participate in religious meetings – their dates are agreed with the administration of the centre.

X. Principles of doing shopping

1. Shopping is done at least twice a week: on Tuesdays – for the first floor, and on Thursdays – for the second floor and the custody suite.
2. Purchases cannot be paid for using payment cards or credit cards.
3. Detainees report their shopping lists to an officer on duty or the designated officer by 12:30 on the day preceding the shopping day.

4. In justified cases, the manager of the guarded centre may permit shopping on another date.
5. The purchases and their confirmations are issued if possible on the shopping day.

XI. Issuing and accepting parcels

1. Parcels must not contain any foodstuffs or objects that are not allowed in the centre for reasons of security and order.
2. Parcels are issued, once their content has been checked in the presence of the detainee.
3. Parcels issued to the detainees are subject to control also with the help of the appropriate technical means and devices.
4. Foodstuffs contained in parcels are returned to the sender at his/her cost or destroyed.
5. Objects which are not allowed in the centre for reasons of security and order are sent back to the sender at the cost of the detainee or are transferred to the deposit.

XII. Principles ruling correspondence

1. Correspondence (official, private or internal correspondence addressed to the administration of the centre) is dispatched/collected with the help of correspondence boxes.
2. Correspondence is collected from correspondence boxes by employees of the Educational Section at least twice a day between 8:00 a.m. and 7:00 p.m.
3. Official correspondence with confirmation of receipt is issued after the detainee confirms the receipt with his/her own signature and date. If the detainee refuses to confirm the receipt of official correspondence, the fact is recorded on a/the return receipt.
4. Official correspondence without confirmation of receipt is issued after the detainee confirms the receipt with his/her own signature.
5. If a detainee refuses to collect any correspondence other than official one, it is sent back to the sender.
6. Envelopes with official correspondence are without delay marked with the date of receipt and address of the guarded centre.
7. Detainees are provided with a written confirmation of receipt of the official correspondence sent by them.

XIII. Principles of the organisation of meetings with institutions and external organisations

1. Meetings with representatives of Polish state authorities, diplomatic missions, consular offices, non-governmental and international organisations dealing with the provision of assistance, in particular legal ones, take place on working days between **7:45 a.m. and 3:45 p.m.** or at other times agreed with the manager of the guarded centre.

2. The meetings take place in the visiting room or in any other room indicated by the manager of the centre, in the conditions guaranteeing order and security.

XIV. Principles of the use of medical/psychological care

1. Medical consultations are provided Mondays-Fridays, 10:00 a.m.-12:00 p.m.(midday), in compliance with a predetermined schedule.
2. The ambulance service is called for life-threatening emergencies.
3. If a further stay of the detainee in the centre might pose a threat to his/her health or life, the manager of the guarded centre takes a decision on referring him/her to hospital in consultation with a doctor.
4. Consultations with specialists and diagnostic examinations are carried out outside the centre in compliance with a predetermined schedule.

$. The medical staff is on duty Mondays-Sundays, 7:30 a.m. – 9:30 p.m.

6. Medicines are issued solely by the medical staff.
7. Consultations with a psychologist take place as necessary, after a request, in compliance with a predetermined schedule.
8. Consultations with addiction specialists take place on the basis of the requests, in compliance with a predetermined schedule.

The order approved on 18.10.2017 loses its effect.
Issued in one copy.
AT: tel. 6643039
Date: 14.02.2019

Doc. 3. Order of the day in the guarded centre – pictographic version (source: materials made available by the Border Guard)

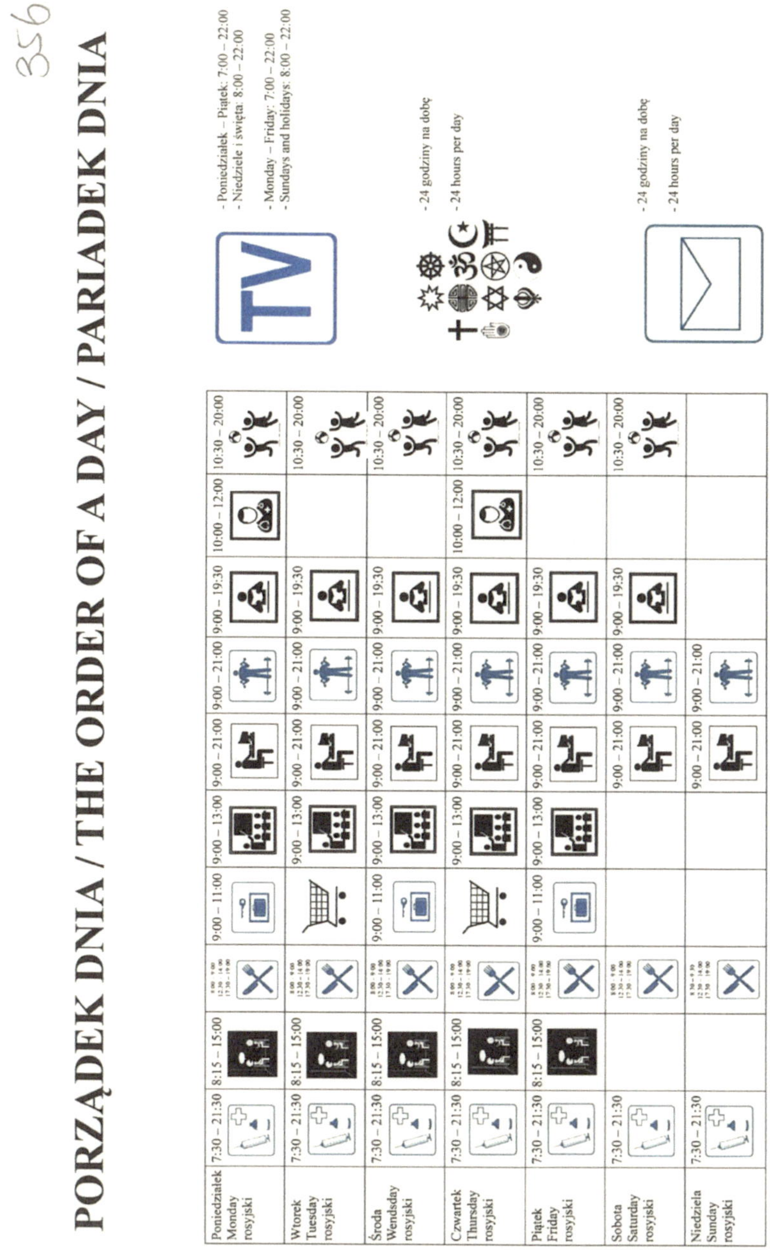

356

PORZĄDEK DNIA / THE ORDER OF A DAY / PARIADEK DNIA

- Poniedziałek – Piątek: 7:00 – 22:00
- Niedziele i święta: 8:00 – 22:00
- Monday – Friday: 7:00 – 22:00
- Sundays and holidays: 8:00 – 22:00

- 24 godziny na dobę
- 24 hours per day

- 24 godziny na dobę
- 24 hours per day

Poniedziałek Monday rosyjski	7:30 – 21:30	8:15 – 15:00	8:00 – 9:00 12:30 – 14:00 17:30 – 19:00	9:00 – 11:00	9:00 – 13:00	9:00 – 21:00	9:00 – 21:00	9:00 – 19:30	10:00 – 12:00	10:30 – 20:00
Wtorek Tuesday rosyjski	7:30 – 21:30	8:15 – 15:00	8:00 – 9:00 12:30 – 14:00 17:30 – 19:00		9:00 – 13:00	9:00 – 21:00	9:00 – 21:00	9:00 – 19:30		10:30 – 20:00
Środa Wendsday rosyjski	7:30 – 21:30	8:15 – 15:00	8:00 – 9:00 12:30 – 14:00 17:30 – 19:00	9:00 – 11:00	9:00 – 13:00	9:00 – 21:00	9:00 – 21:00	9:00 – 19:30		10:30 – 20:00
Czwartek Thursday rosyjski	7:30 – 21:30	8:15 – 15:00	8:00 – 9:00 12:30 – 14:00 17:30 – 19:00		9:00 – 13:00	9:00 – 21:00	9:00 – 21:00	9:00 – 19:30	10:00 – 12:00	10:30 – 20:00
Piątek Friday rosyjski	7:30 – 21:30	8:15 – 15:00	8:00 – 9:00 12:30 – 14:00 17:30 – 19:00	9:00 – 11:00	9:00 – 13:00	9:00 – 21:00	9:00 – 21:00	9:00 – 19:30		10:30 – 20:00
Sobota Saturday rosyjski	7:30 – 21:30		8:00 – 9:00 12:30 – 14:00 17:30 – 19:00			9:00 – 21:00	9:00 – 21:00	9:00 – 19:30		10:30 – 20:00
Niedziela Sunday rosyjski	7:30 – 21:30		8:30 – 9:30 12:30 – 14:00 17:30 – 19:00			9:00 – 21:00	9:00 – 21:00			

Doc. 4. Rules and regulations concerning the use of the computer room (source: materials made available by the Border Guard)

Rules and regulations concerning
The use of the computer room

1. The computer room can be used by all adult detainees of the GCF from 9:00 a.m. until 9:00 p.m.
2. The use of the computer room is free of charge.
3. Users of the computer room are obliged to remain quiet.
4. Only one person can stay by one computer station.
5. Only preinstalled programmes can be used.
6. It is prohibited to install any programmes and introduce changes to the already existing ones.
7. A user of the computer station may work for the maximum of 60 minutes, unless there are no people waiting for a free computer.
8. Only adults may use the internet.
9. Children may use the computer room only when supervised by adults.

Computer users are obliged to:

1. comply with all guidelines of the officers on duty and civil employees of the GCF;
2. report all incorrect operation of the computer station and mechanical damage;
3. familiarise themselves with the rules and regulations concerning the computer room.

Computer users must not:

1. damage computer and multimedia equipment or expose it to danger;
2. use any private data carriers (e.g. CD, DVD, PENDRIVE, etc.);
3. use the software or the hardware for commercial purposes;
4. install any programmes without the consent of the administrators;
5. start any software which may disturb the stability of the system's work;
6. introduce any changes to the configuration or system files;
7. make other users' work difficult or misinform them;
8. disturb others with noisy behaviour;
9. drink, eat or smoke, which also applies to e-cigarettes.

If the person supervising the computer room discovers an infringement of the principles in force, they are entitled to stop the user's work without delay and make it impossible for him/her to use the computer equipment any further. Financial responsibility for mechanical damage to the computer equipment and software shall be borne by the user. If such user is minor, the responsibility shall be borne by his/her parents or guardian.

Doc. 5. Rules and regulations concerning the use of the fitness room (source: materials made available by the Border Guard)

Rules and regulations concerning the use of the fitness room

1. Individuals using the fitness room are obliged to comply with its rules and regulations.
2. The fitness room can be used by adults and people of at least 15 years of age under the care of their parent. Unaccompanied minors can use the fitness room only with the consent of the officer on duty.
3. Only one person may use each device.
4. The fitness room can be used from **9:00 a.m. until 9:00 p.m.**
5. Shoes must be changed in the fitness room.
6. Before starting to exercise, carry out a warm-up.
7. All devices in the fitness room and exercising equipment can only be used in consistence with their intended purpose.
8. Officers on duty must be immediately informed about all discovered irregularities.
9. Individuals destroying equipment or devices in the fitness room shall bear material responsibility for the caused losses to the amount of 100 % of the value of the loss.
10. Users of the fitness room are obliged to leave it in good order after completing their exercises.
11. Exercising without a top is prohibited.
12. Sudden dropping of the weight plates onto the stack of other plates is prohibited.
13. Vulgar vocabulary and noisy behaviour are prohibited.
14. Food and drinks must not be brought into or consumed in the fitness room (does not apply to bottled water).
15. Exercising using damaged or out-of-service devices is prohibited.
16. The users use the fitness room at their own responsibility.
17. After finishing exercises, mobile devices should be put back into their place.
18. Individuals not complying with the rules and regulations of the fitness room shall be excluded from participation in exercising in the fitness room.

C a t e g o r y 4 – documents concerning the organisational structure of the BG (see Fig. 7), including full-time/part-time jobs and positions with their assignment to the particular sections and teams, vacancies, and division into BG officers and civil employees.

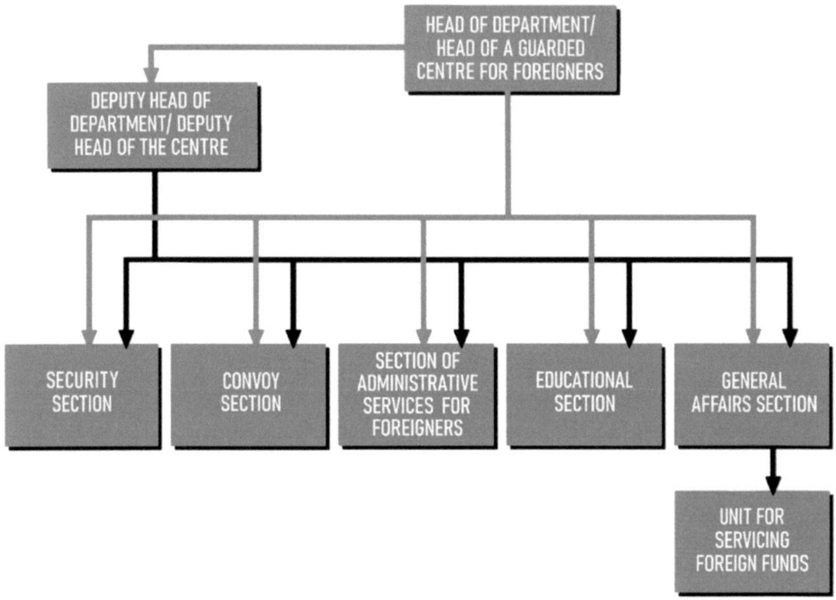

Fig. 7. Sample organisational structure of the guarded centre (own elaboration on the basis of materials made available by the Border Guard)

Category 5 – documents concerning the detailed scope of duties and rights ascribed to the positions/functions of BG officers/civil employees.

Doc. 6. Detailed scope of duties and rights of the security section employees in the guarded centre (materials made available by the Border Guard)

Copy No. 3

Detailed scope of duties and rights of the assistant of the security section of the Guarded Centre for Foreigners in Kętrzyn (rank, full name)

1. Assistant of the Security Section of the Guarded Centre for Foreigners in Kętrzyn reports directly to the Manager of the Security Section of the Guarded Centre for Foreigners in Kętrzyn. While being on duty, he/she reports to the Shift Manager of the Security Section of the Guarded Centre for Foreigners in Kętrzyn and performs his/her orders.
2. The detailed scope of the duties of the Assistant of the Security Section includes:
   1. the knowledge and application in practice of the legal acts in force and internal regulations of the commanding officer of the unit, constituting the basis for the performance of professional tasks related to the position in question;

2. doing service in consistence with the plan of duties and the tasks related to the position in question, in the place determined by the Shift Manager of the Guarded Centre for Foreigners;
3. familiarity with the rights and duties of the sentry guard, officer of the interventions team, provost and shift manager assistant;
4. execution the professional duties of the sentry guard and officer of the interventions team, and, if necessary, execution in compliance with the relevant regulations, of the duties of the Provost and Shift Manager Assistant;
5. knowledge of the current headcount of the foreigners detained in the centre;
6. protection of documents and messages covered by professional secrecy;
7. serving duty in the Guarded Centres for Foreigners in such a way as to prevent escapes of foreigners without endangering the health and life of foreigners and the officers on duty and all other extraordinary events and situations:
8. reporting for duties early enough to start executing tasks at the time specified in the CBD SG SWK [BG database – management support system];
9. serving duty in external medical facilities in such a way as to prevent escapes of foreigners without endangering the health and life of foreigners and the officers on duty;
10. serving home duties in compliance with the regulations;
11. participating in activities as a part of the NPO W-MOSG [supernumerary backup subunit of the Warmińsko-Mazurski Border Guard Regional Unit] in the case of being appointed as a member of the subunit by the superior;
12. collecting and using internal email in compliance with the regulations;
13. using the EZD online system of documentation management in compliance with the regulations;
14. documenting the course of one's duty at the CBD SG SWK database reliably, diligently and in compliance with the regulations;
15. before finishing each duty, checking via the CBD SG SWK database the Officers' Timetable for the date and time of the commencement of the subsequent duty;
16. controlling and observing the detained foreigners, also with the help of devices for the observation and recording of images, with a view to preventing prohibited contact and behaviours infringing the order and security of the guarded centre for foreigners, and constantly supervising foreigners detained in the guarded centre, and in particular:
    (a) undertaking measures in consistence with the procedure for extraordinary situations;
    (b) controlling the detained foreigners and places used by them in compliance with the regulations in force;
    (c) respecting the rule of law in contact with the detained foreigners;
    (d) enforcing the performance of the foreigners' duties in compliance with relevant regulations;
17. drawing up memos and official notes and other documents in connection with the events taking place while on duty;

18. executing projects preventing any loss and damage on behalf of the Warmińsko-Mazurski Border Guard Regional Unit, and documenting them should they take place;
19. checking the headcount of the detained foreigners when taking over one's duty, upon the commencement of the night quiet hours and as necessary;
20. informing the detained foreigners about the principles of behaviour and movement in the area of the guarded centre;
21. controlling the condition of the technical security arrangements of the Guarded Centre for Foreigners:
22. supervising the protection of the official spaces, in the scope covered by the duty, to prevent unauthorised access (of foreigners);
23. identifying information on the detained foreigners and providing it to the superiors as well as findings concerning the moods and atmosphere among the detainees;
24. performing activities related to the admission/release of foreigners to/from the guarded centre for foreigners and escorting foreigners and detained individuals:
25. complying with the regulations and principles of safety and hygiene of work, as well as fire protection;
26. reporting all events and circumstances affecting the functioning of the centre and the stay of the detainees to officers on duty of the guarded centre for foreigners;
27. duly performing measures related to the admission and release of foreigners to/from the guarded centre:
28. using direct coercion in compliance with the regulations;
29. participating in escorts and convoys;
30. keeping official documentation both on paper and in IT systems – reliably, in a timely manner and appropriately;
31. familiarising oneself with new legal acts, letters, guidelines and orders concerning the execution of professional tasks in the guarded centre;
32. preventing negative phenomena in the scope of the infringement of the law and principles of safety by individuals detained in the guarded centre;
33. securing the observation of the order of the day and rules and regulations in force by the foreigners detained in the guarded centre;
34. participating in local and central training organised for the officers of the guarded centre with a view to the effective execution of tasks;
35. complying with professional discipline and regulations concerning clothing;
36. whilst on duty, having the documents authorising to drive service vehicles;
37. complying with the regulations related to the protection of confidential information, and in particular to the production and circulation of documentation;
38. preventing negative phenomena in the area of the infringement of professional discipline of the officers of the section;
39. in the case of being appointed a guardian of an officer commencing his/her duty in a new position:
    (a) assisting the officer in his/her preparations for serving in a given professional position,

(b) familiarising the officer with the regulations concerning the manner of serving in a given professional position,
(c) performing other activities should they be necessary for the officer's due performance of the tasks entrusted to him/her;

40. applying and complying with work protection, health and safety and other regulations in the scope indispensable for the performance of the entrusted duties, including:
    (a) using personal protective equipment in compliance with its designation,
    (b) caring for the safe and healthy condition of the official space,
    (c) implementing the recommendations of the doctor covering officers with medical care;
41. performing activities other than the ones mentioned above if their performance is related to the occupied position or was ordered by the Manager of the Security Section of the Guarded Centre for Foreigners or his/her superiors.

3. The Assistant of the Security Section is authorised to:

1. process personal data processed in connection with the execution of professional tasks in compliance with the authorisations granted by the Local Administrator of the Security of Collections;
2. drive service/special vehicles on an ad hoc basis – provided he/she can produce the due certificate;
3. in justified cases check individuals entering the area of the centre and their luggage:
4. depending on the executed task, give relevant orders to the subordinate officers while being on duty.

……………………………………..
(rank, full name, position of the person determining the above)
……………………………………..
(rank, full name, position of the person familiarising themselves with the document)
……………………………………..
I have read the above and was provided copy no. 1
(date, rank, full name of the officer this document applies to)

<u>Drawn up in three copies:</u>
Copy no. 1 – the interested party
Copy no. 2 – the officer's personal file
Copy no. 3 – direct superior
Drawn up by:
Date:

C a t e g o r y 6 - general/detailed documents/instructions concerning the performance of official duties (such as instructions pertaining to serving duty in the GCF, descriptions of procedures applied in the case of parents abusing their children in the GCF, principles of the treatment of vulnerable foreigners, algorithms in cost procedures, etc.).

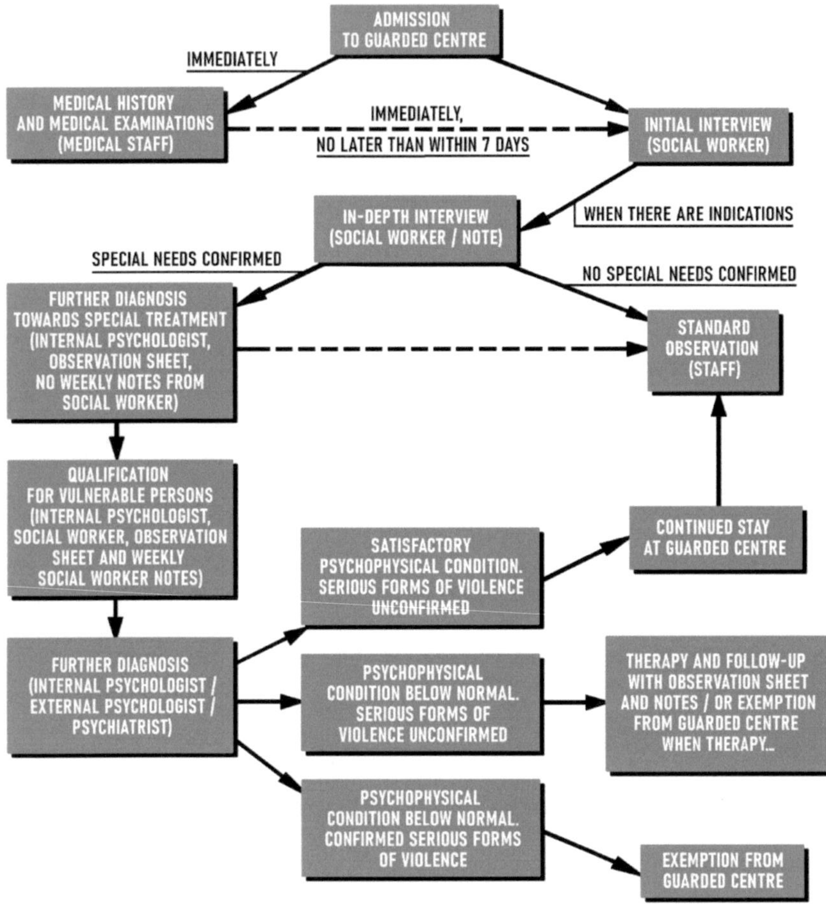

Fig. 8. The Border Guard's rules of conduct in relation to special needs/vulnerable foreigners (own elaboration on the basis of materials made available by the Border Guard)

Doc. 7. Guidelines concerning the provision of information by way of conversation with the foreigners (materials made available by the Border Guard)

Guidelines concerning the provision of information by way of conversation

As for discussing issues related to the foreigners' social needs and the rules in force in the Guarded Centre for Foreigners, I recommend that the following be discussed with the foreigners:

- their clothing-related needs
- rules applying to visits
- rules applying to the use of the internet
- rules applying to shopping
- mode of submission of applications, complaints and requests
- possibility to select one's diet
- possibility to be provided with legal assistance
- organisation of free time
- use of the local deposit
- possibility to use medical and psychological care
- way of sending and receiving parcels
- rules related to correspondence
- religious practices
- possibility to participate in cultural and educational activities
- rules of the use of the library.

Additionally, the newly admitted foreigner should be informed that he/she shall find useful information concerning the stay in the centre, contacts to diplomatic missions and non-governmental organisations, etc. displayed on information boards. I also order that the foreigner be reminded that upon admission, he/she is provided with *Information on the detainees' rights, duties and principles of stays in the guarded centre* in a language understandable to him/her, in a written form.

As for issues related to special needs, I order that the following issues/topics be discussed with the foreigner:

* the need to meet a psychologist;
* the conversation should be guided towards the identification of victims of violence, human trafficking and tortures;
* in the case of a language barrier, the possibility to appoint an interpreter not being an employee of an officer/civil employee of the Border Guard for psychological and psychiatric consultation;
* possible physical disabilities and mental deficits;
* possibility to participate in addiction treatment.

While discussing the particular needs of the foreigner, please be guided by special sensitivity taking into account the detainee's psychophysical state and cultural background.

Drawn up by:

[an illegible signature and a seal with the following contents:] MANAGER of the Educational Section of the Guarded Centre for Foreigners in Białystok, Podlaski Unit of the Border Guard

Category 7 – templates of documents used by the GCFs and sample filled-in documents (deposit slips, parcel provision protocols, notes from conversations with foreigners, shopping cards, catalogues and library cards, memos on the foreigner's aggressive behaviour, foreigner's shopping settlement card, foreigner's observation sheets, notes from in-depth interviews with the foreigner, applications for prolonging the foreigner's stay in the GCF or change of a preventive measure, decisions of authorities concerning applications for release, applications for visits or virtual contact, etc.).

Doc. 8. Application for a 'virtual visit' (materials made available by the Border Guard)

„ZATWIERDZAM"
„УТВЕРЖДАЮ" / „I APPROVE"

WYPEŁNIA OSOBA WNIOSKUJĄCA O WIDZENIE
ЗАПОЛНЯЕТ ЗАЯВИТЕЛЬ / TO FILL OUT WITH PERSON REQUESTING VISIT

WNIOSEK WYPEŁNIAMY PISMEM DRUKOWANYM
ЗАЯВЛЕНИЕ ЗАПОЛНЯЕМ ПЕЧАТНЫМ ПИСЬМОМ / REQUEST TO FILL OUT WITH BIG LETTERS

WNIOSEK
ЗАЯВЛЕНИЕ/ REQUEST

o zezwolenie na „widzenie wirtualne" za pomocą komunikatora Skype
на разрешение на „виртуальное свидание" с помощью коммуникатора Skype / for consent for a „virtual visit" by Skype instant messenger

w Strzeżonym Ośrodku dla Cudzoziemców w Kętrzynie
в Охраняемом центре для иностранцев в Кентшине / in a Guarded Centre for Foreigners in Kętrzyn

w dniu ……………………, **w godzinach: od** ……. **do** ……..
дня/in время с/between до/-

I. DANE DOTYCZĄCE „WIDZENIA WIRTUALNEGO":
ДАННЫЕ, КАСАЮЩИЕСЯ „ВИРТУАЛЬНОГО СВИДАНИЯ" / VIRTUAL VISIT" DATA

1) dane rozmówcy lub rozmówców:
персональные данные собеседника или собеседников / interlocutor's or interlocutors' data

imię i nazwisko……………………………………………………………………………
имя и фамилия / name and surname

obywatelstwo……………………………………………………………………………
гражданство / citizenship

imię i nazwisko ……………………………………………………………………………
имя и фамилия / name and surname

obywatelstwo ……………………………………………………………………………
гражданство / citizenship

Login rozmówcy do konta Skype: ………………………………………………
Логин для учетной записи Skype / Login to Skype account

2) dane osoby wnioskującej o „widzenie wirtualne":
данные заявителя на „виртуальное свидание" / person's requesting „virtual visit" data

imię i nazwisko ……………………………………………………………………
имя и фамилия / name and surname

obywatelstwo……………………………………………………………………
гражданство / citizenship

data urodzenia……………………………………………………………………
дата рождения / date of birth

Login i hasło do konta Skype:
Логин и пароль для учетной записи Skype / Login and password to Skype account

Login:…………………………………………………
Логин / Login

Hasło:…………………………………………………
Пароль / Password

UZASADNIENIE WNIOSKU
ОБОСНОВАНИЕ ЗАЯВЛЕНИЯ / JUSTIFICATION OF REQUEST

……………………………………………………………………………………………………

Doc. 9. Rules and regulations of the 'virtual visit' (materials made available by the Border Guard)

Approved

Rules and regulations of 'virtual visits' via a computer station with an installed skype app

1. 'Virtual visits' takes place in a designated room (the library – room no. 209) via a computer station with an installed SKYPE app and access to the internet using an internet camera, microphone, loudspeakers or headphones with a microphone.
2. 'Virtual visits' last up to 90 minutes.
3. 'Virtual visits' may take place 7 days a week 09:00 a.m. – 12:00, 2:00 p.m. – 5:00 p.m. and 7:00 p.m. – 9:00 p.m. (excluding mealtimes).
4. 'Virtual visits' are available to adults, families with children (children under the care of an adult) and minors above 15 years of age.
5. The detained foreigners may use 'virtual visits' once a day (24h) in the situation when the number of detainees in the GCF is increased.
6. The manager of the guarded centre may make exceptions to the mode of organisation and time of 'virtual visits'.
7. Individuals wishing to participate in a 'virtual visit' must meet the following conditions:
   (a) enter their name on the list of sequence, specifying the time of the commencement and completion of the 'virtual visit'; the list is made available by officers on duty;
   (b) a day prior to the 'virtual visit' – by 13.00 – the foreigner needs to fill in an application for a 'virtual visit' via Skype in the Guarded Centre for Foreigners in Kętrzyn, obligatorily providing their Skype account data: login and password, and submit it to the officer on duty, who shall forward it by 2:00 p.m. to the manager of the guarded centre or another person authorised by him/her;
   (c) having been granted permission, the foreigner may participate in the virtual visit in compliance with the submitted application;
8. The individual who was granted permission for a 'virtual visit' should report to the sentry guards of the family-women's ward a quarter of an hour beforehand to take their place in the queue and appear in the room designated for the 'virtual visit'.
9. Individuals participating in the 'virtual visit' make sure that they begin and end their 'virtual visit' at the time specified in the application.
10. Supervision over the organisation and execution of 'virtual visits' is performed by the sentry guard designated by the Shift Manager of the guarded centre.
11. After the completion of the virtual visit, the sentry guard checks the condition of the equipment and allows another person in. If damage or irregularity is discovered, he/she closes the room until the defect is repaired.

Doc. 10. Memo from a conversation conducted with the foreigner (materials made available by the Border Guard)

Lisówek, 29 January 2018

Memo

Concerns: a conversation with a foreigner

On 29 January, I held several conversations with a detainee, a citizen of Iran, …, concerning the information he sends to the email address of the facility and several assistance foundations regarding his personal and administrative situation as well as the living conditions in the Centre.

The detainee keeps describing his personal situation and underlines that he does not want to go back to Iran, where he is exposed to religious persecution and persecution due to his refusal to participate in research aimed at the extension of the chemical weaponry of the Iranian army. He also indicates that no one in the European Union appreciates his peace-promoting behaviours, for which he is supposedly detained in the guarded centre. Additionally, I asked the detainee about the alleged limitations towards the visit of an employee of the Helsinki Human Rights Foundation in the centre on the part of its authorities which he discussed in the information he sent us.

Once again, I explained the procedure and the premises the court was guided by when issuing its decision on admitting the foreigner to the Centre and I provided extensive answers to his questions. As far as the potential visit of an employee of the foundation was concerned, I explained that no application for visiting the detainee has been submitted so far and that hence his accusations addressed to the management of the Centre are groundless.

The detainee also said that he had not been eating for the last few days due to the deep stress he has been experiencing due to staying in the centre. It is not a form of a hunger protest, although he admitted that on the occasion he wants to turn attention to himself. I explained the health-related consequences of a refusal to eat on a longer-term basis. I also discovered when talking to security officers of the centre that the detainee sporadically appears for his meals, although he is rather often seen cooking and eating his own meals, outside the dining room. This information was confirmed by several other detainees.

I also informed the foreigner that it is his duty as a detainee to comply with the principles of stay and the order of the day, to which he stated that he is a researcher, someone more important than all other detainees and because of this these rules do not apply to him, and that he demands to be released immediately and talk to the commanding officer of the centre. Since the detainee wanted to talk to the commanding officer once again about his formal-legal situation related to his detention in the Centre, I reminded him that all doubts are explained on a continuous basis during the daily conversations with the return guardian, and that thus involving the commanding officer is not justified here. I also reminded him that he already had an opportunity to talk to the commanding officer and dispel his doubts.

During each conversation, the detainee was clearly nervous, he was shouting and experienced in turn euphoria and anger, and he did not allow any explanation. He was nervously waving his arms, causing a real danger of striking someone or something. When we finished talking, he did not want to leave the library, thus disturbing my work. The detainee was again instructed that his behaviour may be interpreted by the officers in the centre as aggressive and breaking the rules in force, resulting in the consequences provided in the rules and regulations of the centre, including placement in the isolation room. The detainee arrogantly answered that no on can do anything to him, since he is a researcher, and every attempt at using coercion in relation to him would be interpreted as persecution.

The memo was drawn up for further official use.

Drawn up in one copy. Drawn up by

29.01.2018

Doc. 11. Medical questionnaire as a part of the preliminary check-up of the foreigner admitted to the guarded centre (materials made available by the Border Guard)

Medical questionnaire as a part of the preliminary check-up of the foreigner admitted to the Guarded Centre for Foreigners

1	Communicable diseases in childhood:			
	(a) rubella	o yes	o no	o I do not remember
	(b) chickenpox	o yes	o no	o I do not remember
	(c) scarlet fever	o yes	o no	o I do not remember
	(d) whooping cough	o yes	o no	o I do not remember
	(e) mumps, measles	o yes	o no	o I do not remember
	(f) diphtheria, tetanus	o yes	o no	o I do not remember
2	Were you vaccinated in consistence with the calendar of vaccinations of your country of origin?	o yes	o no	o I do not know

III Personal interview

1	**What is your general health condition:**	o good	o rather good	o poor
2	**Any surgical operations?**	o yes (what kind?)	o no	o I do not remember
3	**Have you ever suffered from any of the following heart conditions:**			
	(a) congenital heart disease	o yes	o no	
	(b) heart attack	o yes	o no	
	(c) coronary heart diseases	o yes	o no	
	(d) hypertension	o yes	o no	
	(e) arrhythmia	o yes	o no	

4	**Have you ever suffered from any of the following respiratory diseases:**		
	(a) tuberculosis	o yes	o no
	(b) asthma	o yes	o no
	(c) pneumonia	o yes	o no
	(d) chronic bronchitis	o yes	o no
	(e) other respiratory diseases	o yes	o no
5	**Have you ever suffered from any of the following gastrointestinal diseases:**		
	(a) peptic ulcer disease	o yes	o no
	(b) liver diseases or pancreatic conditions	o yes	o no
	(c) gastrointestinal diseases	o yes	o no
6	**Have you ever suffered from any of the following urinary tract diseases:**		
	(a) nephritis	o yes	o no
	(b) urinary tract infection	o yes	o no
	(c) prostatic hyperplasia	o yes	o no
7	**Have you ever suffered from any of the following nervous system diseases:**		
	(a) epilepsy	o yes	o no
	(b) stroke	o yes	o no
	(c) vertigo	o yes	o no
8	**Have you ever suffered from any of the following bone disorders:**		
	(a) spinal pain	o yes	o no
	(b) arthritis	o yes	o no
	(c) fracture	o yes	o no
	d) head injury	o yes	o no
9	**Have you ever suffered from any of the following psychiatric diseases:**		
	(a) depression	o yes	o no
	(b) schizophrenia	o yes	o no
	(c) neurosis	o yes	o no
10	**Have you ever suffered from neoplasm?**	o yes	o no
11	**Have you been diagnosed with poor vision? Do you wear glasses?**	o yes o yes	o no o no
12	**Have you been diagnosed with poor hearing?**	o yes	o no
13	**Do you have any disability? If so, what kind?**	o yes ……………………	o no
14	**Do you smoke?**	o yes ……cigarettes per day	o no

15	**Do you have a history of alcohol abuse?**	o yes when last? ……………… ………………	o no
16	**Have you ever taken any drugs, including designer drugs?**	o yes (what sort?) ……………… ……………… when last? ……………… ………………	o no
17	**Do you take any medicines on a permanent basis?**	o yes (what sort?) ……………… ………………	o no
18	**Have you ever been diagnosed with**		
	(a) food allergy?	o yes (what to?) ……………… ………………	o no
	(b) airborne allergy?	o yes (what to?) ……………… ………………	o no
19	**Are you allergic to any medicines or substances?**	o yes (what sort?) ………………………	o no
20.	**Have you ever experienced:**		
	physical violence	o yes (what sort?) ……………	o no
	psychological violence	o yes (what sort?) …………….	o no
21.	**Have you ever experienced a trauma?**	o yes (what sort?)	o no

<u>*Statement*</u>

I hereby certify that the information I provided above is true and that I have not hidden any data concerning my health.

…………………………………………

(date and foreigner's signature)

…………………………..…………………………………………………………..

(stamp and signature of the person conducting the medical history interview)

Category 8 – documents related to the work of the particular teams or sections of the GCFs (e.g. action programmes and reports on their execution, schedules of activities and events for foreigners, chronicles of events).

Doc. 12. Sample schedule of cultural projects organised in the guarded centre for foreigners in the first six months of 2019 (source: materials made available by the Border Guard)

No.	Date	Project	Execution
January 2019			
1	11	Carnival party	Preparation of carnival costumes and a party with music
2	18	Winnie-the-Pooh's Day	Making a poster, reading fragments of the story, watching a cartoon
3	21	Grandmother's Day and Grandfather's Day	Celebrations with invited guests (Association *Golden Autumn*)
4	29	Puzzle Day	Joint fun with puzzles
February 2019			
1	8	World Radio Day	Preparation of a radio programme about the centre
2	14	Valentine's Day	Preparation of Valentine's day decorations
3	26	Dinosaur Day	Preparation of figures and a talk about the existence of dinosaurs
4	28	First Aid show	A show based on the equipment used in the BG
March 2019			
1	8	International Women's Day	Preparation of a ceremony
2	15	St. Patrick's Day	Preparation of green hats, a party with music
3	20	International Day of Happiness	Taking photographs/making a poster
4	21	First Day of Spring	Change of the decorations in the room, traditional playing 'truant'
5	27	World Theatre Day	Preparation of a play

April 2019			
1	1	April Fools' Day	Theoretical and practical activities related to the topic
2	12	Chocolate Day	Preparation of a poster, small chocolate treat
3	18	Day of the Arabic Language	The basic rules of the Arabic language (an interpreter)
4	21–22	Easter	Art competition
5	29	International Dance Day	Dance show with invited guests

May 2019			
1	2	Polish Flag Day	Making the Polish flag and the flags of the detainees' countries
2	6	International Firefighters' Day	A show of firefighting equipment
3	6	First Day of Ramadan	Learning about the customs
4	26	Mother's Day	Preparation of a ceremony
June 2019			
1	1	Children's Day	Joint fun with small gifts and treats
2	6	Day of the Russian Language	Learning the basic rules of the Russian language (an interpreter)
	20	World Refugee Day	Ceremony and a talk
3	21	Father's Day	Preparation of a ceremony
4	24	End of the school year	A relevant ceremony

Doc. 13. Sample weekly framework plan of work with the foreigners (materials made available by the Border Guard)

	Mon	**Tues**	**Wed**	**Thurd**	**Fri**	**Sat**
10:00–12:30	Preparation of celebrations of the commencement of the new school year Ceremonial beginning of the school year 2018/2019 Making equipment for fun and games in the open to the foreigners – K. Czopiński, S. Krasuska Promotion of reading, issuing books, press and DVDs – K. Czopiński, S. Krasuska	Obligatory education at the level of the primary and lower secondary school – teachers from Primary School No. 3 Making equipment for fun and games in the open to the foreigners – B. Baymert, K. Czopiński Promotion of reading, issuing books, press and DVDs – B. Baymert, K. Czopiński	Obligatory education at the level of the primary and lower secondary school – teachers from Primary School No. 3 Making equipment for fun and games in the open to the foreigners – S. Krasuska Promotion of reading, issuing books, press and DVDs – S. Krasuska	Obligatory education at the level of the primary and lower secondary school – teachers from Primary School No. 3 Making equipment for fun and games in the open to the foreigners – S. Krasuska, M. Sadowska Promotion of reading, issuing books, press and DVDs – S. Krasuska, M. Sadowska	Obligatory education at the level of the primary and lower secondary school – teachers from Primary School No. 3 Making equipment for fun and games in the open to the foreigners – B. Baymert, K. Czopiński Promotion of reading, issuing books, press and DVDs – B. Baymert, K. Czopiński	Making equipment for fun and games in the open to the foreigners – S. Krasuska, M. Sadowska Showing a cartoon – S. Krasuska, M. Sadowska Promotion of reading, issuing books, press and DVDs – S. Krasuska, M. Sadowska
12:30–13:20	The Polish language for foreigners – group 1: beginners, group 2: advanced – K. Czopiński, S. Krasuska	The Polish language for foreigners – group 1: beginners, group 2: advanced – B. Baymert, K. Czopiński	The Polish language for foreigners – group 1: beginners, group 2: advanced – S. Krasuska	The Polish language for foreigners – group 1: beginners, group 2: advanced – S. Krasuska, M. Sadowska	The Polish language for foreigners – group 1: beginners, group 2: advanced – K. Czopiński, B. Baymert	The Polish language for foreigners – group 1: beginners, group 2: advanced – S. Krasuska, M. Sadowska

	Mon	Tues	Wed	Thurd	Fri	Sat
15:00–17:50	Art activities for children 'First day at school' – S. Krasuska Showing a cartoon – S. Krasuska Monitoring the foreigners' needs in the social/living standards aspects – S. Krasuska	Obligatory education at the level of the primary and lower secondary school – teachers from Primary School No. 3 Fitness for women – B. Baymert Monitoring the foreigners' needs in the social/living standards aspects – B. Baymert	Obligatory education at the level of the primary and lower secondary school – teachers from Primary School No. 3 Showing a cartoon – S. Krasuska Monitoring the foreigners' needs in the social/living standards aspects – S. Krasuska	Obligatory education at the level of the primary and lower secondary school – teachers from Primary School No. 3 Showing a cartoon–S.Krasuska, M. Sadowska Monitoring the foreigners' needs in the social/ living standards aspects–S.Krasuska, M. Sadowska	Obligatory education at the level of the primary and lower secondary school – teachers from Primary School No. 3 Fitness for women–K.Czopiński, B. Baymert Monitoring the foreigners' needs in the social/ living standards aspects–K.Czopiński, B. Baymert	Help in doing homework-S.Krasuska, M. Sadowska Making equipment for fun and games for the foreigners-S.Krasuska, M. Sadowska Monitoring the foreigners' needs in the social/ living standards aspects–S.Krasuska, M. Sadowska
18:00–22:00	Duty of officers and civil employees of the Educational Section – S. Krasuska	Duty of officers and civil employees of the Educational Section – B. Baymert	Duty of officers and civil employees of the Educational Section – S. Krasuska	Duty of officers and civil employees of the Educational Section–S.Krasuska, M. Sadowska	Duty of officers and civil employees of the Educational Section–K.Czopiński, B. Baymert	Duty of officers and civil employees of the Educational Section–S.Krasuska, M. Sadowska

Doc. 14. Sample information on medical services for the foreigners in 2017 (source: materials made available by the Border Guard)

Nursing care is provided by qualified intermediate level medical staff (3 persons employed on a full-time basis by the Nadodrzański Unit of the Border Guard), seven days a week, holidays inclusive, from 8:00 a.m. until 8:00 p.m. Their tasks include the execution of doctor's orders, the apportioning, issuing and administering of medicines, performing nursing interventions, providing patients with nursing care, providing first aid services.

Doctor's care as a part of the basic health care is provided by doctors from the medical entity selected – in consistence with the Public Procurement Law (*Dz.U.* from 2015, It. 2164 with amendments) as a part of a public procurement procedure for medical services. A contract for these services is concluded for one year. The doctors examine the patients in the centre for two hours, three times a week. The scope of the provided services includes examining the detainees whose health has deteriorated, determining the fitness of the detainees for staying in the guarded centre and the fitness of the individuals staying within the centre for convoy, examining individuals applying for international protection, periodical check-ups of people staying in the guarded centre for foreigners, referring such individuals for specialist, in-patient, diagnostic or laboratory examinations, and consulting as a part of their specialisation.

Separate services are offered by the psychologist, who also has been selected by way of a public procurement procedure for social services in the area of psychological services (in consistence with the above-mentioned Public Procurement Law). The contract is also concluded for a year. The psychologist provides services (in keeping with the recommendation of the Border Guard Headquarters) for four hours once a week. The scope of the provided services covers psychological consultation in the situation of suspected acute stress, post-traumatic stress disorder (PTSD), adjustment disorder, identification of individuals experiencing physical or psychological violence, incl. victims of human trafficking, support in solving difficult situations, crises, psychological guidance, provision of psychological opinions, providing psychological support, crisis intervention, participation in interviewing foreigners – victims of human trafficking and/or individuals applying for international protection.

Medical assistance is provided to all the foreigners detained in the GCF.

Statistics for 2017:

1. 701 advices from doctors were issued in the GCF;
2. 58 visits to the psychologist were performed at the request of the doctor;
3. nursing services;
   - 767 non-invasive services (such as measuring blood pressure);
   - 597 invasive services (such as measuring blood sugar).

Doc. 15. Sample lists of cultural events in the guarded centre in the years 2019–2021 (source: materials made available by the Border Guard)

Plan of events for 2019

No.	Date	Event	Type of services
1.	04.2019	International Sports Day (sports-recreational event)	Catering services with back-up Fitness show with instructions on CrossFit and strength exercises (CrossFit instructor)
2.	06.2019	World Refugee Day (cultural-recreational event)	Catering services with back-up A magician's show
3.	09.2019	International Day of Foreign languages (cultural event)	Catering services with back-up
4.	12.2019	Night film marathon (cultural event)	Catering services covering the provision of meals and making Christmas parcels for 73 foreigners

Plan of events for 2020

No.	Date	Event	Type of services
1.	04.2020	International Sports Day (sports-recreational event)	Catering services with back-up Fitness show with instructions on fitness exercises (fitness instructor)
2.	06.2020	World Refugee Day (cultural-recreational event)	Catering services with back-up A chess or cards champion show
3.	09.2020	International Day of Foreign Languages (cultural event)	Catering services with back-up
4.	12.2020	International Immigrant Day (cultural event)	Catering services covering the provision of meals and making Christmas parcels for 73 foreigners

Plan of events for 2021

No.	Date	Event	Type of services
1.	04.2021	International Sports Day (sports-recreational event)	Catering services with back-up Fitness show with instructions on CrossFit and strength exercises (CrossFit instructor)
2.	06.2021	World Refugee Day (cultural-recreational event)	Catering services with back-up An origami master show

No.	Date	Event	Type of services
3.	09.2021	International Day of Foreign languages (cultural event)	Catering services with back-up
4.	12.2021	European Day of Healthy Food and Cooking (cultural-recreational event)	Catering services covering the provision of meals and making Christmas parcels for 73 foreigners Training by a catering firm in the area of the preparation of healthy food with actual food preparation

Category 9 – documents concerning the improvement of qualifications of BG officers and civil employees (monthly, quarterly and annual plans in this scope, both for the entire GCF and the particular teams/sections; national-level training of the particular teams/sections, etc.).

Doc. 16. Sample monthly plan of the improvement of qualifications of BG officers and civil employees – January 2019 (source: materials made available by the Border Guard)

Part I – Local improvement

No.	Topic	Date	Duration
1.	Reporting breakdowns and needs concerning information and communications equipment through the Maximo system.	11.01.2019 18.01.2019	1 x 45 minutes 1 x 45 minutes
2.	Organisation of admission and consideration of petitions, complaints and applications (managerial staff)	11.01.2019	2 x 45 minutes
3.	Investigation aimed at the identification/prevention of infringements of regulations of the entry and stay of foreigners in the area of the Republic of Poland in the scope of the features of the division and the circulation of documentation to do with the disclosing of the offender	11.02.2019	1 x 45 minutes
4.	Familiarisation with the current products of Risk Analysis in the Centre	11.01.2019	1 x 45 minutes
5.	Functioning of the managerial control taking into account the task-specific budget	25.01.2019	1 x 45 minutes

No.	Topic	Date	Duration
6.	Legal conditions and determinants of stay in the Republic of Poland of Ukrainian citizens crossing the border on the basis of biometric passports	25.01.2019	1 x 45 minutes
7.	Ways of performing the duties of BG officers while escorting	11.01.2019	2 x 45 minutes
8.	Timeliness and correctness of the performance of professional duties related to the admission and release of foreigners to/from the Centre	11.01.2019 25.01.2019	1 x 45 minutes 1 x 45 minutes
9.	Changes in the area of the adjustment of the rights of the BG officers to perform personal searches to constitutional standards (in the light of the statutory changes from 14.12.2018)	11.01.2019 18.01.2019 25.01.2019	1 x 60 minutes 1 x 60 minutes 1 x 60 minutes
10.	Operation of the CCTV system	16.01.2019	3 x 45 minutes

Part II – Physical education, sports activities, shooting

No.	Topic	Date	Duration
1.	Development of endurance – 3,000 m run	4.01.2019	2 x 45 minutes
2.	Development of general fitness – running and playing	11.01.2019	2 x 45 minutes
3.	Development of endurance – endurance march of 1,000 m	18.01.2019	2 x 45 minutes
4.	Development of general fitness –extended running and playing	25.01.2019	2 x 45 minutes
5.	Shooting practice – static shooting no. 1, 2, 3 and fast gun shooting no. 1	17.01.2019	1 x 60 minutes
6.	Shooting practice – static shooting no. 1, 4, 6 and fast gun shooting no. 2	31.01.2019	1 x 60 minutes

Doc. 17. Sample monthly plan of professional improvement of BG officers and employees – February 2019 (source: materials made available by the Border Guard)

Part I – local development

No.	Topic	Date	Duration
1.	Principles of calculation of short-term stays. Principles of changing long-term stays into short-term ones	8.02.2019	2 x 45 minutes
2.	Results of managerial control in the Centre	15.02.2019	1 x 45 minutes

No.	Topic	Date	Duration
3.	Control of the legality of foreigners' work, including their own business	15.02.2019	1 x 45 minutes
4.	Observation of principles of equal treatment by BG officers	15.01.2019	2 x 45 minutes

Part II – Physical education, sports activities, shooting

No.	Topic	Date	Duration
1.	Exercises strengthening leg muscles	1.02.2109	2 x 45 minutes
2.	Endurance march in the form of a warm-up over 800 m	8.02.2019	2 x 45 minutes
3.	Stretching exercises and exercises increasing spinal flexibility	15.02.2019	2 x 45 minutes
4.	Alternating running speeds over 1,000 m	22.02.2019	2 x 45 minutes
5.	Shooting practice – static shooting no. 1, 2 and 3 and fast gun shooting no. 1, 6, and 7	14.02.2019 28.02.2019	2 x 45 minutes 2 x 45 minutes

Doc. 18. Framework specification of training of BG officers and employees connected with the preparation for their performance of tasks in guarded centres (source: materials made available by the Border Guard)

Preparation of officers and employees for the performance of tasks in the GCF

Linguistic and multicultural training, such as:

- identification of individuals belonging to vulnerable groups, victims of human trafficking, people with PTSD or mental disorders;
- solving conflicts in officer-foreigner relations in the multicultural environment;
- strategies of communication with foreigners;
- team management in extraordinary situations involving foreigners;
- mastering competences in the scope of the performance of tasks in the multicultural environment;
- socio-cultural identification of foreigners from different parts of the world;
- linguistic courses and training: English, Russian – different levels.

Other areas of training for officers of the centre:

- advanced first aid;
- performance of tasks of the border guard and assistance in voluntary return in the light of the regulations specified in the new Aliens Act;
- tasks from the area of the pending administrative procedure concerning the foreigner;
- use of intervention techniques, including direct coercive measures.

C a t e g o r y 10 – statistical documents (such as statistics concerning the number of foreigners staying in the GFC, taking into account their gender, country of origin, time of admission, etc.; information on the frequency and scope of the use of medical care by foreigners).

Doc. 19. Medical services related to foreigners in the guarded centre in Lesznowola in 2019 (source: materials made available by the Border Guard)

Statistics for 2018
Guarded Centre for Foreigners in Lesznowola
Headcount of newly admitted foreigners: 191

ECG	230	ECG during the preliminary check-up and at doctor's request
Laboratory analyses	344	Upon admission: HIV, HBsAb, HCV and at doctor's request
Total examinations by doctor	2485	incl. monthly check-ups, preliminary check-up by doctor, general examination by doctor, final check-up upon release
Permanent orders	2033	Administration of medicines, blood pressure measurement, wound dressings, other – at doctor's request
Ad hoc orders	2140	Assistance as necessary and as required by the foreigners
Dental treatment	180	Upon admission to the Centre and treatment in the Nadwiślański Border Guard Regional Unit
Ambulance/hospital treatment	225	Hospital treatment in the PCM hospital in Grójec or as prescribed by the doctor in his/her referral
Medical consultations and specialist examinations	225	Carried out outside the Centre: X-ray, CT, ultrasound, etc. Consultations: ophthalmological, surgical, dermatological, laryngological, cardiological, neurosurgical, etc.
Psychiatric/ psychological consultations	64/ 109	Consultations in the area of the GCF
Surgical operations	3	Performed at the hospital

Doc. 20. Report of the guarded centre for foreigners in Kętrzyn concerning admissions, releases and other procedures involving foreigners in the period 1 January – 31 May 2019 (source: materials made available by the Border Guard)

Detainees in the GCF in Kętrzyn

The number of foreigners detained in the GCF in Kętrzyn in the period 01.01 – 31.05.2019 – 44 (69 foreigners stayed in the centre without being detained), including: men – 8; women – 16; accompanied minors – 10; unaccompanied minors – 10.

[Pie chart showing:] Russia 15, Afghanistan 10, Vietnam 6, Syria 5, others 8

Individuals detained in the GCF and covered by identification procedure

In the period 01.01-31.05.2019, identification procedure covered 33 individuals (75 % of detainees), including citizens of: Afghanistan – 10; Russia – 7; Vietnam – 6; Syria – 4; Iran – 2; Eritrea – 1; Ukraine – 1; Georgia – 1; Cameroon – 1.

1. Among the 33 individuals covered by the identification procedure, 29 were covered by the procedure concerning an obligation to return (the final decision obliging the detainee to return was issued for 11 individuals):

* identity was confirmed for 18 individuals:
(a) decision on the obligation to return was executed for 3 individuals;
(b) 5 foreigners were released in connection with the lapse of the period of their stay;
(c) 1 foreigner was released due to the fact that it was impossible to execute the decision on the obligation to return;
(d) 1 foreigner continues to stay in the centre;

* the final decision on the obligation to return was not issued for 7 individuals;
(a) 4 foreigners were released due to the discontinuation of the reasons justifying their detention in the guarded centre;
(b) 3 foreigners were released to be admitted to educational-care facilities after declarations for the granting of international protection were filed;

* identity was not confirmed for 11 individuals:
(a) 6 foreigners were released to be admitted to educational-care facilities after declarations for the granting of international protection were filed (unaccompanied minors);
(b) 3 foreigners were transferred under a court decision to another facility (after verification of their age with the help of an X-ray and confirming their full legal age);
(c) 2 foreigners continue to stay in the centre (identification measures are in progress).

2. Foreigners covered by the procedure to be granted international protection – 4; their identification has not yet been confirmed.

Individuals released from the GCF in Kętrzyn

In the period of 01.01 – 31.05.2019, 51 foreigners were released from the GCF:

(a) due to the lapse of the time of stay in the centre – 13 (including 3 individuals with a prolonged appeal procedure concerning an obligation to return conducted by the office for Foreigners);

(b) under a decision of the Commanding Officer of the Warmińsko-Mazurski Border Guard Regional Unit – 17, including:
   - releasing unaccompanied minors to be admitted to educational-care facilities after declarations for the granting of international protection were filed – 9;
   - releasing in connection with the identification of other reasons – (Syria) – 4;
   - releasing for health reasons – 3;
   - releasing due to the impossibility to execute the decision on the obligation to return – 1;

(c) execution of the decision on the obligation to return – 14;
(d) execution of the decision of the Head of the Office for Foreigners on transfer under DUBLIN III – 1;
(e) execution of the decision of Head of the Office for Foreigners on releasing from the centre – 1;
(f) execution of the court decision on changing the centre – 5.

Individuals released from the GCF in Kętrzyn covered by the identification procedure

The number of foreigners released from the GCF in the period 01.01-31.05.2019 covered by identification procedure: 42 (82 % released), including citizens of:

Afghanistan – 10; Russia – 10; Vietnam – 5; Syria – 4; Pakistan – 4; Iran – 2; Ethiopia – 2; Eritrea – 2; Ukraine – 1; Georgia – 1; Turkey – 1.

I. individuals covered by the procedure concerning an obligation to return – 31;
   * identity confirmed – 22:
   - the final decision on the obligation to return was issued for 15 individuals:
     (a) the decision on the obligation to return was executed for 8 foreigners;
     (b) 5 foreigners were released in connection with the lapse of the period of stay (according to the Russian party, it was impossible to determine the family relationship between an adult citizen of Russia and his minor brother remaining under his care the application for readmission was left unconsidered);
     (c) 1 foreigner was released due to the fact that it was impossible to execute the decision on the obligation to return (impossibility to obtain a travel document to the country of origin);
     (d) 1 foreigner was transferred to another centre under a court decision (after reaching legal age, he was transferred to the ward for men in the GCF in Białystok – a travel document was to be issued only after his reaching of the legal age);
   - the final decision on the obligation to return was not issued for 7 individuals:
     (a) 4 foreigners were released in view of the discontinuation of the reasons justifying their stay in the guarded centre (Syria – there are grounds for granting a consent to stay for humanitarian reasons);
     (b) 3 foreigners were released to educational-care facilities after declarations for the granting of international protection were filed (unaccompanied minors).
   * identity unconfirmed – 9 individuals:

(a) 6 foreigners were released to educational-care facilities after declarations for the granting of international protection were filed (unaccompanied minors);
(b) 3 foreigners were transferred under a court decision to another facility (after verification of their age with the help of an X-ray and confirming their full legal age);

II. foreigners covered by the procedure for granting international protection – 11:

* identity confirmed – 1;
* identity unconfirmed – 10.

Identified risks:

1. prolonged appeal procedures concerning cases for obliging already identified foreigners to return (3–4 months of waiting for a determination of officers handling the case in the Office for Foreigners!);
2. prolonged identification procedures – in 10 cases (out of 33 foreigners detained in 2019 and covered by identification procedure), the period from detention to submission to diplomatic missions was longer than 2 weeks;
3. necessity to release the foreigner from the centre before the completion of the identification procedure (unaccompanied minor!). An escape of the foreigner from the educational-care centre before the submission of the declaration for the granting of international protection makes it impossible to finish the procedure;
4. difficulties with the identification of foreigners from East Africa (Ethiopia, Eritrea) and Asia (Vietnam).

Doc. 21. The number of foreigners staying in the guarded centre – state as at 1.02.2019 (source: materials made available by the Border Guard)

GCF	Citizenship	No. of individuals	Adults		Children		Covered by compulsory schooling
			M	F	Accomp.	Unaccomp.	
Guarded Centre for Foreigners in Lesznowola	Afghanistan	1	1	0	0	0	0
	Armenia	1	1	0	0	0	0
	Bangladesh	1	1	0	0	0	0
	China	1	1	0	0	0	0
	Egypt	4	4	0	0	0	0
	Gambia	1	1	0	0	0	0
	India	4	4	0	0	0	0
	Iraq	1	1	0	0	0	0
	Iran	5	5	0	0	0	0
	Jordan	1	1	0	0	0	0

GCF	Citizenship	No. of individuals	Adults		Children		Covered by compulsory schooling
			M	F	Accomp.	Unaccomp.	
	Morocco	1	1	0	0	0	0
	Moldova	2	2	0	0	0	0
	Mongolia	1	1	0	0	0	0
	Unidentified/ Other	2	2	0	0	0	0
	Nigeria	1	1	0	0	0	0
	Pakistan	4	4	0	0	0	0
	Russia	2	2	0	0	0	0
	Sri Lanka	2	2	0	0	0	0
	Tajikistan	1	1	0	0	0	0
	Vietnam	10	10	0	0	0	0
	Total	46	46	0	0	0	0

Doc. 22. The number and age of foreigners staying in the guarded centre – state as at 29.05.2019 (source: materials made available by the Border Guard)

The number and age of the detainees in the GCF in Krosno Odrz., state as at 29.05.2019

Citizenship	NUMBER	AGE
Afghanistan	1	27
Algeria	3	35, 37, 60
Bangladesh	3	27, 40, 41
Belarus	1	44
Georgia	1	25
India	2	29, 29
Iraq	3	22, 22, 27
Iran	1	23
Kazakhstan	1	56
Lebanon	2	24, 31
Moldova	2	34, 45
Pakistan	2	19, 19
Russia	5	19, 20, 56, 56, 68
Syria	2	20, 22
Turkey	1	26

Citizenship	NUMBER	AGE
Vietnam	13	19, 19, 20, 21, 23, 25, 27, 30, 30, 40, 41, 47, 49
Total	43	

C a t e g o r y 11 - documents addressed to the foreigners (e.g. information on their rights and duties, information clauses in different language versions, instructions for individuals subjected to personal search, etc).

Doc. 23. Information clause concerning persons at the Guarded Detention Centre for Foreigners (source: materials made available by the Border Guard)

Information clause concerning persons staying at the Guarded Detention Centre for Foreigners

Dear All,

In connection with the entry into force of the Regulation (EU) 2016/679 of the European Parliament and of the Council of 27 April 2016 on the protection of natural persons with regard to the processing of personal data and on the free movement of such data, and repealing Directive 95/46/EC (General Data Protection Regulation), hereinafter referred to as the GDPR, we advise that with respect to the processing of the personal data of persons staying at the Guarded Detention Centre for Foreigners in Krosno Odrzańskie :

1. The Controller is the Commander in Chief of the Border Guard:
    - Address: Al. Niepodległości 100, 02-514 Warszawa [*Warsaw*],
    - Tel.: +48 22 500 40 00 (head office),
    - e-mail: gabinet.kg@strazgraniczna.pl.
2. The supervision of the proper processing of personal data at the Border Guard is conducted by the data protection officer:
    - Director of the Information Protection Bureau of the Main Headquarters of the Border Guard
    - Address: Al. Niepodległości 100, 02-514 Warszawa,
    - e-mail: boi.kg@ strazgraniczna.pl,
    - tel. 22 500 40 35.
3. The contact person with regard to personal data protection is the deputy data protection officer:
    - Head of the Information Protection Department Nadodrzański of the Border Guard Branch
    - Address: ul. Poprzeczna 1, 66-600 Krosno Odrzańskie,
    - e-mail: iod.woi.noosg@strazgraniczna.pl
    - Tel.: 68 3582102
4. Purpose and legal basis for personal data processing.
    - Personal data is processed pursuant to Article 6(1) point c) of the GDPR, in order to manage your stay at the Guarded Detention Centre for Foreigners in Krosno Odrzańskie and in order to ensure order and safety. Providing personal data is required by the provisions of the Act of 12 December 2013 on Foreigners and the Act of 13 June 2003 on granting protection to foreigners within the territory of the Republic of Poland.
    - The centre is equipped with CCTV cameras that cover the majority of rooms (except for bathrooms), the exterior of the centre as well as its immediate neighbourhood. The use of the surveillance system is among others caused by the necessity to ensure the protection of information processed at the centre, maintain order as well as the safety of all persons at the centre and it results from Article 5a(1) of the Act of 16 December 2016 on the Rules for Managing State Property, i.e. the duty to ensure the safety of property.
5. Recipients of personal data.

    The recipients of your personal data may be public authorities and entities performing public services or acting on behalf of public authorities, within the scope and in purposes resulting from the provisions of the generally applicable law.

6. Providing personal data to a third country or international organizations.

Personal data may be provided to third parties or international organizations pursuant to the provisions of the law or with your consent.

7. Time during which the personal data will be stored at the Border Guard.

Your personal data will be stored for the time required by the law, and the CCTV records will be stored for a time that does not exceed 3 months or until a final and valid conclusion of proceedings conducted pursuant to the law, to the extent that the video recordings may constitute evidence in such proceedings.

8. Rights of natural persons whose personal data is processed by the Border Guard.

You are entitled to the following rights in connection with the processing of personal data by the Border Guard:

a) right to access personal data and receive a copy of such data;
b) right to rectify (correct) personal data;
c) right to erasure of personal data (right to be forgotten) in cases when:
- data is no longer required for the purposes for which it had been collected or otherwise processed,
- personal data is processed illegally,
- personal data must be erased in order to fulfil a requirement resulting from the provisions of the law.
d) right to demand restriction of processing of personal data;

9. Right to lodge a complaint with the supervisory authority.

In the event of learning of illegal processing of personal data at the Border Guard, you have the right to lodge a complaint with the supervisory authority that is competent for matters connected with personal data protection (President of the Personal Data Protection Office, ul. Stawki 2, 00-193 Warszawa).

10. Profiling

Your personal data is not processed by automated means, it is not subject to profiling, and the decisions are not made by automated means.

11. Obtaining personal data from other entities.

In connection with your stay at the Guarded Detention Centre for Foreigners in Krosno Odrzańskie no personal data is obtained from other entities.

Doc. 24. Template of the foreigner's statement of confirmation of having been informed about the rights and duties in force in the guarded centre[72] *(source: materials made available by the Border Guard)*

OŚWIADCZENIE

Ja .... - oświadczam, że zostałem/am pouczony/a o przysługujących mi prawach i obowiązkach oraz zostałem/am zapoznany/a z przepisami regulującymi pobyt w strzeżonym ośrodku dla cudzoziemców w Krośnie Odrzańskim w zrozumiałym dla mnie [illegible]. Zostałem/am również poinformowany/na o tym, że tekst „praw [illegible] oraz przepisów regulujących pobyt w strzeżonym ośrodku dla [illegible] Krośnie Odrzańskim" dostępny jest w bibliotece ośrodka.

....

([illegible])

DECLARATION

I .... hereby declare that I have been [illegible] on my rights and obligations and that I have been acquainted with rules governing [illegible] in the Guarded Centre for aliens in Krosno Odrzańskie in the language that I can [illegible].

I have also been [illegible] Rights and Obligations and of Rules [illegible] the Stay in the Guarded Centre in Krosno Odrzańskie" is available in the centre's library.

....

(date and signature of the alien)

Declaration

I .... hereby declare that I have been informed on my rights and obligations and I have been acquainted with rules governing stay in the Guarded Centre for Foreigners in Krosno Odrzańskie in the language that I can understand.

I have also been notification that text of Rights and Obligations and Rules of the Stay in the Guarded Centre in Krosno Odrzańskie is available in the centre's library.

....

(date and signature of the alien)

72 The text is given in its original form/wording.

Doc. 25. Information about the rights, duties and rules of stay of persons placed in the Guarded Centre (source: materials made available by the Border Guard)

Information about rights, duties and rules of stay of persons placed in the Guarded Center

Rules of stay in the Guarded Centre

1. A person admitted to the Guarded Center must submit to detail checking. This consists of a body inspection, checking of clothing including underwear and footwear, and items owned by or belonging to him/her. Detailed checks may also be carried out during the persons stay in the Guarded Center when justified on grounds of safety and order.
2. A person placed in the Guarded Center is obliged to lodge in the deposit of the Guarded Center on the basis of a written confirmation:
   - documents confirming identity, money and valuables as well as technical devices that would serve to record images;
   - items that may pose a threat to the order or the safety in the Guarded Center;
   - objects the dimensions or quantity of which may limit the surface of a room for foreigners.
3. A person placed in the Guarded Center shall be responsible for any items not lodged in the deposit of the guarded center;
4. Within 14 days of admittance to the Guarded Center the lump sum to cover the cost of issuing and carrying out a decision about obligation to return is determined. The lump sum shall be excluded from the money turned over to the deposit. The amount of money left in the deposit shall not be less than 500 Polish Zloty.
5. The person admitted to the Guarded Center is subjected to medical examination as soon as possible and, if necessary to sanitary treatment.
6. The person admitted to the Guarded Center is placed in a room for foreigners. People of a different sex shall be placed separately.
7. A person placed in a Guarded Centre together with his/her family members or with a minor remaining under his/her care, shall be provided with a common room. Upon their written request people who declare that they are in close relations shall be placed in one room.
8. A person placed in a Guarded Centre is provided with bed linen and personal hygiene items.
9. Rooms for person placed in the Guarded Center, and other rooms in which placed persons are staying are subject to ad hoc checks carried out by the head of the Guarded Center or other persons designated by the head of the Guarded Center.
10. A person placed in the Guarded Center can have in their room all necessary personal possessions which are not prohibited because of constituting a threat to the security and internal order of the Guarded Center.
11. The amount and type of personal items that a person can have in their room depends on need, hygiene requirements, living conditions and safety rules.
12. A person can have a mobile phone which does not have the function of image recording. Phones that have factory-installed cameras recording image may be returned temporarily with the authorization of the head of the Guarded Center provided that this feature is disabled.
13. The number of persons staying in the Guarded Center is counted as specified in the order of the day.
14. A person in the guarded center is subject to supervision with use of technical equipment and through the use of CCTV monitoring.
15. If necessary a person in the Guarded Center can be moved at any time to another room.

16. Persons, who do not observe the duties and bans imposed on them and to ensure a person's safety, can be placed in an isolation room.
17. A person placed in a guarded centre uses their own clothing, underwear and footwear. If these items are not suitable for use or if their clothing is inappropriate for the season or if required by safety or sanitary reasons, a person may receive clothing, underwear and footwear for free.
18. A person is entitled to a haircut at least once every two months.
19. A person receives three meals per day (including one hot) and drinks. In case when temperature exceeds 28 C° additional drinks are provided, not less than one liter per day. Meals are served according to a schedule described in the Order of the Day and shall take into account the religious and cultural requirements.
20. Meals not taken on a particular day during the meal times are not served later and cannot be exchanged for a cash equivalent.
21. A doctor may order individual meals for a person whose state of health requires a diet.
22. If a person's life is in serious danger as a consequence of refusing meals he/she can be submitted to necessary medical treatment without his/her agreement.
23. While in the recreation and sports areas persons may take part in team games provided that they observe Guarded Center safety and order rules.
24. Smoking is permitted only in smoking rooms or places designated by the head of the Guarded Center.
25. the Guarded Center staff includes :
    - a return assistant - responsible for informing a person about the current situation as to the state of administrative proceedings,
    - a social assistant - responsible for ensuring the appropriate conditions and for early identification of individuals who are classified as belonging to groups with special needs, in order to provide them with the necessary assistance or with special care.
26. Detailed rules of stay are set out in the order of the day which is placed on at least the bulletin board and in the library.
27. A person placed in the Guarded Center can lodge a request for release from the Guarded Center to the Commander of the Border Guard Regional Unit (in the case of Guarded Center in Biała Podlaska to the Commander of the Border Guard Post). In the event of a decision refusing to release, the person is entitled to appeal to the Court against the refusal, provided that the request for release was submitted at least one month from the date of placing the person in the Guarded Center or one month from the extension of the period of stay.
28. A person placed in the Guarded Center is released in case of :
    - the expiry of the period of stay specified in a decision of a court ;
    - the issuing by a body of the Border Guard or a competent Court a decision or order to release a person from the Guarded Center;
    - the issuing of a decision about obligation for foreigner to return;
    - the delivery of the decision about revoking of the decision about obligation for foreigner to return, or the granting refugee status, or of subsidiary protection, or of asylum, or of the granting of a residence permit on humanitarian grounds or of a permit for tolerated status.
29. A person released from the Guarded Center will have returned from the deposit:
    - documents confirming identity;
    - money excluding deducted costs of issuing and executing the decision about obligation to return on the basis of the decision about establishing the costs;
    - items unless they are necessary to cover the cost of issuing and executing the decision about obligation to return.

30. Upon the request of the person released from the Guarded Center, items put into deposit may be handed to a person authorized in written form or to the indicated institution or organization. The costs of sending items from the deposit to any third party are to be covered by the person released.
31. When a person is released from the Guarded Center and the decision about obligation for foreigner to return is executed forcibly, the deposit is given back at the Border Guard Post where foreigner crosses the state border , or at the airport or maritime port of the country to which foreigner is convoyed.

Entitlements:

A person placed in the Guarded Center has right to:

1. contact Polish state bodies, representatives of diplomatic missions or consular offices of his/her country of origin or permanent residence, appointed proxy and representatives of non-governmental or international organizations involved in foreigner issues.
2. use the items turned into deposit (technical devices, money and other valuables, unless they have been secured to cover the cost of issuing and executing the decision about obligation for foreigner to return);
3. use of medical assistance. The use of medical assistance, the costs of which are covered by the person placed in the Guarded Center, requires the permission of the Head of the Guarded Center;
4. uninterrupted sleep between 10:00 p.m. -7:00 a.m. and on holidays until 08:00 a.m.
5. possess objects of worship, perform religious practices, use religious ministries as well as to listen and watch religious ceremonies transmitted by the mass media provided it does not disrupt the established order of stay in the Guarded Center;
6. read the press and use their dormitory and the library;
7. use the culture and sports equipments according to rules determined by the administration of the Guarded Centre;
8. purchase at own expenses foodstuffs, items for personal use, personal hygiene products, stationery materials , books, games, tobacco products and keeping them in their room.
9. receive packages with clothing, shoes and other items for personal use, medical dressing, hygiene products and medications (which will only be given to the person placed in the Guarded Center with the permission of the doctor), after the contents have been checked in the presence of the person.
10. to correspond and to use communications means at their own expenses (in exceptional cases to use the means of communications or send correspondence at the expense of the Guarded Center).
11. submit requests, complaints and applications to the Head of the Guarded Center.
12. visits of close persons in specially designed premises upon the permission of the Head of the Guarded Center.
13. move around the Guarded Center between 7:00 a.m. - 10:00 p.m. and on holidays between 08.00 a.m. - 10:00 p.m. with exception of places where the administration of the Guarded Center has a ban on entry.
14. use other entitlements than those listed above upon authorization of the Head of the Guarded Center or a person authorized by him.
15. compensation and reparations from the State Treasury in case of unjust detention or placement in the Guarded Center.

Duties:

The person placed in the Guarded Center is obliged to:

1. obey the rules of the Guard Center and carry out the orders its administration.
2. respect the lights-out period between 10:00 p.m. -7:00 a.m. and on holidays until 08:00 a.m.
3. respect the rules of appropriate social behavior.
4. take care of personal hygiene and keep rooms and public space clean.
5. use furnishings and equipments in the Guarded Center for the purpose what which they are intended.
6. Inform immediately the administration of the Guarded Center of any diseases or other situations with potentially serious consequences.

It is forbidden to:

1. Arbitrarily leave the area of the Guarded Center or stay in places where there is a ban on entry.
2. Violate the rules of safety and of stay in the Guarded Center.
3. possessing devices outside deposit intended to record images as well as items that may pose a threat to internal order or safety in the Guarded Center.
4. possessing inside rooms items the size or quantity of which may limit the surfaces of the room.
5. Drink alcohol and take intoxicants or psychotropic drugs.
6. Smoke tobacco products outside the designated areas.
7. Cause or urge any actions likely to result in injury of body or loss of health.
8. arbitrarily change rooms and places designated for sleeping.
9. Organize gambling games and participate in them.

Disciplinary responsibility:

1. Persons are liable to disciplinary penalties for violating bans and ignoring imposed obligations.
2. Disciplinary penalties consist in deprivation for a period of up to 7 days of rights to:
    - participate in cultural, educational or sports activities (with the exception of access to the library and reading the press);
    - purchase of foodstuffs and tobacco products.
3. The decision about penalizing a person is issued by the Commanded of the Regional Unit of the Border Guard or the Border Guard Post on the basis of a request of the Head of the Guarded Center.
4. Persons shall have the right to lodge a complaint to the competent penitentiary court on any decision to impose a disciplinary penalty which should be submitted within 7 days from receipt of the decision.

C a t e g o r y 12 - documents concerning cooperation with external entities and audits performed by external institutions (non-governmental organisations, the Polish Ombudsman, the Ombudsperson for Children, EU entities, etc.).

Doc. 26. A list of organizations providing assistance to foreigners (source: materials made available by the Border Guard)

LISTA ORGANIZACJI ZAJMUJĄCYCH SIĘ UDZIELANIEM POMOCY CUDZOZIEMCOM

THE LIST OF ORGANIZATIONS ENSURING ASSISTANCE TO FOREIGNERS

ПЕРЕЧЕНЬ ОРГАНИЗАЦИЙ ЗАНИМАЮЩИХСЯ ОКАЗАНИЕМ ПОМОЩИ ИНОСТРАНЦАМ

Centrum Pomocy Prawnej im. Haliny Nieć
Center of Legal Aid named after Halina Nieć
Центр юридической помощи им. Г. Нець
www.pomocprawna.org

Centrum Wsparcia Imigrantów i Imigrantek
Center of Support for Immigrants
Центр поддержки мигрантов и мигранток
www.cwi.org.pl

Helsińska Fundacja Praw Człowieka
Helsinki Foundation for Human Rights
Хельсинский Фонд по Правам Человека
www.hfhr.pl

Stowarzyszenie Interwencji Prawnej
Association of Legal Intervention
Общество Юридической интервенции
www.interwencjaprawna.pl

Fundacja "Multiocalenie"
Foundation "Multiocalenie"
Фонд Мультиоцалене
www.multiocalenie.org.pl

CARITAS Polska
CARITAS Poland
КАРИТАС Польша
www.caritas.pl

Fundacja "Ocalenie"
Fundacja "Ocalenie"
Фонд Оцалене
www.ocalenie.org.pl

Centrum Migranta Fu Shenfu
Center for Migrants Fu Shenfu
Центр Мигранта Фу Схенфу
www.migrant.pl

Doc. 27. Agreement on collaboration between the Jagiellonian University and the Podlaski Unit of the Border Guard.

Agreement on collaboration

Concluded on ....

by and between:

Jagiellonian University in Kraków, ul. Gołębia 24, 31-007 Kraków,

represented by His Magnificence Vice-Chancellor prof. dr hab. med. Wojciech Nowak,

hereinafter referred to as 'JU',

and

Podlaski Unit of the Border Guard in Białystok, ul. Gen. Józefa Bema 100, 15–370 Białystok

represented by the Commanding Officer of the Border Guard, brigadier general Grzegorz Biziuk,

hereinafter referred to as 'PUBG',

hereinafter jointly referred to as '**Partners**':

General purpose

Partners intend to cooperate with each other, providing one another with subject-related and organisational mutual assistance.

Obligations of the partners

§ 1

JU and **PUBG** shall collaborate in the area of the execution of the particular obligations resulting from this Agreement.

§ 2

JU shall:

1. carry out presentations and training for officers and civil employees of the Guarded Centre for Foreigners in Białystok in the area of a comprehensive training programme developed by the Jagiellonian Centre of Migration Studies and the Institute of European Studies, JU and the state of research into the phenomenon of immigration in Poland and the immigration policy of the Republic of Poland;
2. support the work of BG officers in Białystok by involving its employees and students in the organisation of the free time of the foreigners staying in the Guarded Centre for Foreigners in Białystok, as well as informing the foreigners about different aspects of life in Poland.

§ 3

PUBG shall:

1. provide consultations related to the activity of the Guarded Centre for Foreigners in Białystok in the scope of the projects indicated in Art. 2 hereof to the employees and students of JU;
2. make it possible for employees and students to participate in short-term visits to the Guarded Centre for Foreigners in Białystok in compliance with jointly agreed arrangements.

§ 4

1. **Partners** shall support each other as a part of their actual and legal possibilities and take into account the other Partner's businesses and interests in their own actions.
2. The scope, dates and details of the execution of the Partners' obligations referred to in § 2 and § 3 shall be subject to separate arrangements between Partners in the working mode.
3. Collaboration between **Partners** shall not be related to any financial obligations in relation to them.

§ 5

1. On the part of **JU**, the person responsible for an efficient course of the collaboration shall be **dr hab. Dariusz Niedźwiedzki, prof. UJ**
2. On the part of **PUBG**, the person responsible for an efficient course of the collaboration shall be **ppłk SG Jacek Dederko**

Duration

§ 6

1. The Agreement is concluded for three years as of the date of its signing.
2. Each **Partner** has the right to terminate the Agreement at any time, without giving reasons.

Final provisions

§ 7

Changes and supplementations of the Agreement require a consent of both **Partners** and must be made in writing, otherwise they are null and void.

§ 8

This Agreement has been drawn up in four originals, two for each of the **Partners**.

JU **PUBG**

Category 13 – other (e.g. descriptions of the employees' foreign missions, their experience related to visiting other guarded centres).

Doc. 28. Foreign missions in which officers of the guarded centres in Białystok participated in the years 2016–2019 (source: materials made available by the Border Guard)

Foreign missions in which officers of the guarded centres in Białystok participated in the years 2016–2019

No.	Rank	Full name	Section	Grade	Type and place of the mission
1	BG non-commissioned officer	Emil [surname deleted]	Convoy	03	Greece (Frontex) Malko Tarnovo, Bulgaria (Frontex) Malko Tarnovo, Bulgaria (Frontex) Lesvos, Greece (Frontex) Agrigento, Italy (Frontex) Kos, Greece (Frontex)
2	BG ensign	Mariusz [surname deleted]	Administrative Services	04	Kos, Greece (Frontex)
3	BG non-commissioned officer	Krzysztof [surname deleted]	Security	02	Greece (Frontex) Kos, Greece (Frontex) Malaga, Spain (Frontex) Spain (Frontex)
4	BG major	Bogusław [surname deleted]	Convoy	08	Lesvos, Greece (Frontex)
5	BG ensign	Karol [surname deleted]	Security	04	Bulgaria (Frontex) Kos, Greece (Frontex) Alexandropoulis, Greece (Frontex) Chios, Greece (Frontex)
6	Major	Marcin [surname deleted]	Security	08	Svilengrad, Bulgaria (Frontex) Levros, Greece (Frontex) Sardiani, Italy (Frontex) Lampeduaza, Italy (Frontex)
7	BG ensign	Jarosław [surname deleted]	Security	04	Macedonia
8	BG non-commissioned officer	Konrad [surname deleted]	Security	03	Lesvos, Greece (Frontex)

Foreign missions in which officers of the guarded centres in Białystok participated in the years 2016–2019

9	**BG ensign**	**Rafał [surname deleted]**	**Security**	**04**	**Kalatina, Bulgaria (Frontex)** **Greece (Frontex)** **Alexandropoulis, Greece (Frontex)**
10.	BG non-commissioned officer	Damian [surname deleted]	Security	02	Macedonia
11.	BG non-commissioned officer	Marek [surname deleted]	Security	04	Macedonia
12.	BG non-commissioned officer	Daniel [surname deleted]	Security	03	Macedonia
13.	BG ensign	Piotr [surname deleted]	Security	04	Macedonia
14.	BG non-commissioned officer	Bartosz [surname deleted]	Convoy	02	Greece (Frontex) Svilengrad, Bulgaria (Frontex) Kos, Greece (Frontex)
15.	BG non-commissioned officer	Piotr [surname deleted]	Security	04	Macedonia
16.	BG captain	Karol [surname deleted]	Independent position	07	Lesvos, Greece (Frontex) Malko Tarnovo, Bulgaria (Frontex) Greece (Frontex)
17.	BG non-commissioned officer	Magdalena [surname deleted]	Convoy	02	Macedonia
18.	BG ensign	Aneta [surname deleted]	Administrative Services	06	Greece (Frontex) Greece (Frontex)

Category 14 – materials acquired before the commencement of the project's execution: observation journals and reports drawn up by students during their internships in the guarded centres.

Doc. 29. A fragment of a journal of a student on a study visit to the guarded centre in 2019 (source: repository of the Institute of Anthropology and Ethnography, Adam Mickiewicz University, Poznań)

We encounter rules and regulations as well as codes all around us; they rule the place. The foreigners perform a lot of activities together – they eat together, they have common bathrooms, joint separate time for entertainment, nothing individual. It goes as far as providing each person with a number (as clearly exemplified when people wishing to enter for a chess competition, signed themselves with their number instead of their names). This is a sort of deprivation of attributes of a separate identity. Discipline and bans – taking away belts and even shoe laces, taking away phones with a camera, rationing time for using computers – and there is no access to the majority of websites, coercive measures, isolation rooms… A ban on moving not only outside the institution, but even within it (no access to the administrative part, specific hours for using some of the places or going out) is another important element

Officers treat the detainees with significant distance and not very seriously, as if they were not adults (at least the majority of the encountered employees). They do not show much empathy. They treat the foreigners as if they were 'transparent', like a job which needs to be done. The foreigners say that their cases keep being postponed, and the officers-guardians keep answering 'next week' or 'one week' to their questions about when the decision will be taken. And they have to wait for the subsequent weeks in this futile hope. Why do not the officers simply say 'I do not know when your decision will be taken, this does not depend on me. You do not have another option, you have to wait'. Such a frank attitude might strengthen the guardians' authority and the foreigners' trust in them.

The foreigners' contact with the guards/sentry guards is much warmer. In the presence of the guards, foreigners are much more relaxed; they talk to each other. They openly joke with them; they say that the guards are all right. It was significant when one of the foreigners patted the guard on the shoulder as a joke, like an old friend. The guards' attitude to the foreigners is also quite friendly and more personal.

Erving Goffman writes that using speech in total institutions is purely rhetorical. It is possible to spot manifestations of this also here: many officers cannot or do not want to talk to the detainees in English (according to the foreigners and my observations). Normally, they are spoken to as if they were children or halfwits and show them with gestures where to go to. This way of communication deprives the foreigners of some agency; it is difficult for them to express themselves, to protest, and present their own convictions. They are forced to passively subordinate themselves to the orders.

I have changed my view on the relations between the managerial staff and the foreigners a little; I have objectified it. Despite mistrust, the former do not purposefully make things difficult to the latter. The officers have specific rules of treatment of the foreigners: they do not want to make friends with them or establish closer relations, as X says, they do not want them to 'walk over them'. They have to be consistent and decisive to maintain order and stick to the rules and regulations. However, I still do not understand why access to the walking yard or common room has to be limited.

Goffmanian features	Realities of the centre
1. Two-element management – clear division into staff and the managed	1. There is a very clear division into officers + guards and the detainees. Examples: the use of the antagonisms WE and THEY, completely different rights, duties, principles concerning these two groups, clear power relations, use of physical violence and, above all, symbolic violence towards the group of foreigners, etc.
2. Group rather than individual treatment of group members, joint activities, rights, etc.	2. Easily noticeable– detainees are treated as one group to which the same principles apply (in the majority of cases). Examples: there is a prescribed common rhythm of the day, similar diet (which might seem adjusted, but all meals are issued at the same time), everyone has similar rights, are required to comply with the same rules and regulations, referring to foreigners as THEM, rarely talking about them as individuals, giving them serial numbers, treating people from the same country as a rather homogenic group (the 'Vietnamese'), all rooms look similar, have the same furnishings, potentially everyone has equal rights, e.g. as far as access to computers is concerned (if there is no internal hierarchy or if someone has not been punished)
3. Formal regulation of the principles ruling in the institution	3. Functions very strongly: everything is regulated with top-down regulations and there are internal codes of principles – their significance is stressed at every step; in the case of the majority of activities, officers refer to these regulations (although they also interpret them)
4. Managerial staff's specific language of communication with the subordinate group	4. It exists – normally, the foreigners are spoken to in Polish; they are often given orders with hand gestures (depriving of agency); only in some cases the managerial staff makes the effort to speak other languages (Russian was observed for I and sometimes English for D)
5. Creation of idealised vision of the institution to external persons	5. Initially, when we were shown round the centre, it was presented as an excellently, properly functioning institution having well-educated, competent staff
6. All spheres and activities of life take place in one place and are controlled by one managing team	6. Yes, eating, sleeping and other activities are performed within a single centre and are controlled by a team of officers
7. All activities take place according to a predetermined, top-down scheme	7. Yes, there is an enforced schedule of meals, activities, quiet hours (e.g. TV is switched off at 10:00 p.m.)
8. Everything taking place in the institution is ruled by specific assumptions and goals behind the existence of the centre	8. Yes, the goal of all things happening in the centre is the decision concerning the future of the detainees and its execution (release, deportation, etc.)
9. It is a bureaucratised, formalised institution	9. Yes, every activity is recorded in the 'papers'
10. The institution is incompatible with the family functioning model	10. The centre is a facility for men only, which means that family members are separated, and the detainees live in artificially created groups (although it is possible to hold visits and there is a room for a family)

The above set, with the exclusion of category 1 with its legislation, contains 467 items. This does not reflect the actual number of the collected documents, since the particular inventory items contain from a couple to several dozen documents (such as packages of archival photographs of the BG, library catalogues, packages of internal rules and regulations). Hence, the acquired set is *de facto* composed of a dozen or so thousand individual documents.

This extensiveness of the set of sources calls for some explanation. We collected complete packages of analogical documents in each of the six centres under study. This measure was guided by the need to perform a comparative analysis of the documents at a later stage from the point of view of the identification of similarities and differences in the mode and style of the staffs' work, and on this basis to diagnose the integrity, the degree of uniformity, of the detention system in Poland. In view of the different profiles of the individual local institutions, this measure was of significant importance. Moreover, we wanted to take a close look at analogical documents generated within each of the centres separately. The scopes of the rights and duties of individuals working in the same positions are a good example here.

The group of first-hand sources included materials which were divided into eight categories:

Category 1 – recordings[73] of individual interviews. We conducted 155 interviews, which were divided on a working basis/for working purposes into problem-specific (114) and supplementary (41) interviews.

Category 2 – recordings of group interviews. We conducted 6 interviews of this type.

Category 3 – photographic material. We collected several thousand photographs taken by all the project participants. The documentation concerns all the spaces and places (open and closed) in the guarded centres and the specifics of their 'buffer zones' (the outposts within which they are located and their nearest surroundings).

Category 4 – observation notes concerning behaviours and social interactions. It is impossible to count the materials of this type exactly, as in many cases, as a part of the preliminary ordering, we decided to draw up the so-called collective notes, which covered the entire records of the particular types of

73 All the recordings were deleted after being transcribed.

behaviour/interaction throughout our study visit in a given guarded centre. For more information on the types of observations, see Section 2.4.3.

Category 5 – notes on the so-called social situations. A description of this category can be found in Section 3.4.3.

Category 6 – notes of the so-called daily reflections. They were drawn up by the research team during the meeting closing each daily research session. They contained the most important immediate insights concerning various issues related to the functioning of the centre and its actors, which were discussed by the team.

Category 7 – research journals (6). Every project participant was obliged to keep their own research journal.

Category 8 – other materials. The collection also included recordings and protocols of informal conversations with the staff and the detainees, all the recorded conversations carried out in these groups, as well as presentations of the centres performed by the officers for the research team on the first day of the study visit.

Information on our research tools, including sets of guidelines concerning the acquisition of first-hand sources from the particular categories and templates for their recording, can be found in Section 2.4.3.

The above description documents both the richness and the diversity of the collected source materials. The accumulation of this set did not lie in spontaneous data collection, but was related to carefully thought-out decisions based on predefined information-related needs of the project team. In connection with the multiplicity of the undertaken research threads and their different profiles, it is impossible to describe the status and usefulness of the particular sources in the entire project. However, it is worth highlighting two general features of the source resource under discussion. First, we are dealing with a complementary set, which should result in a multi-aspect source triangulation, as discussed further on in this chapter. Secondly, observational data as a source immanently integrated with other first-hand sources, one best suited for verification and complementation of all other types of sources, will act as a universal binder of the set in question.

2.4.2. Research subjects – selection of the sample

Participants of our research included two basic categories of people staying in detention centres: (1) officers of the Border Guard employed in the facilities and civil employees, and (2) foreigners detained in the centres under a court decision. Both these groups were subjected to the technique of observation, becoming the 'protagonists' of different types of reporting notes. Also the documents collected during our work were related to both these categories of the subjects.

The applied technique of in-depth problem-specific interview called for a different treatment of the research subjects as defined in this way. As already mentioned, during our fieldwork, we interviewed officers and civil employees of guarded centres for foreigners. The reason behind this selection was the basic goal of our research, i.e. the identification and description of the detention centres as institutions with a specific organisational culture and a description and explanation of the socio-cultural aspects and consequences of the organisation of space in these centres. This required an identification of the agential subjects who might provide us during interviews with the maximum quantity of data necessary to achieve the research goal. Detention centres assemble foreigners who are the object of the administrative procedure aimed at obliging them to return to their country of origin. However, we have no doubt that by an order of the courts they find their way to the centres in which the space is organised in the material and legal dimension by officers and civil employees of the BG. It is these particular people whom we identified as the specific 'hosts' of the space constituting the object of our considerations. In the centres, foreigners play the role of temporary 'guests'. Our conversations with them had the nature solely of free interviews; what is more, they were conducted on the initiative of the foreigners themselves.

Because the category of people employed in the detention centres is internally varied, it was each time an analysis of the employment structure which was the starting point for the selection of our interlocutors. It is worth pointing out that it is different in each of the centres under study, which results from many factors such as their capacity, character of the material space, profile (for men, for families) and other factors. The most important differences in the employment structure are related to the manner of organisation of the centres, their location as a part of either an Outpost of the Border Guard or a Unit of the Border Guard.

An analysis of the employment structure resulted in a determination of several categories of interlocutors originating from among the officers and civil employees employed in the centres.[74] The first one is the top level management of these institutions. In the case of the centres located within BG outposts, they included the commanders and deputy commanders of the outposts who also fulfilled the function of managers of the centres. In the case of the centres

---

74 The guidelines concerning the conducting of interviews in the particular categories of officers and employees can be found in the *Annex*.

remaining directly within the structure of the BG, the top level management covered department heads – simultaneously managers of the centres, and their deputies. We had no doubt that in the case of this category, we had to conduct interviews with the entire sample of our subjects. This is because they play the pivotal role in the organisation of the space of the centres – on the one hand, being responsible for the enforcement of external regulations, while on the other hand for the development of the internal principles and norms of the organisation and use of this space. In total, we conducted 14 such interviews – we interviewed some of the managers of the centres twice: at the beginning and at the end of our visit to the centres. In view of our frequent contact with the top level management during our study visit, we additionally acquired a lot of significant data as a result of informal, spontaneous conversations.

We tried to conduct interviews with the managers of the centres and their deputies at the beginning of our visit in the field – for several reasons. First, these interviews were aimed at making the management familiar with the research team, which, as mentioned above, was subject to suspicions as to its activity extending behind the research. Secondly, during our interviews with the management, we endeavoured to acquire preliminary knowledge on the specific features of the centre, with a view to selecting interviewees for our further interviews. Thirdly, we assumed that the interviews with the management would make our access to the other employees of the centres easier, that they will lower the possible level of aversion to the team or fears of consequences of talking to the researchers. Finally, these interviews were an important source of information concerning the documents we should collect during our visit. They were usually conducted by the entire team of researchers staying on the premises of the centre. These collective interviews were aimed at accumulating data constituting the basis for further research.

Another category of our interlocutors was composed of managers of the particular sections and teams. Just like in the previous case, we had no doubt that we needed to interview the entire sample. We sought to conduct these interviews also at the beginning of our visit, since the managers of sections and teams together with the top level management were for us jointly a group of interlocutors – experts in the area of comprehensive knowledge concerning the organisation and functioning of the centres. In view of the significance of the information we acquired, these interviews were conducted (as much as possible) by the entire research team. Ultimately, we conducted 26 interviews with people fulfilling the function of the managers of sections/teams.

A very significant category of interlocutors was formed by people employed in the educational sections/teams. This is because they play the role of the so-called social guardians, and are the first addressees of the foreigners' requests and demands. They also conduct preliminary conversations aimed at being aware of the detainees' situation – in particular, the identification of the reasons why they should be granted the status of vulnerable individuals.[75] Tasks of the staff of these sections/teams include the organisation of the free time of the foreigners staying in the centres. The offices of these sections/teams are located directly within the space available to foreigners, and their employees are basically in constant contact with the detainees. This makes them an exceptionally valuable source of knowledge on the organisation and use of the space by the people staying in the detention centres. In the case of this category of interlocutors, we decided to carry out interviews with the whole sample. The absence of very few individuals resulted from their refusal to participate in an interview or absence during our study (illness, leave, etc.). We conducted a total of 27 interviews with the employees of these sections/teams.

Another category of interlocutors is officers employed in sentry guard/ security sections/teams. It is the most numerous category of officers in all the centres under study. In view of the constant presence of foreigners in the usable space, they are a precious source of knowledge on the interpersonal relations in the centres. Our interlocutors included people fulfilling the functions of shift managers, assistants of shift managers, provosts and sentry guards. The number of interviews conducted in the particular centres was guided by the principle of data saturation. We conducted a total of 39 interviews with officers employed in the sentry guard/security sections/teams.

In relation to the employees of the remaining sections/teams, we applied the principle of the purposeful selection of interlocutors. Following the principle of proportionality of the sample selection, we interviewed at least two individuals from each of the remaining sections/teams. We conducted a total of 44 interviews. More detailed criteria of the selection of interlocutors concerned two issues. The first one was the daily contact with the foreigners. Our interlocutors included the so-called return guardians, whose basic tasks include co-participation in the administrative procedure related to obliging foreigners to return to their country of origin. Individuals fulfilling this function are in particular mediators between the Office for Foreigners and other institutions participating in the carrying out of this procedure, and the foreigners detained in the centres. This criterion was also a deciding factor in the selection of

75 This is about individuals who experienced traumatic physical or sexual violence, victims of human trafficking, etc.

employees of the convoy sections/teams for research by means of the interview technique. They are responsible for the practical implementation of the foreigners' obligation to leave Poland, i.e. convoying them to the air transport or to the national border in order to hand them over to the neighbouring countries, and collecting foreigners handed over to Poland from these countries (in particular from Germany) under the Dublin agreements. Moreover, they perform daily convoy activities related to transporting foreigners between detention centres, executing various legal activities involving the foreigners (convoying them to courts, prosecution service, etc.) and activities related to the maintenance of their health during their stay in Poland (visits to outpatient clinics, hospitals, etc.). The daily contact with foreigners was also a decisive factor behind the selection of interlocutors from among the individuals employed in the centre in the position of depositaries and healthcare staff (regardless of whether healthcare services were provided by employees of the Border Guard or an external entity). Depositaries are responsible for the safekeeping of the foreigners' property, which for security reasons is deposited upon their admission to the centre, and for making purchases for the detainees in shops. In each of the centres, we conducted one interview with the depositaries (a total of 6 interviews). Health professionals are responsible for the daily primary health care covering the foreigners, including the issuing of medicines prescribed during medical examinations. Just like in the case of employees of the security sections/teams, the number of interviews in this category of interlocutors depended on the data saturation.

The second issue taken into consideration when selecting interlocutors employed in the remaining sections/teams was the participation of their employees in the shaping and maintenance of the space of the detention centres. Hence, our interlocutors included employees responsible for the acquisition of external funds (including EU funds) for the reorganisation and furnishing of the material space of the centres, and maintenance technicians responsible for its upkeep.

The last category of interviewees covered outsiders requested to work in the centres under different types of collaboration agreements. The most significant group was composed of teachers teaching children covered by compulsory education in the centres for families. Interviews were also conducted with auxiliary staff executing various services for the benefit of the guarded centres. They included individuals employed in the BG (kitchen staff, fitters, cleaning staff), as well as people hired by external entities, such as the health service, with whom the entities concluded contracts for the provision of services to the guarded centre. We conducted a total of 15 such interviews.

While conducting our study, we also decided to carry out focus group interviews. In this case, our interest was concentrated on the cooperation of the people employed in detention centres in working out the desired solutions in the area of the organisation of space and work in those detention centres. Their task during the interview was to construct an ideal model of the guarded centre for foreigners. We invited representatives of all the sections and teams functioning in the centres to participate, making sure that they did not include the subjects who were interviewed individually. We conducted a total of 6 focus group interviews.

2.4.3. Research techniques – ways of collecting materials

Our study was aimed at the understanding of interpersonal relations taking place in the space of the detention centres in Poland. The above required the acquisition of numerous data concerning formal regulations and practical ways of the organisation of this space as well as determinants of behaviours and interactions themselves taking place in the centres under study. To achieve this purpose, we decided to use a number of tools and techniques conducive to contemporary anthropological fieldwork (see Fig 9).[76]

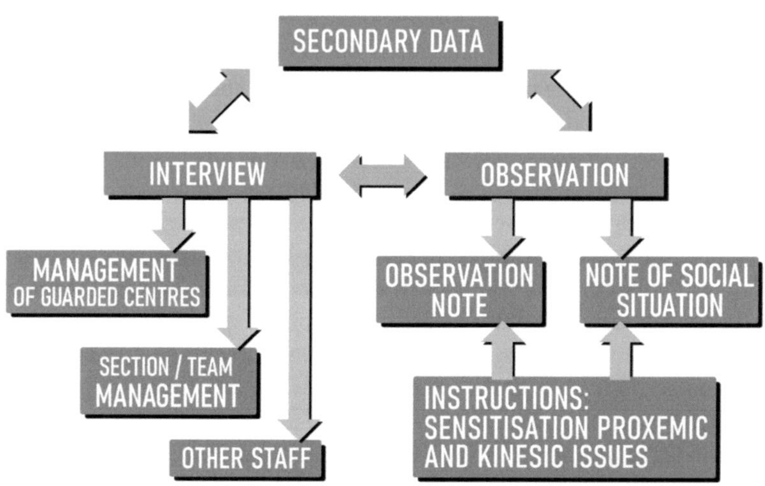

Fig. 9. Triangulation of techniques and auxiliary research tools (own elaboration)

76 All the guidelines concerning the inventory of space, conducting interviews and observation are presented in the *Annex*.

The study conducted by the team was each time commenced with a guided walk around the external area and the premises by a representative of the top level management of the centre. We recorded this reconnaissance in the sound form on a dictating machine, and we were also permitted to make visual records in the form of photographs, which constituted a starting point for visual inventory. This specific trip made it possible for us to orient ourselves preliminarily in the spatial layout and formulate the first reflections concerning a description of this space by individuals having a considerable impact on its organisation. As already mentioned, it was also a good introduction to the further inventory.

As far as the inventory was concerned, we were interested in all the closed spaces (with the exception of the foreigners' residential rooms). These included corridors used by the detainees and the staff, reception areas and visiting rooms, dining rooms, educational rooms for children, rooms for recreation and sports (billiards, computers, rooms equipped in sports equipment). The open spaces which were the subject of our interest included walking areas, areas designated for recreation/sports, and external smoking areas. All the internal spaces and elements of open space were described taking into account their dimensions, furnishings and decoration. The internal and external spaces were viewed both from the micro and macro perspective – as autonomous units, and in the context of the entire space of the centre, respectively.

The inventory covered the organisation of the space of the centre as a whole – the layout of the particular closed and open spaces taking into account a description of their functionality. Moreover, the inventory took into account a description of the 'external' view – the body of the centre and its characteristic features (bars, barbed wire, gates, etc), and its location (autonomous or located as a part of a complex of other BG facilities; the nearest neighbourhood, e.g. an open centre for foreigners, housing estates, natural conditions). Our interests also covered the history of the facility with special focus on its modernisation and adaptations of both the internal and the external spaces.

The inventory was performed on the basis of three basic types of sources. First, we collected iconographic material in the form of photographs, site plans and descriptions of the internal and external spaces of the centres together with comments. Secondly, we used the existing sources such as architectural plans, chronicles, reports, equipment records, catalogues of resources of the educational department with records of the frequency of its use, and the available computer programmes and conditions in the scope of access to the internet. Thirdly, the sources mentioned above were complemented with statements of the staff employed in the guarded centres on the internal and external spaces.

The space-concerning threads of the interviews played an important role in the analysis of the cultural and social importance of the space. Our interest in the social generation of space and the interactions, relations and social processes taking place within it, as well as the searches and interpretation of the cultural meanings of space, called for the recording of the scope and form of the use of the closed and the open spaces by both the detainees and the staff. The above required the conducting of observations in the scope of the individual and group appearance in the particular parts of the space both for the foreigners and members of the staff employed in the centres.

As far as the foreigners' behaviour was concerned, we were interested in the various forms of individual and collective activity (social life, supervision over children in centres for families, phone conversations, etc.) and the performance of these activities in the context of the consistency/inconsistency with the designated purpose of the space. The observations were also aimed at the inventory-taking of different cyclical, daily activities of the foreigners, such as going for meals, placing shopping orders, using medical care, etc. What was important while doing so was taking into account 'props' used by the foreigners and the ways in which they used them. The recording of the detainees' activity in the centres took into account their communication-related attitudes during interactions with other detainees and BG officers and civil employees. We wanted to grasp the attitudes manifested in behaviour such as the avoidance of contact *vs* trying to establish contact, friendliness, indifference, hostility, passiveness *vs* activeness, tendency to isolation, and endeavours to stir a conflict. What was important in this observation was the recording of symptoms of the so-called communication etiquette, i.e. the language of gestures (e.g. hand-shaking, gesticulation, facial expressions) and verbal conventions (the language of communication, using first name terms, greeting formulas and other messages).

Of course, this observation applied above all to the activity of the staff in the space of the centres. We were in particular interested in the forms of their supervision over the detainees, i.e. the interactions between foreigners in the area of assistance and disciplining. Just like in the case of the observation of foreigners, we paid attention to elements of communication etiquette, i.e. the language of gestures, verbal conventions, as well as the equipment which the staff had at their disposal (including means of direct coercion), and, if any, the way it is used. What was important in the case of the observation of individuals employed in the centres was the recording of their attitudes and intergroup behaviours. In particular, we paid attention to the course of interactions between the people employed in different sections/teams and the ones at different levels of the hierarchy of authority.

The said observations were conducted in an extrospective way, i.e. one striving to examine human attitudes as a result of the observation of behaviour. We performed them directly and indirectly from different spaces (such as the guardhouses) enabling this sort of overview and by watching the screens of the monitors recording images from cameras. Nevertheless, the latter cannot be considered disguised observation, since the BG officers and civil employees, as well as the foreigners, were well aware of remaining under constant monitoring, when they stayed in the spaces monitored by the system of cameras. We mostly conducted direct observations, i.e. ones carried out during our presence in a specific internal space or a fragment of the external space. Referring to Angrosino's typology (2007: 54–55), as researchers, we positioned ourselves above all in the role of a complete observer, but sometimes also participant as observer, or even actual participant. The observation activities specified above were accompanied by the acquisition of information on the topic in question from employees of the educational and security sections/teams, i.e. BG employees remaining in direct contact with the foreigners.

The research team conducted observations using two templates of observation notes, which ordered the activity.[77] The first template concerned classically-understood, intentionally undertaken observation. In this case, the note covered data concerning the characteristics of the place of observation, a list of the participants with their detailed description, the chronology of events taking place and descriptions of behaviours and interactions – both verbal and non-verbal. The second template concerned the so-called situations, i.e. events, observed on an *ad hoc* basis, taking place during informal contacts of the researchers and members of the staff or detainees; staff members, detainees or representatives of these two groups, and the events taking place in the course of interactions during which members of the research team were provided with the existing data by staff members. Along with elements taken into account in classical observation notes, this template also covered the researchers' reflections, and their interpretations of the encountered social situations.

A significant role in the conducted observations was played by the guidelines adopted by the team, sensitising themselves to the proxemic and kinesic side of the behaviours of the research subjects.[78] They were aimed at directing the research towards the issues of non-verbal behaviours of the individuals staying in the space of the detention centres, which are hard to perceive and interpret. The

77 A detailed description of observation notes can be found in the *Annex*.

78 Full guidelines in this scope are presented in the *Annex*.

sensitisation concerned the recording of behaviours related to the maintenance of various types of spatial distances and interaction etiquette, including visual, auditory, gesture and olfactory communication. They also covered issues related to the subjects' understanding of the spatial order and disorder, hygiene, attitude to joint property, forms of nutrition and the spending of free time.

Without any doubt, the key technique in obtaining data for us was that of the in-depth problem-specific interview - only in this way could we reach the phenomena taking place in the consciousness of the subjects that were related to the issues of our interest, i.e. the conditions and motivations concerning interactions, relations and bonds developing in the space of the guarded centres. As was already mentioned, this technique was used in relation to BG officers and civil employees. In our study, we used three versions of the partially structured questionnaire.[79] The first one was designed for the top level management of the guarded centres, and we used the second one during interviews with the managers of the sections/teams, and the third one in relation to the other subjects employed in the centres.

In the case of the top level management, we were dealing with the formal leaders of the institution. In connection with the above, we focused in the interviews on the reception and adaptation of external regulations and the generation of internal ones concerning the organisation and functioning of the material and sociocultural space in the centres. Our set of guidelines for interviews with the top level management was divided into three basic blocks of issues. The first one concerned issues related to the inventory of space and its furnishing in the material dimension as well as the formal conditions of the use of this space. It included questions concerning the demand for information in the area of the investments and refurbishments which have been carried out and are planned for the centres, needs in the scope of the changes related to space – also from the point of view of security – internal regulations governing the use of space and the need for external regulations in this scope. Another issue discussed during interviews with the management was their assessment of the detention centre as a tool of internal migration policy. We were interested in their opinions concerning the purposefulness and effectiveness of the functioning of closed centres for foreigners. Moreover, we asked them about their role in the implementation of the migration policy, and, in this context, various 'disturbances' appearing in their activity, as well as ideas concerning a model detention centre. Another significant problem discussed during interviews with

79 All the three sets of interview guidelines can be found in the *Annex*.

the management was the impact of 'external factors' on the functioning of the guarded centre. The questions concerned the impact of the world of politics, organisation of the civil society, as well as a broader European context of the functioning of detention centres.

When interviewing managers of the particular sections/teams, we focused on the issues related to the role of the latter in the organisation of space and ways of its use in the execution of their daily duties. In this case, the guidelines were divided into six blocks of issues. The first three were analogical to the ones applying to the top level management, although their content was narrower. The two subsequent blocks of issues were related to the interpretation and assessment of the space of the centres and the formal and informal conditions of its use. In this case, the questions were related on the one hand to the evaluation of the condition of the equipment of the space, and on the other – the barriers and limitations connected with its use, including the internal and external regulations, as well as the assessment of the state of its safety for the BG officers/civil employees and for the foreigners. Additionally, in this part of the interview, we also asked about the development of individual and collective routines of activity in this space in the context of the existing relevant external and internal regulations. The last block of guidelines concerns the inter- and intragroup relations within the space of the centre, and covers the ones taking place within the staff group and within the foreigners group, as well as between the two of them. The issues we were interested in, in this part of the interviews, were related to the impact of the hierarchy of positions and functions on the relations between the officers/civil employees of the centres, communication barriers between the particular groups of the users of the space, and the conflicts emerging among the officers/civil employees, among the foreigners, and between these groups.

Interviews with other individuals employed in the centres were aimed at the identification of their opinions and attitudes to the space and the interactions taking place within it and the relations between staff members, between the staff and the foreigners, and within the group of foreigners, taking into account the relations among the culturally and socially diverse categories of the detainees. In this case, the blocks of issues again covered questions related to the interpretation and evaluation of the space of the centres, the formal and informal conditions of its use as well as the intra- and intergroup relations taking place within the space of the centre and including relations within the groups of the employed staff and the detained foreigners, as well as the ones taking place between the staff and the foreigners.

The organisation and performance of focus group interviews deserve some remarks concerning the ethical issues. We made sure that the groups of our interlocutors were composed as much as possible from representatives of all the sections/teams functioning in the guarded centres. Naturally, these individuals had to first express their consent to participate in the focus group interview. Additionally, in order to limit the participants' possible discomfort connected with speaking in a broader circle, we excluded individuals employed in managerial positions from this form of interviews. During the focus group interviews, we asked the participants to develop a desired model of interactions and relations between the officers and the civil employees, and the detained foreigners. The second key task facing the subjects was the designing of a spatially, architecturally ideal closed centre for foreigners/ a closed centre for foreigners that would be a model one in terms of spatial, architectural solutions.[80]

Almost all the interviews were conducted in places selected by our interlocutors. Interviews conducted in the places made available to us by the management, to which we could invite our interlocutors, were an exception to the rule. A decisive majority of interviews took place without the presence of the third parties. Interviews conducted with officers from the security sections/ teams in guardhouses were a specific deviation from this rule. The specificity of this place limited the possibility to conduct the interviews in isolation from others, since normally two or three BG officers were staying simultaneously in the space of the guardhouse.

2.4.4. Analyses

Analytical activities are a continuous and multi-stage process, which *de facto* starts with the selection and preliminary conceptualisation, and ends with the last correction of the report or publication (e.g. Rapley 2007). We have already signalled our acceptance for this particular approach to qualitative analysis on the previous pages of this book. At the same time, we believe that analyses are composed of two groups of activities: 'office' work (collating data, creating a repository, transcribing and coding) and work 'proper' (interpretation, explanation, the development of models, etc.) (e.g. Gibbs 2007) - and we shall present them in this particular order. We shall begin our considerations with a presentation of the concept of frame analysis, which binds all others to make a single catalogue of activities ruled by the logic behind it (scheme of our analytical procedure – see Fig. 10).

80 A manual of focus group interviews can be found in the *Annex*.

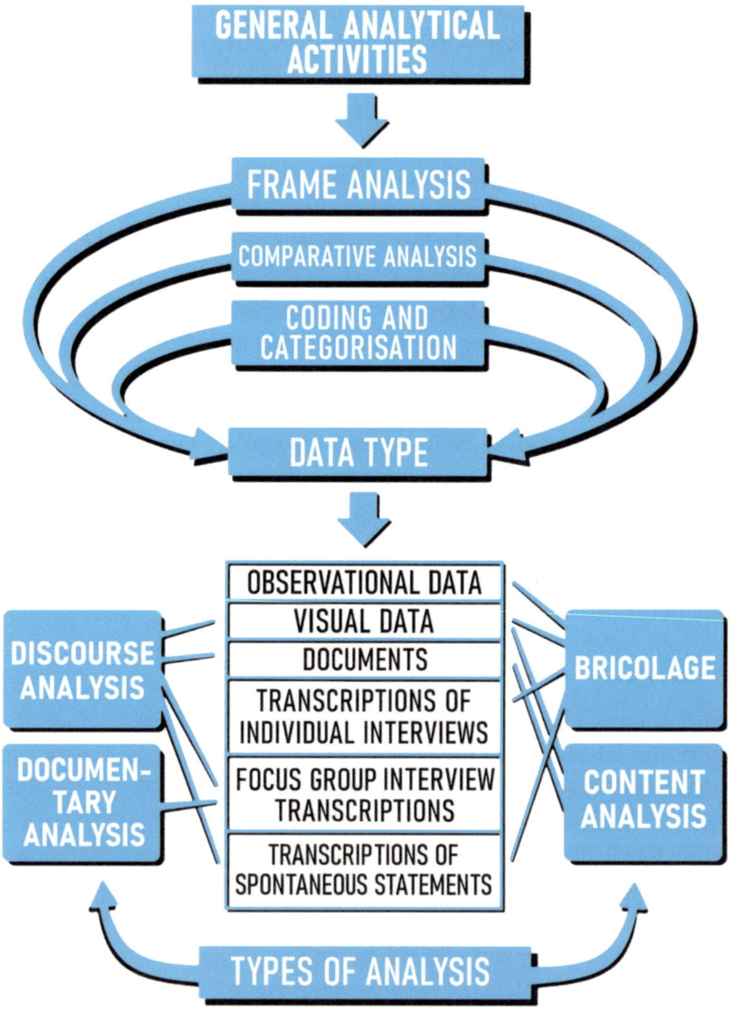

Fig. 10. Scheme of the analytical procedure (own elaboration)

Frame analysis. Frame analysis is the key element of our analytical procedure, largely organising other activities. The concept is strongly associated with Erving Goffman, whose work *Frame Analysis* became one of the most important points of reference in the study of the framing theory. Goffman's achievements were marked by the fact that the basic categories he used, such as 'frame' and 'framing', were not precisely defined (Czyżewski 2010: VIII).

Although the author defined the purpose of his procedure clearly – as the finding of the basic frames of understanding available in our society, enabling the giving of sense to events and analysing the specific weaknesses and challenges to which these frames are vulnerable (Goffman 1986: 10) – his style is marked by a unique multitude of metaphors and notions, including neologisms, which make interpretation of this concept more difficult (Burdziej 2011: 47).

Marek Czyżewski (2010) indicates a double nature of the frame. On the one hand, it is a cognitive scheme owing to which each of us is able to define the situation of a given interaction. On the other hand, it determines the mode of action in the course of such a situation. This means that Goffman's frames allow us to focus on the significant and omit the non-important in a given situation, while indicating which of the possibilities for interpreting the event (discourse, image) taking place is more important than the others (Snow 2004). They also make it possible to identify the way in which the specific events are perceived and interpreted. In this context, frames are indispensable for the possibility to understand the reality around us.

This interpretation is of key importance to us, because it means that frames and ways of framing (the use of the frames) are an effect of the accumulation of the collective experience of a given community, i.e. that their cultural setting is of key significance. This also means that the ability to use the frames is a consequence of the socialisation in the culture of a given community - it is a result of the interaction of individuals with the social environment. What follows is that the cognitive schemes characteristic for framing create particular standards of the perception of reality and behaviours consistent with this perception. In consequence, frames not only make it easier to understand what is taking place – they also determine the normative expectations related to human behaviour. Frames and framing determine the way of adoption and fulfilment of social roles. In some specific situations, individuals are required to act in compliance with the frames, because stepping beyond them would expose them to particular sanctions, marginalisation, or, in extreme cases, even exclusion from the community.

K n o w l e d g e   b a s e. jIn the case of team research, the need to create a safe, complete data repository available to all the researchers is of particular importance. Hence, we decided to keep our project materials in a specially protected, dedicated cloud administered by the Jagiellonian University.[81] Every

81 The information collected in the cloud was ordered in several folders: legislation, examination of detention centres, relevant literature, methodology, and research tools. The folder 'examination of detention centres' with data acquired during fieldwork was divided into folders assigned to the particular locations of the detention centres (Biała Podlaska, Białystok, Kętrzyn, Krosno Odrzańskie, Lesznowola, Przemyśl).

project participant could access it using a login paired with their email address, and obtained a one-time password for each instance of logging in. Before entering data, the team developed the architecture of the repository, owing to which individually entered resources were ordered on the basis of templates of thematic catalogues and subcatalogues. The repository also contained 'guidebooks' to the collection: files with inventory lists of documents, interviews and reports, including thematic reports. A package of methodological documentation, relevant literature, etc. were also uploaded to the cloud.

T r a n s c r i b i n g. Due to the fact that we made almost 300 hours of recordings, the question of transcription was a highly important analytical challenge. The research team decided that most of the work would be performed by one person – a trusted collaborator, participant of previous joint research projects, having years-long experience in transcribing and with specialist sound cleaning software. The work lasted for almost a year and took about 1,200 hours. The transcription covered the entire scope of the acquired material, and no stylistic or linguistic interventions were performed. In turn, the interviewers introduced their own comments gathered in their research journals to the gradually acquired materials, along with descriptions of the so-called social situation of the interview (interlocutor's approach to the topic, researcher, etc.).

C o m p u t e r – a i d e d q u a l i t a t i v e d a t a a n a l y s i s. In view of the previous experience of some of the team members, we selected the software MAXQDA (version STANDARD, 2020). All the members of the project team obtained licences to use the programme; workshops devoted to a discussion of its application in relation to various categories of sources were subsequently organised.

Each of them has four subfolders for various types of data: photographic material, existing materials, observations and reflections, and interviews. The subfolder 'photographic material' contains photographs and is internally divided into several sections depending on the architectural (e.g. in the case of multi-storey buildings, a division into sequences of photographs of the particular storeys) and spatial (a division of the photographs related to the functionality of the particular fragments of the external space) specificity of a given centre. The subfolder 'existing materials' was divided into several sections: documents of the sections and teams, architectural plans, rules and regulations of the centre and its spaces, employment structure and scopes of duties of the particular positions, internal laws, and other documents concerning the centre. The subfolder 'observations and reflections' contains various types of observation notes and reflections of the researchers-members of the team. The subfolder 'interviews' was divided by types of interlocutors: management of the centre, mangers of sections/teams, other staff, and focus group interviews.

C o d i n g and c a t e g o r i s i n g. Preparations for coding mainly consisted in the repeated, individual reading of source texts. In connection with the organisational conditions and different profiles of interests of the particular members of the project team, it was agreed that the first stage of coding would be carried out individually. We are referring here to preliminary coding. It consisted in open coding line by line,[82] the preliminary hierarchisation of codes, and comparing data. The significant goals of these measures included a determination whether the acquired data corresponded to the research tasks, what they suggested and what gaps emerged in this set. When this book was forwarded for printing, work in this scope was not yet completed. A subsequent stage – already having a collective character – will consist in project workshops as a part of which we shall discuss the individual findings and proposals of the preliminary coding with a view to the joint drawing up of a package of codes which are marked by the greatest analytical importance for in-depth data categorisation – both from the point of view of segments and as a whole. Such focused coding should not close the possibility to return to the level of preliminary coding. The above description clearly shows that we were inspired by the procedure applied by the supporters of the grounded theory – however, they did not cover all the activities comprising the axial coding or the stage of the creation of theoretical codes (Glaser 1978; Glaser and Strauss 2006; Charmaz 2006).

C o m p a r a t i v e m e t h o d a n d i s c o u r s e a n a l y s i s. It is not accidental that these two procedures are referred to together – they seem to be 'natural' analytical activities – they are applied to various types of source materials in the majority of stages of the research procedure.

The very comparison of phenomena, events, artefacts and behaviours is a rudimentary cognitive process – a manner of daily reflection on the surrounding world as a part of an endeavour to understand it, a source for taking decisions, making choices, etc. We may say that only by referring to a difference and discovering alternatives may we become familiar with both ourselves and the social and physical world around us. This banal statement refers to the same degree to comparisons carried out as a part of the research procedures. Our overriding project goal was a comparison of all the six cases (guarded centres) making up the system of the detention of foreigners in Poland, its organisational

---

82 The proposed standard of work did not exclude the adoption of other solutions such as word-by-word or event-by-event coding. The people performing the coding were sensitised to the issue of the coding of the terms used by the participants of the study – *in vivo* codes (Charmaz 2009: 76–79).

culture. In practice, the comparison covered the entire chain of activities related to the selection and collection of the particular categories of sources, comparing – confronting various types of sources, coding, categorising, etc. As a part of an internal comparative analysis, we discovered formal and homologous analogies, put together extremes, identified case of 'curiosities', etc. As a part of the conducted comparisons, we were inspired both by the classic methodological solutions developed on the grounds of social and cultural anthropology (Sarana 1975), and the guidelines of the proponents of the grounded theory and the documentary method (Glaser and Strauss 2006; Konecki 2000; Bohnsack 2004). We found the concept of *tertium comparationis* (Nohl 2004) a particularly interesting idea, and we used it during our key comparative analyses.

The constructivist perspective assumes that the examination of the social world should be based on discourse analysis. This analysis takes into account both the text itself, the discourse it contains and the context. It is marked by antirealism, i.e. underlining of the versions of the world, society, events and inner psychological states that are created as a part of a discourse, as well as constructionism, i.e. an interest in the participants of the constructions and ways in which they are created, and reflexivity, i.e. a focus on ways in which the text constitutes a version developing, selectively and partially, consistencies and inconsistencies of the history creating the existing reality (Potter 1997: 146).

The texts may take different forms: written, spoken, iconographic, and that of an artefact. Here, we shall concentrate on texts in the form of official documents discussed in Section 2.4.1; we shall talk about an analysis of other types of texts further on in this Section. We have already discussed in this chapter our repository of documents, in which these sources were divided into 12 categories. It is obvious that discourse analysis as a part of the particular categories will have different profiles and scopes. Nevertheless, we decided to develop a package of guidelines - analytical desiderata sensitising one to the significant fields of interpretation of the discourse. It includes the following postulates: (1) the examination of texts as a part of 'interdependent' sets (e.g. rules and regulations of the centres, series of rules and regulations governing the use of spaces/places, regulations of the BG Commander concerning the provision of rules and regulations to the unit commanding offices); (2) identification of the author of the text (institutional, personal, community), determination of goals and intentions related to the drawing up of the document; (3) interpretation of the content of the text (language of the message: rhetoric, persuasion tools, exposed content, overlooked content, etc.); (4) grasping relations between the content of the text and reactions to it by confrontation with other types of sources; (5) grasping the effectiveness of the impact of the text on the basis of sources of other types.

As results from the above, the pivotal idea of the discourse analysis was to grasp the social context of its generation and functioning, its 'dialogicity' manifested by way of putting together the different perspectives of the producers, distributors and recipients of messages (Fairclough 2003; Rapley 2007; Kunter 2012).

Analysis of individual interviews. In relation to this category of sources, we decided to apply the analytical approach referred to as bricolage (Denzin and Lincoln 2018: 45-46; Kvale 2007: 115–117). As a part of this approach, we combined selected elements of meaning-oriented analysis and language-oriented analysis.[83] Analysing the meaning of the interlocutors' statements lay above all in the already discussed coding, and in some way in the simultaneous condensation of meanings in the spirit of the phenomenological approach. In turn, the analysis of the language was focused on two elements: the characteristics of the manner of communication (e.g. personal and impersonal forms, metaphors, phatic expressions, the active and the passive voice, terms used in the context of the self-positioning of the speaker and other actors in the hierarchical social space of the institution) and the already discussed discourse.[84]

Analysis of group interviews. In relation to this type of data, an approach developed as a part of the documentary method was applied. We are referring here to the formulating interpretation and the reflecting interpretation (Bohnsack 2004: 47-48; Krzychała 2004: 56–62). The former consists in describing and summarising threads of discussion, and their division into larger thematic fragments. The latter focuses on the ways in which participants of the focus group interviews describe their experience, express their beliefs and conduct discussions. This leads to the identification of the so-called collective models of approaching the reality (or their absence) and the specificity of interactions, social communication. During our study, we also acquired drawings illustrating the interview participants' ideas of a model centre for foreigners, which we analysed separately. These drawings were prepared collectively by the individuals participating in the focus group interviews, which made it possible for us to notice the different preferences in the scope of the organisation of the space of

---

83 Because of the extensiveness of the collected source materials and the laboriousness of transcription requiring the taking into account of the package of specialist guidelines, we resigned from the valuable conversation analysis in this approach (Rancew-Sikora 2007: 36-38; Kvale 2010: 180-181).

84 As a part of preparations for discourse analysis in the interviews, a catalogue of 'sensitising' notions such as securitisation, authority, domination and subordination, formalisation, empathy, and identity was drawn up.

the model centre, and an observation of the process of the negotiating of these preferences in the final version of the model.

Analysis of visual data. In connection with the provisions contained in the regulation on the protection of personal data (RODO), photographs taken by the research group were above all a tool for the inventory of the specificity of the guarded centre for foreigners. They are records of all the places and spaces as well as the furnishings. Here, we very often used the researcher's triangulation: two individuals executed two independent photographic sessions of the same facilities, places and spaces. Owing to this mode of work, we sought to avoid threats related to the adoption of an imperfect perspective created by an individual overview or an omission of important details. The complete set of the collected materials was grouped into thematic blocks and subjected to comparative analysis. The photographic images were confronted with the information on the functionality and aesthetics of places and spaces provided by the users from the groups of the staff and the detainees. We also managed to acquire a substantial set of photographs from the resources of the Border Guard. They documented both the transformations of the places and spaces resulting from the performed renovations and modernisations, and educational and cultural events taking place in the centres over the years. Owing to the above, we acquired an insight into the social interactions taking place locally, which we then confronted with our observations, reports and data from our interviews with the staff. Our analytical approach related to the category of sources in question, as a part of which we referred to content analysis, the materiality of images and the entire package of purely experimental actions, can be described as eclectic and reflexive (Rapley 2007).

3 Research project – 'scene two'

3.1. Space – place – non-place

> 'Space' and 'place' are familiar words denoting common experiences. We live in space. [...] Space and place are basic components of the lived world; we take them for granted. When we think about them, however, they may assume unexpected meanings and raise questions we have not thought to ask. (Tuan 2001: 3)

Inter alia in connection with the above, space constitutes the central category both on the grounds of the formal sciences (in particular mathematics/geometry), the natural sciences (geography, physics, biology), and philosophy, socio-cultural anthropology, sociology, architecture and literary criticism, and the various subdisciplines and theoretical orientations as a part of them. This set should also include considerations of representatives of the world of art. It is worth stressing that the particular reflections on the phenomenon of space are not autarkic, developed in the 'ebony towers' of the disciplines. They are often based on inspirations borrowed from other fields and are hence interdisciplinary. The group of the most frequently mentioned thinkers – inspirers of the diverse contemporary reflections on the spatial determinants of human functioning – include inter alia Wilhelm Leibniz (1969), Martin Heidegger (1977, 2005), Michel Foucault (1987, 1993, 2005). Michel de Certau (2008), Maurice Merleau-Ponty (2001), Alfred Schütz (1964, 2008), Jean Baudrillard (2005), Gilles Deleuze (2014), Henri Lefebvre (1991), and Edward Soja (1996).

The so-called connotative semantic features of the notions of 'space' and 'place' and the relations between them call for an additional commentary. Let us quote again the words of Yi-Fu Tuan:

> In experience, the meaning of space often merges with that of place. 'Space' is more abstract than 'place'. What begins as undifferentiated space becomes place as we get to know it better and endow it with value. Architects talk about the spatial qualities of place; they can equally well speak of the locational (place) qualities of space. The ideas 'space' and 'place' require each other for definition. From the security and stability of place we are aware of the openness, freedom, and threat of space, and vice versa. Furthermore, if we think of space as that which allows movement, then place is pause; each pause in movement makes it possible for location to be transformed into place. (Tuan 2001: 6)

Analogical thoughts appear in the reflections of other researchers, for instance Michele de Certau:

> A place (*lieu*) is the order (of whatever kind) in accord with which elements are distributed in relationships of coexistence. It thus excludes the possibility of two things being in the same location (*place*). The law of the 'proper' rules in the place: the elements taken into consideration are *beside* one another, each situated in its own 'proper' and distinct location, a location it defines. A place is thus an instantaneous configuration of positions. It implies an indication of stability. A *space* exists when one takes into consideration vectors of direction, velocities, and time variables. Thus space is composed of intersections of mobile elements. It is in a sense actuated by the ensemble of movements deployed within it. Space occurs as the effect produced by the operations that orient it, situate it, temporalize it, and make it function in a polyvalent unity of conflictual programs or contractual proximities. On this view, in relation to place, space is like the word when it is spoken, that is, when it is caught in the ambiguity of an actualization, transformed into a term dependent upon many different conventions, situated as the act of a present (or of a time), and modified by the transformations caused by successive contexts. In contradistinction to the place, it has thus none of the univocity or stability of a 'proper' (Certau 1984: 117).

Let us now have a look at the third notion, which appeared in the eponymous triad of this subchapters, i.e. that of the 'non-place'. The concept of non-places, put forward by Marc Augé (2010), was one of the guiding ideas in our conceptualisations of the research project. Places which can be referred to as anthropological are a starting point for our considerations. They are 'only the idea, partially materialized, that the inhabitants have of their relations with the territory, with their families and with others' (Augé 1995: 56). Non-places are located on the other extreme:

> If a place can be defined as relational, historical and concerned with identity, then a space which cannot be defined as relational, or historical, or concerned with identity will be a non-place (Augé 1995: 77).

According to Augé's qualification, they include transitory places of stay such as refugee camps, squats, means of transport, transit routes, and communication hubs (motorways, airports) or shopping centres. All these non-places are fast-passing (temporary) – they are a product of the supermodern world 'surrendered to solitary individuality, to the fleeting, the temporary and the ephemeral'[85] (Augé 1995: 78).

Non-places are 'no-one's places'. The term 'no-one's' excellently expresses their perception by the people who find themselves in them. Referring to the context of the guarded centres under study: this refers both to the foreigners who are

85 An excellent description and analysis of non-places in the form of a literary message was provided by the Nobel-prize winner Olga Tokarczuk (2017).

detained there without their consent and who find themselves in the trajectory of migration events (temporarily stopped in motion), and in some scope to the staff – officers (often) temporarily posted to work there from other places of work under an order. A significant marker of such non-places is also a frequent change of the composition of the people who stay there. It is hard to talk about one's identification with such places, to perceive them as one's own.

Non-places fulfil a transitory function – one's appearance and functioning in them is not a choice but a necessity. The use of non-places is controlled by legislation and precise (local) order-related provisions, which exclude individual habits of activity. We also deal here with the anonymity of the users, depriving them of their own identity (e.g. numbers instead of names), as an effect of which they are all similar to each other. This forces a limitation in the form of 'taking up a position' and '[striking] the pose' (Augé 1995: 87).

Simultaneously, non-places seemingly resemble anthropological places, because their architecture and furnishings are very similar. If we visit a non-place belonging to the same category and fulfilling analogical functions (e.g. a hospital), we may assume that we shall effectively find ourselves familiar with another one.

The ideas of this researcher correspond very well with the concept of 'other spaces' (heterotopias), which was presented in 1967[86] by Michel Foucault (1986). An important place in his classification is occupied by heterotopias of deviation 'those in which individuals whose behaviour is deviant in relation to the required mean or norm are placed' (Foucault 1986: 25). By nature, spaces of this kind are located in isolation from other spaces; additionally, they are very specifically related to time. There is no question here of an accumulation of time (as in the case of museum objects or library items) or 'timelessness' (e.g. cemeteries) – there is only transitoriness, impermanence, ephemerality. Moreover, the heterotopia of deviation seems to be an integrated combination of numerous, often incomparable places.[87] Foucault's concept

86 The idea of heterotopia enjoys unfailing popularity inter alia among representatives of different areas of philosophy (aesthetics, phenomenology), architects, literary critics, geographers, anthropologists and sociologists – it is often creatively modified, and combined with other concepts of space (e.g. G. Deleuze – 'spatial folds'; P. Norra – 'places of space'; E.W. Soja – 'third space'). Interestingly, Foucault himself did not use this category in his works devoted to space in prison systems and hospitals.

87 This state of things can be well exemplified by the location of such spaces as penal isolation rooms and fitness rooms next to one another in the detention space.

also fits the already mentioned topic of the relation between space and place.[88]

The spatial and environmental aspects have always been taken into account in classical anthropological studies – still, they had there the status of an indispensable background for a presentation of the local specificity of social life and culture - they were not problematised. During the last several decades, this state of things underwent a significant change as a result of a variety of factors both within and outside science. We are witnessing a specific decomposition of geography as a spatial, territorial base of cultures. The relation between culture and space ceases to be essential, and frees itself from the barriers of topography, borders, political and territorial units, etc. There is no question here of a complete detachment ('deanchoring') of cultures from local contexts (including places) – it is about the flows of people and ideas in the age of globalisation, in which deterritorialization, understood as the intermingling of ethnic, technological, ideological or economic markers of modernity (postmodernity or late modernity) plays a significant role (e.g. Appadurai 1996; Giddens 1991; Bauman 1998).

Setha M. Low and Denise Lawrence-Zúñiga (2003: 1-47) reviewed reconceptualisations of the perspective of the spatial determinants of anthropological studies which emerged in the 1990s and distinguished six thematic categories ('embodied spaces', 'gendered spaces', 'inscribed spaces', 'contested spaces', 'transnational spaces' and 'spatial tactics') being the most significant areas of studies. Our project considerations best dovetail the category of 'spatial tactics', which refers to the study of 'space as a strategy and/or technique of power and social control' (Low and Lawrence-Zúñiga 2003: 30). Although without any doubt this perspective also appears in other thematic categories/areas mentioned above, in this case it is the pivotal point of reference based on the ideas of the aforementioned Foucault, de Certau and Baudrillard.

As a part of the conceptual project works, we referred to a number of selected ideas, typologies and tools developed on the grounds of proxemics, kinesics, the anthropology of the senses and the anthropology of emotions. A very significant element of the proxemic concept of Edward T. Hall (1990: 101-112) is the

88 The translator of Foucault's lecture comments on the terminological complexities related to his use of the terms 'place' and 'space'. The former (*lieu*) is a real place, a fragment of the space of a given whole; the latter (*emplacement*), i.e. location, 'implies movement and the possibility of translocation– also the movement of meanings determining a given space' (Foucault 2005: 118). It is a movable (dynamic) space containing the sense of both space and place, integrating them.

division of space into fixed-feature space, semi-fixed-feature space and informal space. 'The important point about fixed-feature space is that it is the mold into which a great deal of behavior is cast' (Hall 1990: 106). Settlement topography, the layout of towns and settlements, all closed spaces (such as structures: their appearance, layout and functions), as well as the ecological landscapes that divide them – all the manifestations of fixed-feature space are always culturally-determined models, appropriate for the different times and culture. Differences in their perception show mainly on the grounds of intercultural contacts.

In turn, the semi-fixed-feature space, which Hall analyses by referring to public places (such as hospitals, railway stations or cafés), can affect individual and group behaviour. Following Humphry Osmond, the scholar distinguishes sociofugal and sociopetal spaces. The former incline people to maintain physical distance and limit the scope and forms of communication, while the later facilitate integration – physical closeness and intensification of communication.

Hall believes that it is the informal space which plays the most important role. It is experienced through the use of a variety of non-codified and also usually non-conscious codes regulating interpersonal distances: intimate, personal, social and public (Hall 1990: 113–129). These four universal, even fundamental forms of activity of the individual in the social world, are a spectacular exemplification of the translation of the aspect of the physicality of space and human corporeality into the symbolic aspect, which the researcher metaphorically calls a 'hidden dimension'.

When we put the above together with the context of the spaces and places of the detention centres under study, we shall easily notice a specific complexity of the relations within them. On the one hand, we are dealing here with a crossing of the detainees' cultures, which in many cases are based on different, sometimes exclusive habits and interpretations of interpersonal distances organising social life. Practising them in daily life, as a part of functioning in the enforced physical space with all its limitations, is sometimes difficult and often leads to misunderstandings or even conflicts in this multicultural group. On the other hand, there is also the organiser of this space, i.e. the representatives of the supervising institution, referring to detailed, codified rules of its use, with its primary principle of its full surveillance. In consequence, this enforced physical space is home to significant 'disturbances' manifested inter alia in the violation of the intimate sphere, far-fetched limitation of the personal sphere, and arbitrary shifts of boundaries between the personal, the social and the public.[89]

---

89 The many examples of this state of things may include humiliating procedures of admitting foreigners to the centres, regular searches in residential rooms, the

The problem discussed earlier can also be viewed from a broader perspective offered by Hall (1989: 105–116 et al.), i.e. the division into high- and low-context cultures.[90] Their representatives differ by the way they concretise objects of cognition. These differences are expressed for instance in the sphere of the development of the self-other and the superior-subordinate relations, and in a preference for different forms of social communication (directness *vs* veiled message, ritualization).

The above-mentioned, generally familiar divisions of space are analytical – what one culture perceives as permanent, another sees as semi-permanent. In turn, interpersonal distances which in one cultural context are considered appropriate for intimate relations, are perceived as personal or social in the other, etc. Additionally, the perception of space is influenced by many other factors such as the personality traits of the people who function within it, environmental determinants (e.g. noise, level of light/visibility), types of social relations between users of the space, and modes and styles of their activity.

Since many spatial behaviours have the nature of non-verbal manifestations,[91] Hall's proxemic ideas are obviously connected with the kinesic reflection of Ray Birdwhistell and continuators of his work, as well as researchers investigating other aspects of this type of communication (e.g. Dul 1995; Brocki 2000). One of the significant elements of the considerations in this scope is the issue of the synchrony of people's behaviours as a part of interactions (Hall 1983: 140–160, 1989) – more broadly speaking, the functioning in the same socio-spatial contexts. This is not about the little examined physiological areas of the functioning of the central nervous system, but modifiers of socio-cultural group behaviours. Hall characterises the gist of synchrony in a vivid way:

> People in interactions either move together (in whole or in part) or they don't and in failing to do so are disruptive to others around them. Basically, people in interactions

---

limitation of access to personal belongings, which are considered dangerous (such as cigarette lighters and shaving tools), or supervision at meal-time.

90 In Hall's concept (1989: 85–128), the notional category of 'context' ('contexting') plays a significant role – speaking in broad terms, it refers to selecting, associating, and then using information resources. Contexting should be considered in close association with the giving of meanings.

91 This is about, for instance, pantomimic expressions (gestures) and other body movements, facial expressions and haptic behaviours. They may replace verbal messages or complement them, give them special meanings, take the form of the manifestation of emotions, and provoke particular reactions replacing verbal messages or highlighting one's attitude to them and to the showing of emotions.

> move together in a kind of dance, but they are not aware of their synchronous movement and they do it without music or conscious orchestration. Being 'in sync' is itself a form of communication. The body's messages (in or out of awareness), whether read technically or not, seldom lie, and come much closer to what the person's true but sometimes unconscious feelings are than does the spoken word (Hall 1989: 71-72).

This synchronisation of behaviours (we might call it a dovetailing of rhythms) in the interpersonal and group dimension requires adjustment.[92] It might seem that in the formalised conditions of detention (based on hierarchy, rules and regulations and strict etiquette), such synchronisation would be controlled top-down and would thus have a limited scope not corresponding to the natural 'rhythmisation' of behaviours of the social actors. Nevertheless, it was already our preliminary findings based on observation which challenged this assumption, directing us to this aspect of the functioning in space in the course of the research proper.

The organisation (experience – 'interpretation') of space, with a subsequent effective functioning within it is based on a synthesis of 'traditional' receptors: eyesight, hearing, smell and touch,[93] as well as the sense of the perception of time (Hall 1983). In connection with the above, only through an examination of the scope of their use, including integration during the perception[94] of space, that one can draw up complete ethnographic descriptions of the principles of its organisation.

The detention space under study, which we shall describe below, triggers many verbal and non-verbal manifestations of an emotional nature in all the groups of social actors. Since they were the subject of our special interest, it is necessary to refer to our understanding of 'emotions'. Emotions should be perceived as a phenomenon connected with both bodily sensations and cultural meaning. Hence, we must not lose from sight the obvious fact of the 'generation' of emotions as a physical phenomenon delineating the privacy and integrity of the individual, while remembering that 'the body does not call out its own interpretations of internal somatic states [...]. The body adjusts itself to the emotional interpretations persons place upon it' (Denzin 1983: 403–404).

---

92 This term was coined by William Condon, and is used by E.T. Hall (1983: 161-175) with reference to processes which enable synchrony.

93 An extensive review of the concept of the study of the senses/perception in the cultural context can be found in a work by Dorota Angutek (2013: 152-202).

94 Merleau-Ponty's (2001) reflection on synesthesia proved very inspiring in this scope – nevertheless, his ideas turned out to be hard to operationalize during the collection and subsequent analysis of the source material.

Hence, we treat them as ideas inseparably connected with knowledge, co-coding the most significant senses of cultural behaviours and meanings of the majority of social interactions (Lutz and White 1986: 407; Lutz 2012; Leavitt 2012).

We may point out several features of the detention space under description, which are its most spectacular distinguishing marks and which were specified at the stage of the conceptualisation of the research project and the earlier visits to the guarded centres for foreigners. Firstly, this space is in an obvious way separated as one isolated from the other parts of the BG outpost/unit (see Photo 13),[95] not mentioning the spaces located outside the jurisdiction of the services. Access to it as well as contact with the outside world is closely controlled, requires complex procedures and is subject to extensive limitations.[96] These limitations include contacts via mobile phones and the internet (inaccessibility of the social media, impossibility to send photographs, etc.).

95 The very guarded centre is divided into the administrative part, incorporating the management and the entire administrative services, and the part for foreigners, which is the place of work for the majority of the people responsible for contact with the detainees (the sentry guard and educational sections). These parts are very often located in separate buildings standing away from one another.

96 These limitations also apply to the employees – only some of them bear permissions (cards and codes) allowing them to move through the subsequent security passages and reach all the places in the centre.

Photo 13. The fence separating the GCF in Biała Podlaska from the space of the BG Outpost on the grounds of which it is located (photo by Dariusz Niedźwiedzki)

Secondly, this space is imposed upon the foreigners – and they are euphemistically referred to as 'detainees' [in the Polish language, the word – *umieszczeni* – translates literally as 'the placed'].

Photo 14. The computer room in the GCF in Biała Podlaska (photo by Dariusz Niedźwiedzki)

Thirdly, this space is entirely alien to foreigners (see Photo 14-15), which makes it necessary for them to become familiar with the principles of its organisation and ways of its use, and is connected with the experience of unknown situations, often incomparable to their past cultural habits (rules and standards), and the practised styles of community life.

Photo 15. A walking yard between residential buildings in the GCF in Przemyśl (photo by Dariusz Niedźwiedzki)

Fourthly – and closely related to the previous feature – this space is arranged top-down by the managing entity (see Photo 16), giving no possibility for the detainees to adapt it or modify it in any meaningful way for their comfort.

Photo 16. A TV room in the GCF in Białystok (photo by Dariusz Niedźwiedzki)

Fifthly, this space is ceaselessly and comprehensively supervised[97] (monitoring network – see Photo 17), one-way mirrors, direct observation by the security staff). Basically, almost all the places apart from toilets, bathrooms and residential rooms, which are controlled periodically, are subjected to 24-hour surveillance. Hence, we may talk about a far-fetched minimisation of privacy, as a part of which even smoking, walking through the yard or exercising in the fitness rooms take place under supervision.[98]

---

97 The sight of the guardhouses equipped with a row of large-scale monitors recording the image from about 30 cameras brings to mind an unintentional association with panopticon – a model of an ideal prison authored by Jeremy Betham (Foucault 1993: 240–244 and Fig. 17 in the *Annex*).

98 Additional discomforts include a ban on the possession of the so-called dangerous everyday objects, such as shaving accessories and cigarette lighters (they are kept in the deposit in the guardhouse and need to be collected each time for the duration of their use). The ban on wearing trouser belts or braces, which forces the detainees to constantly hold their trousers up or wear tracksuit bottoms is an even greater interference in the foreigner's privacy and dignity in some of the facilities.

Photo 17. Monitoring in an official space in the GCF in Lesznowola (photo by Dariusz Niedźwiedzki)

Sixthly, we are dealing with a rationed access to some fragments of space defined under internal rules and regulations (see Photo 18). This results in the necessity to subordinate one's daily activity to the regulations specified in the order of the day.

Photo 18. Information concerning the limitation of availability of the computer room in the GCF in Przemyśl (photo by Dariusz Niedźwiedzki)

Seventhly, this space is an arena of an intersection, even the clash of cultures (see Photo 19): representatives of the managing institution and the foreigners *en bloc*, foreigners originating from the particular ethic groups, as well as - within the group of foreigners - people representing different races and cultures.

Photo 19. A room designated for the practising of different religions and denominations in the GCF in Kętrzyn (photo by Dariusz Niedźwiedzki)

Eighthly, within the space itself there is a considerable dynamics of change of the composition of its users.[99]

Finally, ninthly, the space in which foreigners are detained is in a very special way connected with the time during which individuals need to exist here. Individuals detained in the guarded centres do not know how long they will be obliged to stay there. Descriptions of the detention space for foreigners can be justifiably associated with the features attributed to the total institutions – and we shall analyse this issue more closely in Section 4.3.

It is worth summing up the above findings concerning the specificity of the space/place in question by pointing out sensitising terms – profiling the directions for further in-depth studies into their understanding and application. These terms include: isolation (isolated space), compulsion (imposed space), alienness (unknown space), completeness (existing/ready space), supervision (controlled space), rationing (rationed space), multiculturality (space of the

99 It is sometimes the case that a group of a dozen or so foreigners is brought to the detention centre on a single day.

intersection of cultures), changeability of the composition, unclearness of the relation with time (space with 'suspended time').

The first, routine step of the exploration of space consists in its inventory:

> [...] we measure and map space and place, and acquire spatial laws and resource inventories for our efforts. These are important approaches, but they need to be complemented by experiential data that we can collect and interpret in measured confidence because we are human ourselves (Tuan 2001: 5).

The above conclusions (the preliminary specification of apparent, objective features of the studied space/place and compiling an inventory of its material substrate) can be classified as the so-called thin description (Geertz 1973: 3–32, 412–454). Its thickening will consist in its 'filling' with social actors: the recording and endeavouring to understand their spatial practices, including preferences for or avoiding particular places in the space, maintaining specific interpersonal distances, gestures, facial movements, body movements, producing sounds and the emotions manifested through them. The recording will be carried out at the micro-level (the individual), the mezzo-level (groups and subgroups of the users of the space), and macro-level (intergroup profiles), in all the situational contexts.

Bodily manifestations are a form of narration about the world, they unveil the sense of meanings given to space, i.e. the process of its creation. When we confront them with verbal narrations in all their scope of articulation (from a single word to autobiographical reflection), and then put them together to make a whole – a single story, which illustrates a whole spectrum of working through and interpreting experience – we have a chance to discover the 'lifeworlds' (Barthes 2004: 12; Rosner 2003: 7).

As much as we found the idea of such proceeding/reflecting on space/creating space obvious, difficulties with its implementation showed themselves at the level of our perception of the experienced area. In contemporary ethnography, the researcher's reflection on the experience of space by its actors must be accompanied by the recognition of his/her own perception of this space and the events taking place within it. Let us begin with recalling the title of the project in question – *The Organisation of Space in Polish Detention Centres for Foreigners*.[100] The decision to point out to space as the central object of our interest was

100 The general formulation of the title without a reference to the pivotal notions such as 'place' and 'non-place' resulted from the need to simplify the message for the purposes of negotiating a permission to perform our study in the detention centres with the managing institution.

conscious and deeply considered. We decided that it was the basic, indispensable key to the interpretation of meanings (senses) of the individual and group behaviours appearing within it, as well as the intentions behind them, ways of their understanding and their socio-cultural determinants.

We intuitively felt the above as early as during our first pre-project visits to the guarded centres, with our students, which were organised for purposes not related to the study (lectures and organisation of free time for the foreigners). It was then that all our routine journals of ethnographers independently featured identical impressions, expressed with such terms as 'wires', 'security passages', 'surveillance', 'control', 'prison', 'sterile place', 'totally ordered place', as well as 'rigour', 'humiliation', and 'trauma'. Functioning in such space was an unhappy, exhausting experience. We were trying to limit the duration of our visits in the centres to the indispensable minimum necessary for the execution of the planned activities – nevertheless, this topic kept recurring during our evening briefings at the hotel. Over time, already during the project's research, we became more 'used to' the described state of things, and even to some extent 'impregnated' with this reception of space. At the same time, we became aware that its examination involves the engagement of different receptors: sight, hearing, smell, touch and the sense of taste.

Ending these considerations, we need to mention the tripartite concept of space proposed by Henri Lefebvre (1991: 33, 38–46 et al.), which we found very useful. First, the author distinguished spatial practice, i.e. everyday, routine practices, interactions taking place in the context of a given space and the artefacts that fill it, coherent actions requiring appropriate competencies and effectiveness. Secondly, he indicated the representation of space, i.e. the space conceptualised by planners, architects, technocrats, lawyers, ideologists and its managers. This space dominates or at least contains the potential for domination. Thirdly, he distinguished representational space – the world of open and hidden meanings and symbols connected with values and the worldview, making up the codes of space.

3.2. Organisational culture

Inspirations with the achievements (ideas, conceptual apparatus, research methodology) of anthropology have been noticeable on the grounds of the management sciences since the 1970s. In 1986, Gareth Morgan wrote that the understanding of the complexity of organisational life and its management calls for referring to a variety of metaphors, which will enable a discovery of previously not assumed perspectives, and ways of thinking about the nature of the organisation. His typology of such metaphors, along with models of the organisation as a machine, organism, brain, political system, mental prison (domination), flow and transformation, includes the metaphor of the organisation as culture (Morgan 2006). Here, it is worth recalling the virtues of this approach:

> One of the major strengths of the culture metaphor is that it directs attention to the symbolic significance of almost every aspect of organizational life.[…] A second major strength of the metaphor is that it shows how organization ultimately rests in shared systems of meaning, hence in the actions and interpretive schemes that create and re-create that meaning […] The culture metaphor points toward another means of creating and shaping organized activity […] A final strength of the culture metaphor is the contribution that it makes to our understanding of organizational change […] The message of the culture metaphor is that change programs must give attention to the kind of corporate ethos required in the new situation and find how this can be developed. Since organization ultimately resides in the heads of the people involved, effective organizational change always implies cultural change (Morgan 2006: 141–145).

Monika Kostera (2013: 30–32) refers, after Linda Smircich, to three ways of using the notion of culture through the prism of the management sciences. In the first one, culture is treated as an independent variable. One canonical exemplification of this approach is a study by Geert and Jan Hofstede (2010) devoted to the impact of national cultures on the management processes in international subsidiaries of the IBM corporation.[101] The second way of examining the organisation lies in treating culture as a dependent variable – an internal variable of the organisation, which can be managed in order to achieve the desired effects (Hatch 2013: 168–172).[102] The third way is referring to culture as a root metaphor. In this approach, culture is 'something the organisation is' (Kostera 2013: 31).

Culture understood as a reality of thought (ideational reality) 'denotes an historically transmitted pattern of meanings embodied in symbols, a system of inherited conceptions expressed in symbolic forms by means of which men communicate, perpetuate, and develop their knowledge about and attitudes toward life' (Geertz 1973: 89). As results from the above, culture is not only a

101 Methodology of studying 'cultural programming' (Hofstede 2010), based on four dimensions (power distance, individualism-collectivism, masculinity-femininity, uncertainty avoidance – Confucian dynamism), which became the basis for distinguishing four types of culture, is among the ones most often referred to in literature and is also used in research contexts other than studies into multicultural organisations (e.g. Żakowska 2011).

102 For instance a very influential model by Edgar Schein.

guiding light, a recipe for a 'way of life', a repository of socially-shared and/or respected knowledge on the nature of ideas, notions and beliefs, as well as an 'organiser' of a set of identification-communication practices (behaviours). The most significant components of cultural knowledge are norms, values and the worldview (Burszta 1998: 50–52). Without going into describing them, we shall seek to indicate several features of culture which are particularly significant in the context of our project's conceptualisations.

First, they include the relation between culture as an ideational order and a behavioural order, which is available to cognition by way of observation. This relation is very complex and cannot always be determined by reference to the model relation of 'regulation–execution' (Burszta 1998: 54–55). Secondly, culture is dynamic - it is not a permanent 'reality' transferred between generations or groups, and seems to be a series of 'inventions' serving ad hoc ideological or political goals (Hanson 1989: 183–184, 197–201). Thirdly, going back to Geertz's definition, culture is thoroughly symbolic, with symbols being carriers of the senses the reading of which, followed by their putting together into larger wholes (such as myths or rituals), is the greatest challenge of the anthropologist and other researchers studying organisations (e.g. Geertz 1973: 89–94 et al.; Kostera 2013: 32–33).

In our investigation of symbols we referred to many anthropological and sociological categories such as the myth, cult, usage, custom, rite, ritual (as a specific category of rite), rite of passage, ceremony, cultural performance, stereotype, prejudice, superstition, ethos, neotribalism, tribalism, cultural identification and identity.[103]

The organisational culture, analogically to the national or ethnic culture, is not a monolith – subcultures can be distinguished as its part. The usefulness of such a measure was discussed for example by Mary Jo Hatch (2013) and Gareth Morgan (2006). In this place, it is worth referring to a conclusion of Sarah Thornton:

> The defining attribute of 'subcultures', then, lies with the way the accent is put on the distinction between a particular cultural/social group and the larger culture/society. The emphasis is on variance from a larger collectivity who are invariably, but not

103 The abovementioned tools of description and interpretation of culture and its extension do not in any way exclude the possibility of a concurrent use of the conceptual apparatus from the area of theatrical metaphor (Gofmann 1959), or referring to the notions and interpretations connected with the narrative approach (*story-telling*). Monika Kostera (2011: 17–19) also points to the fourth possibility, i.e. an approach inspired by the grounded theory.

> unproblematically, positioned as normal, average and dominant. Subcultures, in other words, are condemned to and/or enjoy a consciousness of 'otherness' of difference. (quoted after: Barker 2003: 378).

Our task related to the distinguishing, for analytical purposes, of subcultures making up the organisational culture of detention was to create 'little maps of meanings' in order to determine the relations (connections) between them and the differences within the organisational system in question. There are many 'keys' on the basis of which people create and share these maps of meanings at the subcultural level.

Organisational subcultures may remain in different relations to the culture as a part of which they are distinguished. They may take the form of countercultures contesting the rules in force and the common standards of thinking and behaving; they may function next to them; and finally they may fit the organisational culture – confirm, consolidate the norms and values being a part of its mission[104] (Hatch 2013). Relations between the particular subcultures as a part of a single organisational culture can be equally significant (see Fig. 11-12).

104 Aleksander Posern-Zieliński (1987: 334–336) mentions three types of such relations in his dictionary definition.

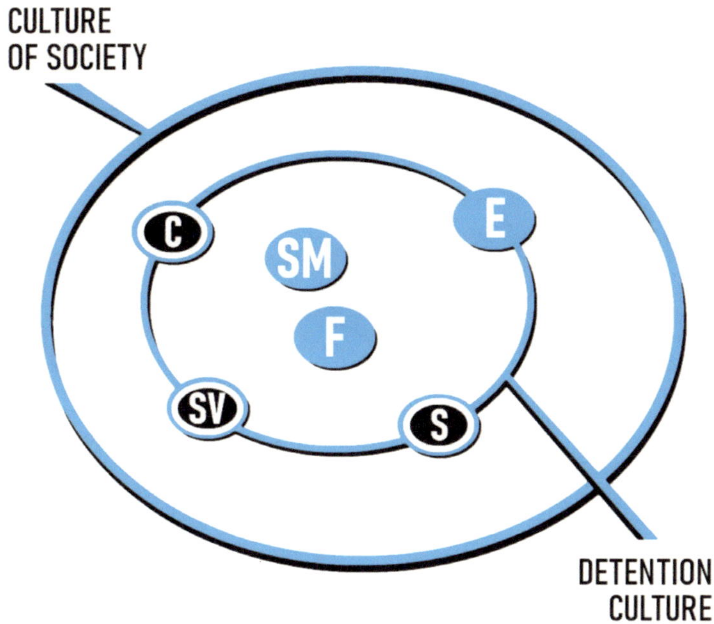

LEGEND:

SM - staff members
F - foreigners
E - escorts
C - cooperation: local government, scientific, legal, cultural and educational organisations
SV - supervision; supervising entities: Commissioner for Human Rights, Ombudsman for Children, UN High Commissioner for Refugees, non-governmental organisations, superior authorities of the Border Guard
S - services: external services for the detention centres for foreigners - e.g. health care, catering, educational services, cleaning services

Fig. 11. Culture of society and detention culture (own elaboration)

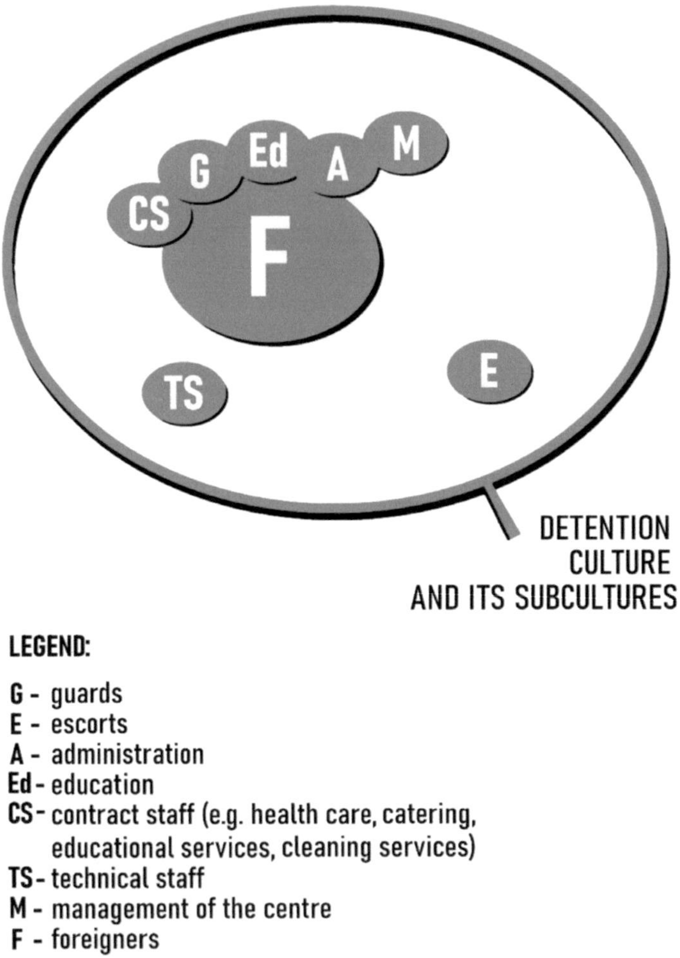

Fig. 12. Detention culture and its subcultures (own elaboration)

The list of reasons behind the creation of subcultures in the conditions of a strongly hierarchised organisation based on rules of domination and subordination is extensive. We shall limit ourselves to indicating a couple of them – ones which seem to be particularly significant in the organisational (including spatial) context under study.

Among the staff there are groups/teams of employees who due to the nature of their tasks are relatively isolated from the other members of staff and remain in constant contact with the foreigners. They include sentry guards - uniformed officers working on a shift basis, having a separate social infrastructure, etc.[105] The second group of 'front men' working with the foreigners are employees of the educational/cultural sections. Both these subcultural groups involved in close contact with the foreigners are challenged with having to cope with the considerable cognitive dissonance which ceaselessly accompanies them at work. On the one hand, they are obliged to respect rules and regulations and the resulting procedures, which enforce distance to the detainees and the formalisation of interpersonal relations.[106] On the other hand, as a part of the daily interactions, they become familiar with the immigrants and the stories of their life and develop empathic abilities, which results in the establishment of certain social bonds.[107] Group three is composed of the employees who work outside the zone demarcated for the foreigners, but who, in connection with their tasks, contact them regularly, albeit briefly (individuals responsible for purchases for the detainees and their deposits, and return guardians). Finally, we have a group of staff isolated from the foreigners, often working in a separate building, also outside the centre itself. Apart from BG officers and civil employees, work on the premises of the guarded centres is also performed by external subjects (teachers and providers of the medical, catering, and cleaning services).

In the above examples, we have referred to just one factor facilitating the development of subculturality, i.e. the intensity of interactions based on the physical closeness resulting from the joint performance of duties and using

---

105 This group is marked by the sense of a particular responsibility of their tasks accompanied by the belief that the other groups of staff and the top-level management treat it, as employees, at the lowest level of the professional hierarchy, people who perform simple tasks of little burden.

106 Until recently, every foreigner was given an identification number, which replaced their full name. This resulted in obvious associations with the unfortunate times of the rule of totalitarian systems, in particular Nazism and Bolshevism, and the justification of this procedure with difficulties to pronounce the foreigners' names was not very convincing (see Lemondżawa 2017).

107 The described state of things resulted in the adoption of different attitudes. Some officers managed to minimise the problem by adopting the strategy of a cognitive and social distance to the foreigners and their problems, while other remained in the state of mental discomfort, which negatively affected their private life and, sometimes, their health condition.

the same infrastructure and work tools. Nevertheless, we should also have in mind other variables, which can be defined by referring to the mutually attracting status similarities (such as similar age, level of education, gender), as well as the posts and the amount of remuneration resulting from the category of employment (BG officers and civil employees).

In turn, the community of foreigners is usually composed of an ethnic, national and religious mosaic marked by the constantly changing number of representatives of their particular categories. Relations between them take different forms depending on many factors such as the dominating number of representatives of a given group/category, the experience of particular intergroup relations originating from the country of origin, broadly understood cultural baggage affecting the scenarios of functioning with both Others and compatriots, individual 'strategies' of adaptation to the encountered situation, experience of a refugee trauma, and, finally, the profile of the centre (for men, for families). At the same time, during situations of crisis, it is possible to notice a tendency of the particular subcultures to integrate on the basis of a community of interests and a search for solutions for all the individuals experiencing a similar life circumstances.[108] Regardless of the above determinants, the subculture of foreigners *en bloc* seems to be a counterculture as a part of the organisational culture. The enforced necessity to fit in with the organisational actions of the totalising institution consisting in the unconditional, minutely defined adjustment to the line of action connected with detention goals that are strictly contradictory to legitimate interests of the detainees, deprives them of subjectivity, violates their dignity, and, in a broader perspective, may endanger their health or life. Hence, we are dealing with a situation as a part of which we may talk about a conflict or even exclusion of the 'identity of organisational action' of both parties (Konecki 2007: 8–9).

No culture is an isolated, autonomous island built on the opposition of us/them (alien). This obvious conclusion appearing in contemporary theories of multiculturality and interculturality (Welsch 1998, 2004) also refers to the characteristics of such separated organisational cultures founded on enforcement (total ones) as the detention of foreigners. Despite the rationing and supervision of contacts with the outside world, which extends behind physical barriers (walls, wires, the forces of law, etc.), these relations are multidirectional.

---

108 We are dealing here with both solidarity in moments of crisis (organisation of protests) and daily situations (such as the exchange of practical information, lending money for shopping).

Examples include regular audits conducted in detention centres by public and non-governmental entities, assistance activities (voluntary services) provided by students and lawyers, events marking special occasions, recreational events, etc. organised in cooperation with local governments, the visits of family members and other individuals (mainly lawyers), video conferences with representatives of diplomatic posts and lawyers, and the daily contact with employees of external entities providing catering and medical services.[109] Assessment of the impact of these relations on the broadly understood identity of organisational culture constituted one of the elements of our project-related research interests.

There are three categories of artefacts distinguished by organisational studies: physical, behavioural, and linguistic (verbal) (Hatch 2013: 171). Physical artefacts include the spatial layout, buildings, their furnishings and interior decoration, clothes and other attributes of human appearance. We have already discussed space and places in Section 3.1, but it is worth indicating several additional trails which can be found in research into this aspect of organisational culture. Studies devoted to organisational architecture, pursued since the very beginning of the management studies, were recently finally the subject of a comprehensive description, which tends to be referred to as a 'spatial turn' in organisational studies (Marrevijk and Dvora 2010). The turn consists in, inter alia, referring to the above-mentioned concepts of such thinkers as Henri Lefebrve and Michel Foucault, and the findings of anthropologists (e.g. Edward T. Hall and Marc Augé),[110] as well as the concept of the trialectics of spatiality, otherwise referred to as 'Thirdspace' by the cultural geographer and urbanist, Edward Soja (1996).

The abovementioned scholar questioned the closed dialectics of a binary perception of space promoting focus solely on 'Firstspace' – the material physical space as experienced by people, which is a foundation of social relations that can be empirically measured or mapped, or on 'Secondspace' – an imagined, subjective space 'produced' in the course of social relations. His proposal includes the Thirdspace – a specific conjunction of the Firstspace and the Secondspace

---

109 Our research team, whose presence in the culture under study affected the organisational reality, should be considered a part of this classification as well (Sułkowski 2007: 26–27).

110 In consequence of these inspirations, a new perspective emerged, focusing on the discovery of strong, dynamic and bidirectional relations between architecture and social structure (such as the materialised relation of power, soulless spaces, spaces of identity, and lost spaces).

and its supplementation with elements not fitting the binary system, located beyond this division – a hybrid structure consisting in a multi-aspect, holistic and critical spatiality (Soja 1996: 74–82 and further). This is accompanied by an awareness that architectural space is marked by a significant feature: it models human behaviours, emotions, beliefs and, more broadly, perceptions of the social world inscribed into the architecture (Hall and Hall 1995; Eco 1997; Toporov 2003). In the case of detentive space, the power and direction of this modelling is inscribed into the system of management in this organisational culture in the form of optimum scenarios containing the desired results related to the ways of their use.

In all the interpretative models of the organisational culture, the 'reading' (discovery of meanings) of artefacts takes place through their symbolisation, as well as references to the world of values through which people try to reach the basic assumptions of culture (Kostera 2013: 36–39).[111] Ethnography is commonly considered an optimum method of the exploration of organisational culture (Kostera 2013: 24–29; Gellner and Hirsch 2001; Wright 1994). When taking a look at studies into organisational culture performed on the grounds of the management sciences, organisational sociology and organisational anthropology, it is easy to spot the mutual inspiration[112] of researchers representing all these research 'niches', the bridging type interdisciplinarity of approaches both in the cognitive and ontological dimensions, as well as the permeation and mutual complementation of the acquired knowledge.

3.3. Other theoretical inspirations

The concepts of space and organisational culture do not exhaust the set of theoretical tools used in our research. We soon realised that the comprehensive approach to examining the process of the development of social relations in the space of detention centres makes it necessary to reach for many theories and concepts. We wanted to avoid a premature closing of our thinking on the research problem as a part of the particular assumptions and conclusions of a single theory. Along with the leading constructivism, our philosophical worldview in this project also covers the activist and the pragmatic paradigm; the latter

---

111 Monika Kostera refers inter alia to Mary Jo Hatch's model of the dynamics of the organisational culture.

112 The ideas of Max Weber (such as the concept of bureaucracy and types of authority and violence) and Émile Durkheim (e.g. formal and informal aspects of organisation, analysis of types of bonds/solidarity) seem to be coming to the forefront here.

inclines one to adopt the analytical opening strategy proposed by Eisenstadt and Curelaru (1976). It recommends stepping beyond the boundaries of particular directions towards solutions proposed by other, competitive theoretical schools. We were also inspired by the planned thinking – avoiding single-dimensional thinking for the benefit of multidimensional thought (Mannheim 1940: 151–153), which would allow us to perceive and examine different factors shaping the construction of behaviours and relations in the space of detention centres in the entirety of their mutual relations.

3.3.1. Symbolic interactionism

Our research project is marked by scientific multidisciplinarity, which naturally resulted in a number of differentiated theories and concepts inspiring our team members at the stage of its preparation and execution. Because of the adoption of constructivism as the leading paradigm of our worldview approach, the theory of symbolic interactionism, grounded in works by James Cooley and George H. Mead, comes to the first plan. What is also important is the relation of this theoretical approach and pragmatism presented by John Dewey, with its key feature of a pressure on the process of the adjustment of people to the surrounding world by giving meaning to different objects during the process of interaction. This meaning has several dimensions: cognitive (knowledge on the object), communicative (exchange of meanings by social actors) and dramaturgical (constructing the social reality of meaningful objects) (Blumer 1969: 11). Seeking to harness the reality, people construct their unique characteristics and shape their processual thinking as a result of their actions in the area of adjustment to other people.

This theoretical approach basically assumes that the world of culture is constructed as a human domain as an effect of social interactions. What is of key importance for their course is the definition of the situation, i.e. determination of the characteristic traits of the perception situation of the interacting individuals. The functional features of the physical space have the decisive importance here. In the conditions of our research, this would translate to a differentiation of the space of centres for foreigners and the internal division of this space connected with access to its particular fragments. Human aspirations and interests related to undertaking interaction are an important factor behind the development of a definition of the situation. In the case of our study, we took into account the employment structure and the functional division into sections and teams in the particular centres as well as the resulting consequences. Competition for controlling the processes of the symbolical coordination of actions was extremely important – along with (because of the focus on a hierarchical, totalising institution) a division into the decision-making and the subordinated peripheries (Shils 1982: 202). Another important aspect of the availability of the space of the centres was the division of their users into BG staff, foreigners and outsiders appearing in the centres for a variety of reasons and having different motivations. Our research team belonged to the last group and we are convinced that the already mentioned unclear approach to the causes and role of our visits affected the interviews.

It is important for the course of the interaction that both parties define the situation in a similar way – and this is largely facilitated by sharing the reality, the common, intersubjective (i.e. similarly experienced) space with others (Schutz 1953).[113] The cultural competences of the actors participating in the interaction are equally significant for its course. They are decisive for the process of the interpretation of messages voiced as a part of the interaction. It seems that this factor is of key significance in the context of the mutual impact of the culturally different groups of Border Guard staff and the foreigners detained in the guarded centres – especially that the latter group is highly heterogeneous, and additionally experiences dynamic changes to its composition, which is in consequence tantamount to its progressing cultural volatility. Finally, a significant role in the course of interactions is also played by the various sorts of disturbances which emerge as the interaction progresses. They may be internal or external. The former are connected with the psychophysical condition of the people participating in the interaction, while the latter with the features of the space in which the parties to the interaction are located, as well as the periodical participation of any third parties. There is no doubt that in the case of our research, our team to some extent played the role of an external factor modifying the internal interactions of the BG staff employed in the centres and their interactions with the foreigners.

Erving Goffman's interactionist concept (1959, 1967, 1971), which serves as our basis of reference in this internally diverse theoretical approach, is composed of three rudimentary notions: interaction, activity and part. Interaction is a mutual impact of individuals staying in close proximity to one another (Goffman uses alternatively the term 'encounter') on their behaviour. Activity (otherwise referred to as performance) is understood as all the activity of a given participant of the interaction in a given situation, aimed at exerting an impact on any of

---

113 For more information on the notion of the 'lifeworld' (*Lebenswelt*), and in particular its interpretative modifications, see Krasnodębski and Nellen 1993.

the other participants. Part (otherwise routine) is a pre-established pattern of activity which progresses during a performance, and which may also be applied to other activities. Parts may be performed cynically (when one does not identify themselves with the activity) or sincerely (when they do).

A very important role during an activity (performance) is played by the front. It is an element of the individual's performance which functions ceaselessly throughout its duration, providing observers with a definition of the situation. The front is divided into the setting (physical artefacts in space), which is relatively unchangeable in the course of the interaction, and the personal front connected with the acting individual. According to Goffman, the setting plays an extremely important role in interactions, as it defines the features of space in which the social actors notice each other and act. This is very clearly visible in guarded centres, where the particular parts of the space constituting the setting – the foreigners' residential rooms, the sports facilities, the guardhouses of the security section or the dining rooms – call for very different features of interaction between the BG staff and the foreigners. Most of them have their own rules and regulations determining the desired behaviours and thus the forms of interpersonal interactions. What is more, within this space, the interacting individuals create and protect different territories they claim to be their own, such as their personal space, the stall, the use space, the turn, the sheath, possessional territory, information preserve, and conversational preserve (Goffman 1971: 29–41). Additionally, since we are often dealing here with public spaces, the social actors, endeavouring to protect their own territories, use different sustaining and repair techniques making it possible for them to function with others in the same social space.

The personal front consists of the appearance, which does not change much in the course of action, and the manner, i.e. behaviour - the most dynamic element of activity. Goffman (1967) devoted a lot of space to this issue, writing about face-work, demeanour, and showing respect or embarrassment during interaction. Nevertheless, we expect a consistence between all the elements of the front in interactions.

Goffman's discovery that the interacting individuals use different kinds of techniques during action (performance) can certainly be considered his huge merit. Their recognition helps us better understand the acting individuals. The said techniques include dramatic realization, idealization, the maintenance of expressive control, misrepresentation, and mystification (Goffman 1959: 19–46). We treat the sentiments appearing in the course of the application of these dramaturgical realizations as social phenomena; as a result, it is the awareness and activity which lead to sensations and gestures expressing emotions rather than the emotions motivating human behaviour. In effect, 'they emerge as a result of real, anticipated, imagined or recalled social relations' (Hałas 2001: 93). It is the social context which decides about the kind of appearing emotions, as well as about when, where and what for they appear, how they are expressed and what social actors express them.

Dramatisation helps highlight in our activity the outlays incurred in connection with the performance of an action which cannot be noticed at first sight. If we present to another individual (e.g. our superior) a half-a-page note, which is a fruit of our poring over various documents for several dozen hours, a question appears as to what to do to make this huge effort noticeable in this short text. This issue, so significant for our everyday life, challenges us with a permanent dilemma: to make a good impression or to act in contact with others? Without any doubt, this technique is often used in all organisational cultures based on strong hierarchical dependencies between people. The organisational culture of the BG is certainly one of them, which means that this technique regularly appears in the internal interactions of the staff employed in the guarded centres for foreigners.

Idealisation helps show one's better self to others in the conditions of work, and show oneself as more competent owing to one's knowledge and experience. This technique is tantamount to acting in a way completely opposite to the already discussed dramatisation. Here, this is about showing that things are easy for me as an officer/employee, because I am very competent – not to say a genius (sic!). Again, we have no doubt that in organisational cultures generating hierarchical relations between their participants, this technique is well-suited for confirming one's usefulness for the functioning of the institution. In particular, it is important from the point of view of the process of promotion within its hierarchical structure. This sort of action is connected with the so-called looking glass self (Cooley 1902; Mead 2015) as a part of which we provide ourselves with an answer to the question: how to act to be acceptable to the social environment? If we want to satisfy our need for social recognition, we should confirm the values appreciated in a given group, institution, etc., i.e. participate in certain ceremonies, rituals, and confirm the prevailing stereotypes even if we do not really like doing so. Idealisation seems to be useful in the organisational culture of the Border Guard also in this dimension.

As a part of idealisation, we may be dealing with the hiding of consumerism (obviously of the type that might weaken the effectiveness of our action), which helps us hide the discrepancy between the impression we want to make with our action and the reality. The spheres of yielding to weaknesses 'undesirable' for our image may be very different: some odd little pleasures, suspicious profitable forms of business, errors and mistakes, etc. In particular, the last ones may play an important role in interactions both among the staff with a different position in the hierarchy of authority and between the staff of the guarded centres and the detained foreigners. Another form of idealisation is calling, which is to justify one's performance of a specific part – the challenge here is to make an impression that one's qualifications fit the adopted part, that we are made for this type of action. This technique is often used together with idealisation. In the conditions of the guarded centres for foreigners, maintaining the *status quo* of the position occupied by a BG officer/civil employee may be beneficial. Finally, idealisation of the moment consists in the introduction of a sacralising element which is to underline, to elevate the significance of the performance. Putting it in a nutshell, the thing is to show that whatever I do at a given moment is my most important activity. This calls for a clear division of the so-called spectators, since highlighting the significance of the performance in the eyes of two groups of people (in our opinion with different members) could end in a loss of credibility in the situation when some individuals would be members of both these groups. In the conditions of the BG organisational culture, this technique may be applied by the officers/employees at the managerial level. The aim is to make the employees of the particular sections/teams or narrowly-specialised groups of employees such as return guardians, sentry guards, etc. feel appreciated.

Controlling expression helps to maintain the uniformity of the performance whenever it is desirable. The emotional and behavioural control of behaviour is to level up disparities between the individual, subjective 'self' conducive to momentary moods, and the socialised, objective 'self', an effect of the socialisation with others, complying with formal-legal and moral norms and standards (Mead 2015). We are certain that this type of technique is used by the staff of the guarded centres, in particular that they remain in constant contact with the foreigners. As a part of these contacts, every uncontrolled emotion is a potential risk of contact between the BG staff and the foreigners. Avoidance of such conflicts is one of the goals of the management of the guarded centres, and is also expected by the higher-level superiors in the BG structure.

Mispresentation is to maintain the good impression in the situation when there are discrepancies between the reality and the desired picture. Here, we have a broad range of tools to be used: open lies, diplomatic lies, exaggerations, understatements, concealments, and giving a wrong identity (manipulating one's status, age, origin, etc.). At the same time, we should remember that presentation always differs from the very action, which unavoidably leads to mispresentation. We feel that this is one of the techniques which can be used by the BG staff employed in the guarded centres to prevent an outbreak of open conflicts. We are also certain that this type of technique is used by the detained foreigners wishing to keep their socio-cultural characteristics secret.

Mystification is a technique which is designed to hide the missing elements. The problem lies in the creation of an aura of secrecy making others embarrassed and shy. 'As countless folk tales and initiation rites show, often the real secret behind the mystery is that there really is no mystery; the real problem is to prevent the audience from learning this too' – as Goffman put it (1959: 46). We have no doubts that similarly to the previous one, this technique can be used in different situations which may potentially result in an outbreak of a conflict, such as the activities connected with the implementation of the decision to oblige the foreigner to leave Poland. We are under an impression that mystification may also be applied by the foreigners in their interactions with the BG staff in order to, just like in the case of the previous technique, hide their own socio-cultural characteristics.

All these determinants of interactions from the Goffmanian model show that people enter interactions being in some way determined by different factors. In the case of the guarded centres for foreigners, these determinants call for in-depth analysis stepping beyond the model of theoretical symbolic interactionism. We are convinced that in order to better understand the activity of people in their organisational culture, it is necessary to refer to a theory explaining the relations between the human individual as an agential subject and the structure of the reality in which they happen to act.

3.3.2. Developed theory of morphogenesis

The theory of morphogenesis describes processes leading to an extension or change of the form, structure or state of a given system in which the human individual happens to act. In the case of our research, the guarded centre for foreigners is such a system, while obviously remaining a subsystem of a broader institutional subject – the Border Guard.

According to Margaret S. Archer (2000), all social systems are marked by one particular feature, which differentiates them from mechanical and organic systems: their ability to undergo rapid restructuring, which may deeply change them, but does not cause their breakdown. The scope and reach of the restructuring depend ultimately on the human subjectivity, which means that interaction is connected not only with exerting an influence on other individuals, but also affects the structures, i.e. relations between elements of the social system, which have several dimensions (Sztompka 2002: 142–143). They are:

1. the normative structure, i.e. relations between the rules of activity of different individuals and groups occupying different social positions in the social system. Such structuring may be harmonious when the rules of activity are complementary, consistent with each other and symmetrical. It may also be chaotic when the rules are mutually incompatible, block each other or when the competences of the particular individuals overlap. In reality, the actually existing systems are somewhere between these two stages. In connection with the above, we were also expecting to discover features indicating harmony and chaos in the normative structure of the guarded centres for foreigners under study;
2. the ideal structure, i.e. networks of relations between the existing beliefs and views. We are dealing with the homogeneity of this dimension of structure when the network of relations is rooted in one specific system of norms and values, and with the heterogeneity when different and diverse system of norms and values are referred to. We were certain that in the case of our research we would be dealing with a relative homogeneity of the web of internal relations of the staff and a relative heterogeneity of the web of relations between the BG staff employed in the centres and the foreigners on the one hand, and between the foreigners themselves in view of their far-fetched cultural diversity on the other hand;
3. the structure of interests, i.e. relations determining the possibility of access to socially valued goods; in the European cultural setting, these are: tangible goods, power, prestige/social recognition, knowledge/education, and health. Again, we may be dealing with a convergence or divergence of chances for such access. We assumed that in the case of the guarded centres, we would deal with a far-fetched divergence in this scope: first, in view of a deeply hierarchical nature of the social system, and secondly because of the divergence between the structure of interests of the BG staff employed in the guarded centres and that of the detained foreigners;
4. the interactive structure, i.e. relations determining the network of forms of communication between individuals and social groups. It is open when we deal with accessibility across the subjects in the system, and closed when there is no accessibility. We were convinced that in the case of the guarded centres, the interactive structure would be marked by far-fetched closeness.

The notion of morphogenesis refers to complex exchanges between structures and actions, which leads to the changing of the existing form, structure and state of the system. If interaction is connected with exerting an impact on the structures, the structural determinants of human actions are inseparably grounded in interaction. Examination of such exchanges between structures and actions calls for the adoption of the principle of 'analytical duality' (Archer 1995). This means that actions (agency) and structure are understood as analytically dividable, since the new structural properties marking the systems imply a non-continuity between the initial interactions and their result in the form of the structure of the system. Although all the structural properties of every society are permanently dependent on action, the analytical dualism makes it possible to separate 'structure' from 'agency' and to examine their mutual interactions in order to explain the structuring and restructuring of the social order. This is basically possible: first, as the 'structure' and 'agency' are independent of each other, as evidenced by their different properties, regardless of the fact that they are of key importance for their mutual formation, sustaining and development, and, secondly (which is fundamental for the functioning of this explanatory methodology), because 'structure' and 'agency' function diachronically in different periods of time, as the structure necessarily precedes the action or actions which transform it, while the structural elaboration necessarily follows them. This is tantamount to the following sequence of events: structural conditions – social interaction – structural elaboration (Archer 2013: 19).

The agential subjectivity, which transforms the structure of the society, systematically transforms itself – structure is an elaborate result of interaction: subjectivity is shaped by structure and transforms it, which means that it transforms itself in the course of the process of action. Where does subjectivity, agency, come from in the individual? They first of all need to acquire social identity, i.e. become a social actor. Step one is tantamount to personal identity being a symptom of the individuation of a self-aware human being. This leads to the emergence of the 'subjective self' (I), which conducts an internal dialogue with the 'You' constituting a certain expected form of the future 'subjective self'. In turn, the 'objective self' (Me) is developed as a result of a reflection of the expectations of others, which are encountered by the 'I' while acting; it is a peculiar storehouse of the earlier experiences. The internal dialogue takes the following course: The 'subjective self' manifests its situation (aspirations, needs) to the future 'you', because the change may only happen in the future. It strengthens its judgements, referring to the recollections of the 'objective self'. Since the 'subjective self' and 'you' may create contrary scenarios, they have to negotiate which projects to undertake and carry out. The 'subjective self' and the 'objective self' evaluate the strength of the desires of 'you', jointly attributing importance to their concerns, and adjusting the intentions to the practical and emotional possibilities (Domecka 2013: XLVIII–XLIX). According to Archer (2000), we are who we are because of what is important for us, and we give our life the shape which constitutes our internal integrity and the way of being in the surrounding world, thus allowing others to see our individuality (in the form of 'you').

Two issues in Archer's concept seem to be pivotal in the context of our study. Firstly, the maintenance of identity and integrity of the subject is tantamount to the appearance of various kinds of concerns related to internal goods constituting the objects of care. These subjectively determined concerns provide motivation to develop one's life projects which are to lead to the achievement of individual goals. 'If these activities are crowned with success, which is never obvious, our system of goals, if only it is cohesive, is translated into a set of established practices, which constitute our personal *modus vivendi*'. (Archer 2013: 28). We are dealing here with a three-phase process of the mutual influence of structures and subjectivity. The structural and cultural properties objectively shape the limitations and possibilities in relation to the subjectively developed configuration of concerns, which leads to actions having a course consistent with reflexive consideration, to subjective practical projects in relation to objective circumstances. Since the structure of interests in the guarded centres is divergent, such practices are the object of our special interest. Secondly, the most important aspect of 'agency' is Archer's use of the notion in the plural, since the acting subjects are communities which share life's chances and take positions in the unequal distribution of resources in the society (Carter 2013). One of the consequences of this approach that are of importance to us is the existence of the necessary internal relations '...between the community and life opportunities of the ones who belong to it; the individuals who are not in power, are such in view of their relations with the ones who are' (Ibidem: 40).

The agency and reflexivity that are of key importance in Archer's concept, as well as her omission of the cultural conditioning of human actions, including the undertaking of habitual behaviours not accompanied by reflexive considerations, became an object of other scholars' criticism (Elder-Vass 2007; Gronow 2008; Mutch 2004). For us, both categories of factors behind human action that are marginalised in this concept are important. Without any doubt, the cultural determinants are very significant in the reality of detention centres, in which we deal with the heterogeneity of the ideal structure. In effect, the clash of different cultural worlds represented by ethnically and nationally diversified foreigners and the employed staff is a permanent state. In turn, the relatively closed communication structure in the centres, characteristic for hierarchised institutions, certainly contributes to the formation of a broad range of habitual behaviours – above all in the circle of the BG officers and civil employees.

An exceptionally significant context of this self-reflexivity in our research is the specific features of the guarded detention centres as an institution. Hence, we believe that it is necessary to closely examine the foundations of the organisational culture shaped in them. This has led us to our subsequent theoretical inspiration – the concept of the total institution.

3.3.3. Total institutions

The total institution is a living space in which people who share a similar social situation (for example those in need of health and social care, prisoners, foreigners who have illegally crossed the state borders) are cut off from the wider society for a considerable time.

According to Erving Goffman (1961: 5–12), total institutions are marked by several constitutional features. First, it is typical for them to have a relative absence of the division of places for work, play and relaxation. What is even more significant, the physical dimension is important, but what is more important is that in all these places people are subordinate to the same relationally-understood authority – one being a consequence of an imbalance in people's mutual impact on one another. Therefore, in the total institution, we are dealing with the phenomenon of the unity of the authority.

Secondly, total institutions are marked by limiting the physical intimacy of the people they host to the minimum. Obviously, some intimacy does take place, but it is provided in a way greatly divergent from the standards adopted in the culture and civilisation of the West.

Thirdly, this sort of institutions are marked by pervasive scheduling. All activities performed as a part of its operations are scheduled regardless of the extent to which they are later implemented in practice. The planning permeates all the segments of the institution and all its participants – both the so-called staff and the world of the subordinates.

The fourth feature of the total institutions is their separation from the outside world. The limited contact with the outside world is one of the most noticeable features of the functioning of the total institution. To find themselves here, people from outside the world of the staff and the world of the subordinates need to satisfy certain specific, sometimes rigorous conditions. Additionally, the authorities of the total institution have the possibility to rather freely ration access to it to people from the outside world.

Another feature of this type of institution is the binary division of its participants into the superiors and the subordinates, the managing and the managed, the staff and the patients (Goffman 1961: 6–7). These dual categories of people create different sociocultural micro-worlds in the institution although their coexistence, mutual dependence and intermingling are the gist of the social dimension of the functioning of the total institution.

The last basic feature of the total institutions is the omnipotence of authority that pervades them. Additionally, they are marked by the blurring of clearly defined relations of power. The hierarchies of power are usually not very transparent, which makes every member of staff, regardless of their formal position, exercise power over every member of the world of the subordinates. Also, in the institutions marked by the hierarchization of the world of the staff (e.g. in the uniformed services such as the BG), we deal with the spreading of this non-transparency of the relation of power, as a part of which every individual standing higher in the hierarchy of formal positions (ranks/grades) has authority over all individuals who have a lower position.

Goffman was aware of the limitations of his concept. He wrote as follows: 'I would like to mention one conceptual problem: none of the elements I will describe seems peculiar to total institutions, and none seems to be shared by every one of them; what is distinctive about total institutions is that each exhibits to an intense degree many items in this family of attributes. In speaking of "common characteristics," I will be using this phrase in a way that is restricted but I think logically defensible' (Ibidem: 5). The critique of Goffman's concept was focused above all on the excessively generalizing model of total institutions (Davies 1989; Jezierski 2010; Baranowska 2013; Posłuszny 2017). The critical voices were connected with the absence of clear criteria concerning the determination of the degree of totalization of the particular institutions and the necessity to fine-tune the analysis between the two extreme forms, i.e. the permeable and the total institution, which differ from one another in issues such as the length of stay, communication with the outside world, openness to the outside, approach to the question of security, transparency of the institution, social structure, and organisational culture and relations between the staff and the subordinates (Posłuszny 2017: 131). Nick Perry (1974: 346–349) criticizes the non-clarity of the features of the total institution defined by Goffman, omission of their stratification, as well as, in the context of scheduling and purposefulness, the absence of the differentiation between total institutions and institutions which enforce planning and purposefulness of action of their participants as a part of their rationality of action. Christine Davies (1989) pointed to the necessity of an in-depth analysis of features of total institutions indicated by Goffman in the case of every analysed empirical exemplification. In effect, she proposed two model typologies of the total institution, differing in terms of the purpose of the institution and the degree of its openness to the outside world as well as its purpose and the compliance of its assumptions with the implementation (Ibidem: 89–90). In the first case, the degree of closeness/openness allows one to differentiate between institutions that are closed, semi-open and open. In the second case, the adopted mode of consistence with the assumptions of the institution enables a division into coercive, normative and remunerative institutions. It seems that a determination of the degree of totality of a given institution is of the key importance in the situation when the attributes of totality indicated by Goffman may take on different forms and internal solutions, and moreover when their forms depend on the impact of the external environment in which a given institution functions.

We believe that there are many features of the Border Guard which facilitate processes of the totalization of its reality. This is about the predominance of formal rather than personal bonds prevailing in the BG, its bureaucracy strengthened with the hierarchical structure, generating the social environment with its own system of layering (Eisenstadt 1958). Without any doubt, the processes of totalisation are facilitated by the set of norms and traditions existing in the BG as well as the purpose of the calling – the execution of the particular tasks in the area of the ensurance of security for the country and its inhabitants. The Border Guard (just like the police and the army) belongs to the total institutions which gather individuals implementing certain determined instrumental goals.

We are certain that the features attributed to total institutions by Goffman are perceivable in the guarded centres for foreigners (obviously not all of them to the same degree). A constitutive feature of the guarded centre is the isolation of its space from the outside world. It is expressed in both the material aspect (walls, barbed wire, security passages, gates, etc.) and the immaterial aspect in the form of restrictive rules of access to the space of the centre for people external to the institution. Nevertheless, it is worth noticing that this isolation is contemporarily limited by the access of the participants of the space of detention centres (BG staff and foreigners) to electronic means of communication (the internet, mobile phones). Moreover, this isolation has a specific nature. On the one hand, the centres are areas of difficult access for people from outside the institution. On the other, because of the goals they fulfil, contacts with external institutions are numerous and intensive. The procedures conducted in relation to the foreigners (issuing decisions on obliging them to leave Poland or granting one of the forms of international protection) necessitate many relations with the Head of the Office for Foreigners, the courts, diplomatic posts of the foreigners' countries of origin, and lawyers representing their interests. The necessity to provide medical assistance requires numerous contacts with external health service facilities.

The need to provide education to pupils of the compulsory school age in the centres for families results in a lot of contact with educational facilities and teachers. Finally, the organisation of the free time for foreigners leads to frequent relations with cultural institutions, educational facilities and non-governmental organisations.

The limitation of the physical intimacy of the people staying in the centres results, first, from the limitation of the space which the relevant literature refers to as 'personal' (Hall 1990; Goffman 1971; Little 1965; Sommer 1959). Similarly, the space in the centres which Goffman (1971) calls a 'stall', i.e. a place an individual may temporarily claim their own, is limited to the minimum. The second reason is a permanent exposure resulting from the monitoring covering all the space with the exception of the foreigners' residential rooms, toilets and bathrooms. This hierarchical observation (Foucault 1993) is tantamount to organising the space in such a way that it is possible to constantly observe all the individuals who find themselves in it, thus enabling the witnessing of the establishment of relations, functional surveillance, as well as the minimisation of gaps in which the observed could generate anything that would be imperceptible to the staff, the authority of the institution. We are convinced that not only the guarded centres, but also the entire Border Guard is marked by its functioning according to predefined plans. They cover all aspects of activity.

According to Goffman (1961), total institutions are obviously opposed to two principles characteristic for the contemporary society of the Western civilisation. They do not offer a connection between the effort necessary for the individual's daily functioning and the effect in the form of the satisfaction of needs. This discrepancy appears at the level of the so-called charter, i.e. the supreme rules and principles clustering people in the institution and directing their behaviour. Members of the world of the subordinate tend to satisfy certain needs without any effort or independently of the undertaken actions, but they are unable to satisfy their other needs regardless of their effort. The second rule concerns the freedom of family life. Without any doubt, similarly as to the first one, it is broken at the level of the 'overarching principle', since the family either remains in the outside world, i.e. remains outside the total institution, or is within the institution, but its possibilities for an independent development of their life are formally/legally limited.

The world of the subordinate/managed is composed of the individuals for whom the total institution is often established. This is so in the case of institutions gathering the infirm (care establishments), those unable to exist independently and those dangerous to the public, although without their own fault (psychiatric hospitals, infectious diseases hospital departments), individuals considered intentionally dangerous to the public (reformatories, prisons) and people withdrawing themselves from the society (e.g. convents, in particular ones with a closed order). However, in the case of the BG, the issue of the division of people into the staff and the subordinates is more complex. Especially in detention centres, there are two groups of the managed: the detained foreigners, and BG officers and civil employees who do not fulfil managerial functions. This significant finding also indicates the situationality, and contextuality of the social positions occupied by some BG staff in the institution. Depending on the context, the officers and civil employees who do not fulfil managerial functions adopt the roles characteristic for the superiors, those managing (in relations with foreigners) or the subordinates, the managed (in relations with the management of different levels).

The phenomenon of the detachment of the subordinates from their original culture, understood as the one as a part of which their personalities were shaped upon their admission to the institution, is a key variable shaping their world. In consequence, we deal with certain characteristic phenomena – the effects of the subjugation of the subordinates to the total institution. They include a degradation of their personality, which takes place through standardisation,[114] treatment of everyone according to a single model (obviously with the possible extension of the standards to include several types of them), and ultimately depersonalisation resulting from uniformisation, which often leads to the individual's sense of unreality, detachment and alienation to themselves. We may also talk about the phenomenon of the deprivation of personality, which takes place as a result of the loss of the agency by the subordinates, their subjection to the impact of the staff's highly sanctioning group authority applying different types of limitations in the area of the possibility to act and move at leisure.[115] Deprivation is also a consequence of the mental tension prevailing among the members of the world of the subordinates – a result of the absence of the clarity of norms of the culture of the total institution, which is new to them. It is easily noticeable in the case of the guarded centres, where foreigners must cope not only with the differences between their cultures and the Polish culture, but also the specific rigours of the total institution.

---

114 The above can be exemplified by the so-called welcome package handed in to the foreigners upon their admission to the guarded centres. It contains a set of hygiene products and a set for food consumption – the same one for all the foreigners.

115 Forms of such deprivation include a control of mealtimes, the so-called free time, and days in which external shopping for foreigners is ordered or delivered, regardless of their individual needs in this scope.

The world of the subordinates uses different types of techniques facilitating adaptation to the reality of the total institution – some of them seem to be of key importance. A withdrawal from the situation consists in a relative isolation from the reality of the total institution, combined with satisfying, from the formal point of view, the various types of the staff's expectations. In the case of the guarded centres, such withdrawal may apply not only to the detained foreigners, but also the subordinates from the group of BG officers and employees. The tactics of rebellion are tantamount to objecting to the rules and regulations of the total institution and often leads to a successful acquisition of various goods and a satisfaction of needs, since the total institution likes 'peace and order', and all rebellions destroy its desired state of functioning (these tactics can be used by foreigners detained in the guarded centres). Domestication is tantamount to the seeking of good sides to the reality of the total institution and finding loopholes in its formal/legal and lifestyle-related reality, which can be used for one's own purposes. We are convinced that it is used by the subordinates in the guarded centres – both the foreigners and the ones from among the staff. Conversion is a transformation of the identity which leads to an adoption of the attitude tantamount to a comprehensive execution of the principles of functioning of the total institution. This form of adaptation can be sought among the members of the world of the subordinates including officers and civil employees. The tactics of cold calculation are tantamount to premeditated behaviour resulting from the analysis of the 'profitability' of one's own behaviours in the perspective of the satisfaction of one's needs. We expect this sort of adaptation from the members of the world of subordinates: BG officers and civil employees.

A system of rewards and penalties is an important element of the ordering of the everyday life of the world of subordinates in the total institution. The normalising sanction (Foucault 1993) applies above all to the subordinates in the staff group. It covers both the micro-penality in the form of light physical penalties (such as the doing of unexpected physical tasks), the limitation of rights (e.g. no permission to take a leave in a specific period) and petty humiliations (such as ordering individuals to perform tasks degrading their position and status in the institution). What is punished in reality is the non-conformism, which is to be corrected through the authorities' disciplining practices. The normalising sanction is also tantamount to micro-rewarding, i.e. rewards and privileges granted for good behaviour and practices. The basic instrument in the BG and the centres for foreigners which fall within its powers are monies granted to the subordinates by the superiors.

It should also be remembered that the very process of releasing oneself from the power of the total institution or limiting this power is included in the system of privileges. In effect, this leads to a system of secondary adjustment, which allows one to obtain banned gratifications or officially allowed gratifications by prohibited measures without directly opposing the staff. This may lead to the emergence of an informal 'kitchen hierarchy' in the world of the subordinates. In the case of the Border Guard and the guarded centres, such hierarchy may apply to the subordinate foreigners, as well as the subordinates from the world of the staff. This is because the maintenance of proper relations with the particular superiors in the total institution may lead to the acquisition of goods in the form of power and prestige extending beyond the formal place in the staff structure. According to Levis Coser (1974), 'greedy institutions' are ones that seek sole and indivisible loyalty to themselves, thus facilitating the emergence of competitiveness for such loyalty, which usually has a normative nature. Obviously, this competitiveness is strongly grounded in the context of the institution's hierarchy of positions and the related powers and social impact.

As for the world of the staff itself, Goffman turns attention mainly to the specific moral climate and interpersonal norms. This is because there is an essential difference between the norms in force in the world of the total institution and the norms in the external world (obviously, the staff participates in both axionormative orders). The first problem lies in the objectification of other people, in particular the ones from the world of the subordinates - much more extensive in the total institution than in the life outside it. The second problem is the use of norms and standards, which markedly differ from what the staff use in their 'civil' life. For example, this applies to limitations connected with the construction of social bonds with others. These often unaccepted barriers to action frequently result in various problems of a psychological nature such as anxiety, neuroses, depression, and an 'escape' from the reality into different addictions.

The possibility for members of the world of subordinates from among the officers and civil employees to appear in the BG and guarded centres for foreigners raises an important question. In what way are they able to satisfy their needs and aspirations related to the performance of their service/job in the thus determined hierarchy? This question made us consider an implementation of the patron-client concept in our study.

3.3.4. The patron–client concept

Patronage is a specific division of power among social actors – above all individuals, but also collective entities, social groups or institutions. Its definition is based on the inequality of status and the power of the parties to the relation (Kauffman 1974; Gellner 1977; Scott 1977; Eisenstadt and Roniger 1984; Willerton 1992; Tarkowski 1994). On the one hand, this difference makes it possible for one of the parties (the patron) to affect the behaviour of the other party (the client), regardless of their will, but in consistence with their expectations. The individuals taking on the role of the client resign from a part of their freedom and make the execution of their aspirational goals dependent on the patron's will and actions, trusting their competences and possibilities. The client, resigning from a part of their freedom, expects care and protection from the patron. In this way, the patronage is not only a form of power, but also social exchange. It can only persist when the principle of mutuality is implemented. When it is not complied with, the relation collapses and is broken (Kauffman 1974: 285). In a classical situation, the patron provides the client with such goods as: the basic means for living and working, assistance in various crisis situations, protection against external dangers, intermediation and implementation of the client's interests in external contacts. The goods provided to the patron by the client are related to work (very diversified) for the benefit of the patron and promotion of the patron's broadly understood interests (political, economic, etc.) (Scott 1977: 23–24; Weingrod 1977: 45). Summing up, the patron-client relations are 'a special case of a dyad in which the relations between the partners have a permanent nature not limited to a single transaction as well as an asymmetrical character, i.e. they involve differences in the social stratification and/or the owned resources between them. The existence of such a dyad is based on an exchange of goods and services between its participants for the purposes of the satisfaction of their particular interests' (Tarkowski 1994: 54).

Patronalism is a phenomenon strongly related to the individuality of the actors building this relation. It is usually based on norms that are inconsistent with the official morality (of the community or institution), often treating it as false and inadequate in relation to the requirements of the reality. This is tantamount to the actors skirting the edges of law and using the existing legal loopholes rather than to the illegality of clientelism. In the absence of some legislative solutions, clientelism may play the role of a functional equivalent of law (Willerton 1992: 13). What is more, some researchers treat corruption, which increases in contemporary countries, very clearly breaks the law and is penalised, as an indicator of the disappearance of clientelism (Clapham 1982).

The patron–client relation is very common, as it emerges and functions in communities and societies with different historical experience and culture. Being universal, patronalism in individual empirical cases differs from the presented classical approach, as is reflected in a great number of individual realisations (Tarkowski 1994; Lande 1983; Piattoni 2001). Ernest Gellner (1977: 4) indicates three systemic causes behind the appearance of patronalism in a given collective entity (society, social group, institution, etc.): incomplete centralisation, a defective market of goods, and deficient bureaucracy. Incomplete centralisation means that despite its obligations, a given entity is unable to control certain aspects of the life of a collective entity. This leads to an emergence of individuals/entities that begin to control some sources of goods and services as well as spheres of commercial activity. In contrast to our initial assumptions regarding the Border Guard, we became certain that in the case of this institution and the guarded centres for foreigners functioning as a part of it, we are dealing with this particular situation. In particular, personal decision concerning remunerations, positions and functions depend on the opinion of the superiors of the officers and civil employees at the various levels of management. The defective market of goods leads to a search for unofficial ways to reach the goals, including the use of informal relations with others. We are convinced that the BG as a total institution is marked by a deficit of specific socially-desired goods such as prestige, social recognition, power, and financial resources – these ones are best recognisable.[116] Deficient bureaucracy is tantamount to the particularisation and individualisation of principles of operation of all public entities, including institutions. This is one of the features of our contemporary administrative reality. Attempts at the broadening of laws to cover different areas of everyday life usually result in the growth of bureaucracy leading to different types of pathologies in the area of the functioning of collective entities. The BG and guarded centres for foreigners, which in view of their totalising nature are marked by the tendency to control all aspects of their functioning, are particularly prone to the phenomenon of deficient bureaucracy. This potential phenomenon of clientelism in the guarded centres concerns the staff, i.e. the employed BG officers and civil employees subjected to detailed regulations connected with the performance of their official/job-related activities. In consequence, the execution of all the rules of conduct provided by external law and internal orders is in practice impossible.

There are several other factors facilitating the development of the patron–client relation. What contributes to clientelism is a low level of solidarity and social cohesion limiting the possibility of access to the desired goods as a result of collective actions. In such situations, individuals look for favouritism and influences, which may lead to the development of the patron-client relation. Without any doubt, features of the total institution are not conducive to the

116 Managers of the guarded centres for foreigners are authorised to grant selected subordinates special allowances and bonuses on a discretionary basis.

development of the phenomenon of social cohesion. A strong hierarchy of power controlling access to the desired goods enforces competition among the employees relating to the access to promotion. A search for a patron may also take place in systems in which there is an absence of acceptance for the prevailing socio-cultural order. The absence of acceptance for the determined goals and means to reach them is related to the sense of anomie and results in various adaptive reactions (Merton 1968: 198–226) facilitating the development of clientelism. They include innovation, when it is perceived that the official, institutionalised means to achieve the targets are ineffective. In such cases, a search for a patron whose help will lead to becoming successful may be a solution. In the case of an adaptive reaction taking the form of rebellion, patronalism would not only constitute a different road to satisfying the needs, but also achieving the goals inconsistent with the ones officially promoted. Again, we are certain that the total institution and rules of its functioning trigger various adaptive reactions, including the ones mentioned above, which may be conducive to the development of the patron-client relation. We should also mention the factor which is often of key importance for the generation of the relation in question. It is the social awareness of the fact that clientelism leads to success, that it is shrouded in a specific ethos (Gellner 1977: 3).

Along with the increasing complexity of the social structure in the patron-client relation, a third subject appears: a broker, an intermediator (Boissevain 1974: 148). Usually, it is the patron who takes on the role. This takes place as a result of the deepening of the division of work, the progressing bureaucratisation of the reality of collective life. In effect, to satisfy the needs of their clients, the patrons often have to turn to other external entities. In such situations, they basically become an intermediator between their clients' expectations and the entities which have direct access to the desired goods and services. We are certain that a strong hierarchy of power existing within the BG facilitates the appearance of the phenomenon of intermediation.

The patron-client relation involves material and symbolic elements connected with life in the public and the private spheres of both its parties. The exchange taking place as a part of it leads to mutual obligations marked by loyalty, solidarity and the standard of reciprocation. Finally, patronalism is basically a voluntary relation, although sometimes it is bred by situational compulsion.

The above description allows us to conclude that the patron-client relation is composed of many features that are contradictory, as exemplified by the following pairs of sentences:

1. inequality and asymmetry in the area of the power of the parties to the relation *versus* social solidarity expressed in the categories of the identity and interpersonal sentiments and obligations;
2. potential coercion, exploitation, coercion *versus* voluntariness and mutuality of commitments;
3. the public sphere *versus* the private sphere of the parties;
4. pressure on the mutuality of commitments and solidarity *versus* the 'illegal' aspect of the relation (Eisenstadt and Roniger 1984: 277).

We are convinced that the patron-client relation may be analysed from different theoretical perspectives such as the structuralist one, the theory of exchange, interactionism, role theory or functionalism. What is more, they all seem attractive in the context of studies in guarded centres for foreigners. In the structural perspective, one needs to examine the structure created by both parties to the relation and the related system of relations between the patron and the client(s). Such analysis could also cover considerations in the scope of social stratification concerning the most important socially desired goods: power (immanently connected with relation), material goods, prestige, respect, and social recognition. The gist of analysis from the perspective of the theory of exchange would be the transfer of goods/gift, and a response to the gift, i.e. the rule of reciprocation – being compelled to reciprocate. The essence of analysis in the interactive approach lies in grasping the patron-client relation as an effect of interaction taking place in a particular cultural context, examining the specificity of messages between the parties and the possible development of a network of interaction as a part of this relation. From the perspective of research performed from the point of view of role theory, the most significant problems are related to defining the roles by the parties as well as their negotiation and adoption. Finally, the functionalist approach calls for focusing on the functions fulfilled by the patron-client relation in the life of the group, the functioning of the institution, its significance in the determination of the position and social status of the parties, and, above all, investigating the relation as an instrument of satisfaction of human needs.

4 Research project – 'scene three'

These reflections shall constitute a summary, an ordering of the information given in the preceding chapters of the book. As already mentioned, our project consisting in the examination of the detention of foreigners has a pioneering nature (in view of the absence of any earlier studies of the GCFs in Poland, a limited scope of similar research in other countries, and, finally, the limited compatibility of research conducted in other areas of detention). We could not transfer the experience resulting from studies in other difficult access areas, either, since they are specifically marked by the uniqueness of their research conditions. In view of the above, we took on the methodological challenge in the form of the conceptualisation of the research idea covering inter alia a package of research strategies, data acquisition techniques and methods of analysis. We also faced a difficult endeavour to construct a scheme of research procedure, in which we could, on the basis of the acquired experience, suggest a probabilistic algorithm of the procedure not only in the case of detention studies, but also help other researchers design and execute empirical works in other difficult access areas.

In our recapitulation of our experience and the proposal of our research procedure, we consciously resigned from the notion of a research model. We found it too obligating, as regardless of the ambiguity of defining, it suggests a certain solely correct strategy of a 'model' procedure. This is because we are aware that in the case of studies involving difficult access areas, and in particular detention, the situational factors limit the use of any precise models of research procedure both in terms of time and space. Hence, we shall use the notion of a scheme of the research procedure - a scheme, i.e. a construct tantamount to a general, preliminary, sketchy and simplified plan of action. We also do it largely for reasons of our respect for the changeability of the empirical reality, which in particular in the case of areas marked by difficult access from the point of view of research call for an absolute maintenance of theoretical and methodological openness during research.

4.1. Theoretical and methodological schemes

Such a framework of insight and the resulting actions covered the fundamental assumptions concerning the ontic status of the examined phenomena, the epistemic dimension, and, what follows, the research perspectives that were taken into account/adopted, the resulting research strategies, and, finally, techniques of data acquisition and analysis. It is against this background that we shall attempt to expose the most important postulated features of the entire research approach. In this way, we want to indicate one of the possible ways of description and analysis of the phenomenon of the detention of foreigners which is the subject matter of our study – by no means promoting it as the only – the optimum – way of executing such a project. The same can be said about methods of data acquisition, comparison, and, subsequently, interpretation implemented in the project.

Our project was first of all marked by broadly understood multilevel eclecticism as a part of the qualitative approach. It was visible already at the stage of research perspectives resulting from the adopted philosophical worldview. This is about combining an approach directed at the grasping of the point of view of the subjects with one focusing on a description of the construction of social situations. This was related to the distinguishing of both the methods directed at the reading of subjective meanings and the methods useful for describing materials and social artefacts and their spatial determinants. Both these perspectives correspond well with the leading paradigm of our study (constructivism/constructionism) and the theory of symbolical interactionism which we found inspiring.

Constructivism, however, turned out to be a paradigm, which in practice did not exhaust our research approach, since activism conditioned by two factors emerged as a part of it. The first one was the participation of a BG civil employee in the research team – her cognitive and theoretical interests were strongly related to practical goals, i.e. the acquisition of knowledge enabling an improvement of the existing detention centres in the dimension of their space and the interpersonal relations taking place within that space. The second cause behind the appearance of actions characteristic for the activist paradigm was the objectivised conditions of the performed empirical works. In particular, this is about staying for many hours in a closed space and the resulting necessity to interact with the subjects, which steps beyond the research scenario. Without any doubt, this led to a certain involvement and co-participation in the studied environment. In the categories of relations between theory and practice, our actions consisted in the provision of the preliminary conclusions resulting from our study to the circle of BG staff with a view to stimulating reflection on the social situation in their institution (Habermas, 1983). This was manifested, inter alia, in private meetings with individuals from the circle of the subjects, during which members of the research team expressed their opinions and assessments which might have an impact on the functioning of the detention centres under study.

Finally, our eclecticism was reflected in the immersion in the pragmatic paradigm. We are convinced that the most significant factor behind this choice (or, to be more precise, absence of choice) was the pioneering/exploratory nature of our study and the related holistic approach (as discussed below) to the issue of the organisation of the space of detention centres in Poland and the interactions, bonds and social relations taking place within that space. It was not about the fitting of a specific research theory and methodology to the problem under analysis. Our challenge consisted in the question of what to do to explain and understand the issues of our interest related to the functioning of guarded centres for foreigners. It was pragmatism which made us 'run' through theories, concepts and research methods. Nevertheless, we are convinced that we have not broken at any moment the rule of avoiding the use of contradictory philosophical, theoretical or methodological assumptions in our research project.

The keystone of our procedure was the adoption of the strategy of ethnographic research in our study. This choice was not accidental, since the research project concerned a description of a human collectivity, its institutions, interpersonal behaviours, and products of material and symbolic culture and beliefs. We consistently used the ethnographic method of the exploration of the reality, doing research in the field in a personalised way, taking into account multiple factors, inductively, basing our efforts on a dialogue with the subjects (Angrosino 2007: 45–46). It was in particular the multifactorial dimension (different kinds of interviews, observation, collection of documents of social life, drawing up iconographic material) which owing to the procedure of triangulation was to strengthen the certainty of our conclusions, which contributed to our reaching for different theoretical inspirations.

One of the most significant features of the ethnographic method, h o l i s m, lies in conducting research in such a way that it is possible to acquire the possibly complete picture of the community, group, or category of people under analysis. Holism also marks the institutional approach. It aims to study human actions which on the one hand are shaped by and on the other shape institutions understood broadly as social rules with moral and cognitive components (Pawlak, Sadowski 2017: 31). Holism assumes that social fields are interdependent on the political, legal, economic, technological and technical ones. Preferences of the actors' actions are shaped by a broad variety of factors, and institutions have an agential significance – they are not only designed and reconstructed, but also enforce the specified mental models. In our case, holism was dictated by not only the requirements of the method. Rather, it was our belief in the necessity to cover the system of the detention of foreigners in Poland by a holistic insight which led to the adoption of the ethnographic method in our study.

Holism was manifested in several dimensions of the research. First, it covered all the six guarded centres for foreigners functioning in Poland. Secondly, we collected empirical material allowing an analysis of the staff, norms, material substrate, activity and results of the operation of detention centres understood in the categories of an institution. Thirdly, the applied research procedures and tools covered comprehensively the organisation and functioning of the detention centres: from the externally enforced formal/legal framework and internal regulations to the daily behaviours of the people staying in them. Fourthly, we carried out a detailed inventory of the space both inside the buildings and outside them – complete with the buffer zone of the centres for foreigners.

The belief in the comprehensive insight into the system of detention resulted from the already mentioned pioneering and exploratory nature of our project. This also contributed to the already discussed eclecticism resulting from the desire to search for theoretical tools that enabled us best to understand the reality under examination. Another important reason behind our holistic research procedure was the fact that we considered detention centres as a d i f f i c u l t a c c e s s a r e a. What made us qualify them in such a way? In this case, the difficult access could be understood literally. The guarded centres for foreigners are closed spaces and access to them is rationed via a system of permits. Within the centres, one may perform only the activities which are permitted by the management of the centres, and often such a consent has to be approved by their superiors. As already mentioned, our endeavours to obtain a permission to perform scientific research in the detention centres lasted for almost two years, and its granting was related to a positive assessment of the previous cooperation of some members of the research team with the BG.

The treatment of detention centres as difficult access areas also results from the fact that they are a part of the structure of an institution of the total nature. Because of its hierarchical nature and the functioning on the basis of orders, people from outside (in this case members of the research team) are analysed by the so-called ordinary officers and civil employees above all from the point of view of the dangers that may result from contact with them. For them, a meeting with researchers may be perceived in the categories of a risk, i.e. anxiety connected with the possible risk to the cohesion of the system of functioning of the institution within which they work (Douglas 1992). Due to the above, eliciting frank answers to the questions posed during interviews required additional measures on the part of the researchers, including the winning of their interlocutors' trust on every single occasion. Another feature of the totalising institution lies in its limitation of contacts with the outside world. What is self-telling in this context, is that in the case of basically all detention centres in Poland, the BG officers, working almost exactly in the same space of a given seat of the BG unit, usually have no idea about the specificity of the work in the detention centre or its functioning.

The difficult access to detention centres is also related to the process of the analysis of data, in particular the data collected during interviews, at every stage of work. This is because we have to assume that because of the hierarchical nature of the institution, our interlocutors are subjected to forms of shaping ways of thinking aimed at controlling the prevailing forms of discourse (Dijk 2001). This requires the use of critical discourse analysis and a search for the effects of the impact of the people of authority (superiors) on the messages provided by the interlocutors during interviews.

The guarded centres for foreigners are areas of difficult access for research also because of their features related to the organization of the space. High fencing, often secured with barbed wire, bars, security passages and administrative limitation of free movement are a challenge to individuals from outside – in this case, members of the research team. This is because staying in the research area is tantamount to staying in a closed space throughout the research works, which poses a psychological difficulty.

Here, we would like to provide several suggestions concerning the performance of research in detention areas marked by difficult access, which may be helpful to other researchers intending to carry out their projects in the same or similar organisational cultures. It seems not only highly desirable, but indispensable to prepare oneself for such research by participating in an internship in the social environment/detention space. Without such 'familiarisation' with the specificity of the total institution, it is impossible to: (a) articulate even partially accurate research questions to which answers are sought in the field; (b) select adequate strategies and the resulting methods (research procedures and techniques); (c) eliminate traumas, a specific cultural shock experienced by every individual from the external world of freedom when confronted by the world 'with no choice', functioning on the basis of rigid principles unacceptable to them and largely incomprehensible.

At the same time, we are aware that such a specific 'pilotage' of the researcher's personality, preliminary confrontation of their ideas of the future research area with the plan of the research project under development, does not solve the problems indicated above, and only partially minimises them, sensitises them and develops the need for the building of an attitude marked by a sharpened level of reflectiveness. Owing to the fact that most of our research team members had an opportunity to visit detention centres and open centres for foreigners on many occasions (also outside Poland), thus undergoing this specific 'sensitivity training', the issue of the need to include permanent reflectiveness and an autoethnographic perspective as important elements of the future research strategy was obvious to them.

In the literature devoted to the detention of immigrants, research interests are usually focused on the issues related to the breaking of fundamental human rights, the oppressiveness of authorities, non-ethicalness rationalised by the requirements of the security of the state and its citizens, etc. Although we fully agree with these analyses and diagnoses, these important issues appeared at the far end of our plan in our project, which needs to be explained here. Our project was concentrated on an attempt to 'understand' the institution by way of the acquisition and analysis of data which are of key importance for the shaping of the norms, rules and models connected with its functioning. First, they are collected in legal-administrative documents – starting with specific acts and orders of officers of the institutional hierarchy levels, to internal rules and regulations developed in the particular centres. At the same time, we were interested in the level of uniformisation of the institutions in question by the legal-administrative regulations and in the level of their detail. Secondly, our pivotal research issue was the shaping of interactions, and the development of bonds and relations in the space of the detention centres. A significant dimension of this issue consists in the impact of the very material space, its organisation and material and symbolic importance on human behaviour. An answer to the question of who plays the leading role in the shaping of this space became the key behind the selection of our interlocutors. We have no doubt that this role lies above all in the hands of the BG officers and civil employees and applies practically speaking to all the space in the centres which we consider public. Foreigners have this privilege primarily in their private space, i.e. residential rooms, but we excluded them from our study, as we did not want to encroach in any way on their peace. Thirdly, the impact of the foreigners on the shaping of the permanent elements of space and constructing stronger bonds and relations is limited by the fact that their stay in the centres is temporary, often short, and hence their influence on the organisational culture of the institution under study – the detention centre – is limited as well.

The above explanation does not mean that we lost focus on the broadly understood 'interest' of the foreigners. Detention centres could not justify their existence without the presence of foreigners – they are dedicated to them, organised for them. However, the logic of the functioning of this institution has it that the foreigners are the subject of targeted measures, but they basically have no agency in the area of the organisation of the principles and norms of life which they have to comply with in the centres. Hence, one of our intentions in the area of the use of the knowledge acquired in the course of the study was to initiate a transformation of the structural barriers existing in the centres, which often emerge as a result of the routine activities of their employees. The project summary includes educational programmes addressed to both the middle level management of the guarded centres and candidates for work in these institutions. They are to stir the participants' reflection on the desired attitudes and the related good practices in management and development of the appropriate relations with the immigrants. We assume that the foreigners themselves shall be the ultimate beneficiaries of these activities.

The catalogue of the above-discussed features of the project, including its pioneering nature, multilevel eclecticism, holistic character and performance in the conditions of a difficult access area should also be complemented to include interdisciplinarity. On the one hand, this feature was naturally related to the idea of holism and the specificity of the membership of the research team grouping together individuals representing five disciplines of the social sciences. On the other hand, and most importantly, the complex research matter we were dealing with obliged us in many places to undertake collaboration based on the principle of stepping outside the framework of a single science. In effect, 'local analytical alliances' (e.g. lawyer–anthropologist, anthropologist–psychologist, sociologist–representative of security studies) were developed as a part of the project works.

Throughout the course of the theoretical and methodological considerations discussed in this book, we have placed particular emphasis on transparency of the research concept and the related measures, which ultimately was to convince the reader of the due quality of our project, and thus the reliability of its results. There are many indicators of the quality of research, but their practical significance depends on the features of particular projects. Therefore, we shall try to synthetically describe the 'philosophy' behind our thinking about the scientific activity based on projects - the fundamental rules which accompanied our research at all stages of its performance.

First, it is natural for researchers to reach for solutions they used in their previous projects, their baggage of experience, and, consequently, professional competences. Such situations took place in our case as well and were for instance related to the attachment to the ethnographic method as the preferred form of qualitative approach. However, this circumstance was secondary in the face of the fact that it was only after an analysis of *differentia specifica* of all the characteristics of the research area and confronting them with the preliminary research questions, as well as the viewing of the catalogue of the potential qualitative approaches, that it was collectively agreed that the ethnographic method should be the leading work tool. This *nonarbitrary* approach, based on decisions taken by us as a team,[117] made us certain that we were developing a project adequate for the area and the issue under examination.

Secondly, our project and its assumptions had an *open character* – they involved flexibility and simultaneously a certain distance to our settlements, owing to which during the fieldwork and breaks between the study visits in the subsequent locations, we revised the particular elements of the strategies, procedures and techniques, and introduced changes to the directions and ways of our further actions. These changes were possible owing to the permanent control based on reflectiveness.

Thirdly, when deciding to select the specific types of measures, we endeavoured to make their status and mutual connections precise. This attitude can be exemplified by a reference to the list of choices making up the general project research strategy (Section 2.3). Taking a decision on the adoption of a single strategy, as in the example of the ethnographic method, was relatively easy, but it was a much more complex task to decide on a precise nature of the relations between the particular strategies and attributing them to the network of 'tactics' - specific, long- and short-term methodological measures connected with the acquisition and subsequent analysis of data. This course of proceeding was aimed at, inter alia, making sure that our scheme is not a collection of autonomous ideas and measures, but makes up a cohesive, heuristic, *systemic research concept*.

Measures making up the process of the construction of the research project can be grouped as a part of several stages creating a sequence of consecutive activities. In the creation of a project, the *motivations* which are behind its implementation are a natural starting point (stage one). In our case, there were three sources of inspiration. The first one was long-term contacts with representatives of the Border Guard in connection with the carrying out of a research and development project for the benefit of the institution. The second one was the possibility to stay in the detention centres themselves as a part of assistance and educational activities. This type of experience overlapped with our earlier experience of study visits in centres for foreigners in other European countries (such as Germany), providing us with a significant insight into the specificity of the functioning of this type of services and institutions. The third

117 We consider the fact that the project had two leaders-coordinators, who before the commencement of the work defined the style of management and collaboration of the team under the principles of a full partnership, rather than a single author and 'arbiter' in the person of one head, was a circumstance facilitating such collaboration.

inspiration for research, based on the knowledge of relevant literature, was our belief in the significance of this problematics and hardly satisfying state of knowledge in this scope.

Stage two was composed of a series of *organisational actions*. The first one consisted in undertaking efforts to be granted the managing institution's permission to conduct research in detention centres under conditions acceptable to both parties. This was the essential issue – a precondition of the implementation of the planned project. The second action consisted in completing an interdisciplinary research team composed of both researchers and practitioners, people having experience related to the problematics of detention, and the motivation to participate in a project which was not financed from external sources.

The success in the form of an effective completion of the above organisational tasks opened the road to the commencement of stage three of the design work, i.e. *preliminary conceptualisation of research*. It involved the following actions: the team's discussions concerning the research areas emerging from the individually suggested proposals (*credo*) with the possibility of their integration as a part of the joint project, the proposed leading paradigm (paradigms) in the ontological and epistemological context and the resulting perspectives and strategies of doing research. A determination of the list of questions was one of the most important results of these works.

The subsequent, fourth, stage of project design, i.e. the *advanced conceptualisation of research*, was mainly composed of defining source resources and determining the scope and form in which they will satisfy the information needs expressed in the research questions, indicating the optimum research techniques to explore these resources, defining the sample, and distinguishing methods of analysis at all its stages (from archiving and coding to in-depth interpretation). Work at this stage was crowned with technical activities consisting in the elaboration of research tools and auxiliary materials, as well as settlements concerning the style of work in the field (arrangements, coordination of the entire scope of teamwork in the field).

The series of actions described above can be illustrated by the following diagram (Fig. 13).

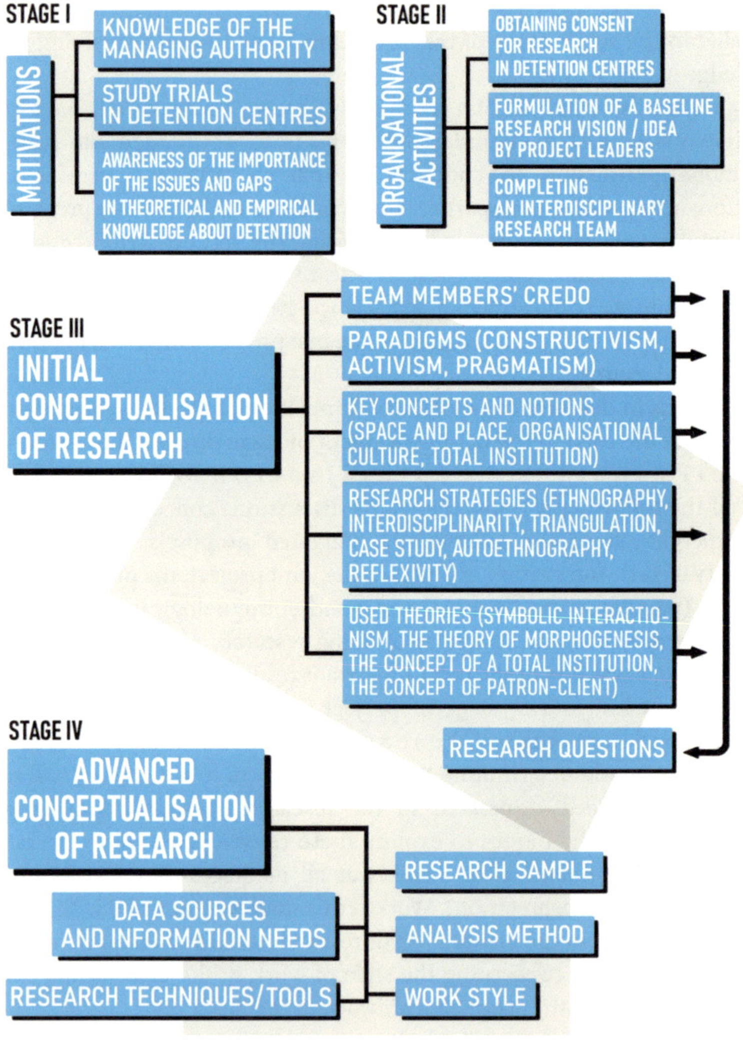

Fig. 13. Scheme of constructing a research project (own elaboration)

Chapter 2 presented six of the most important elements making up our research strategy. This presentation calls for a summary aimed at proving that it is not a set of loose, rather accidently combined elements, but a systematised research perspective, a collection of 'communicating vessels'. From our point of view, in order to meet its targets, a research strategy, which can also be called a research scheme (in this case a qualitative one), should effectively combine theoretical inspirations and research questions with the entire sphere of the project's *praxis*, and subsequently analytical works (see Fig. 14).

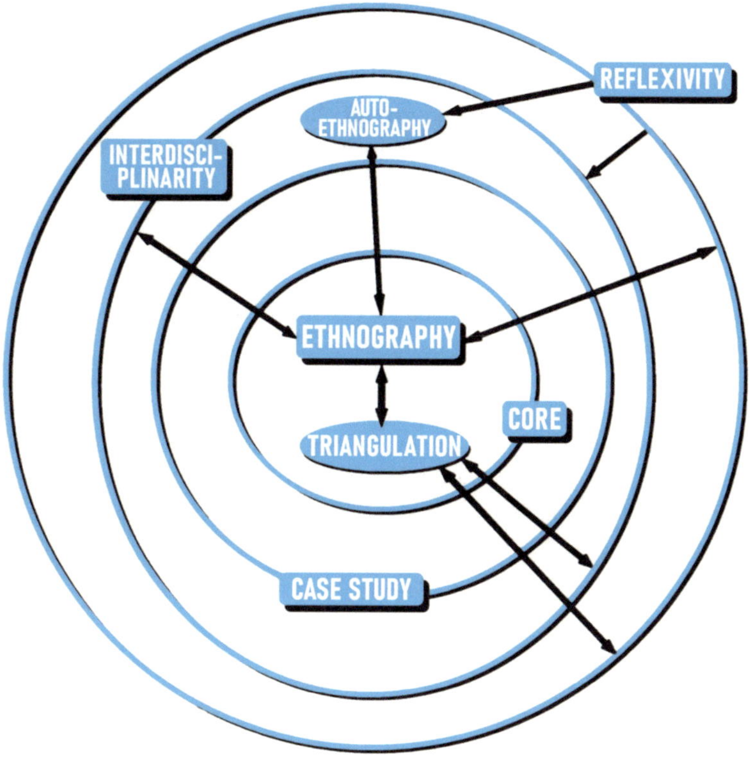

Fig. 14. Systematicity of research strategies (own elaboration)

The entire system is embraced by a 'reflexivity' and 'interdisciplinarity', presented in the diagram in the form of two interconnected external rings. The research attitude attributed to these elements and the related activities are present at every stage of the research procedure – from the moment of taking an interest in the research problem until the elaboration of the resulting works. In turn, the 'core' of the system contains the ethnographic method (ethnography) as our core qualitative approach – its features have been described in Section 2.3.1. It was not accidentally that multidimensional triangulation appeared next to ethnography as a series of measures, which are an important substance in which to practice ethnography and, above all, an indicator of the quality of scientific research. Triangulation requires special reflexivity, as underlined by recording this relation in the diagram. Analogical relations (with ethnography and reflexivity) are marked in the case of autoethnography. The last element of the system is the case study. The diagram highlights its relation with the 'core' (ethnography and triangulation) since the drawing of evidence from many sources and triangulating are permanent elements of the majority of characteristics of this method. The visualisation under discussion has the form of a schematic diagram, which by nature exposes first-plan relations.

The subsequent diagram (Fig. 15) presents a network of theoretical concepts used in the course of the design-related works. The foundation and binder of the system, which is based on the constructivist paradigm, is the theory of symbolic interactionism, which already proved successful on the grounds of the study of organisational cultures, including cultures based on coercion (total institutions). By reading the symbolism enclosed in the interactions inscribed into the space and its places, it is possible to grasp the gist of the organisational culture, i.e. the world of norms, values and worldviews constituting the basis, the sign-post of the of social practices controlling the form and direction. Other theories to which we referred in our interpretations have a 'practical', local nature, while fully corresponding with the idea of interactionism.

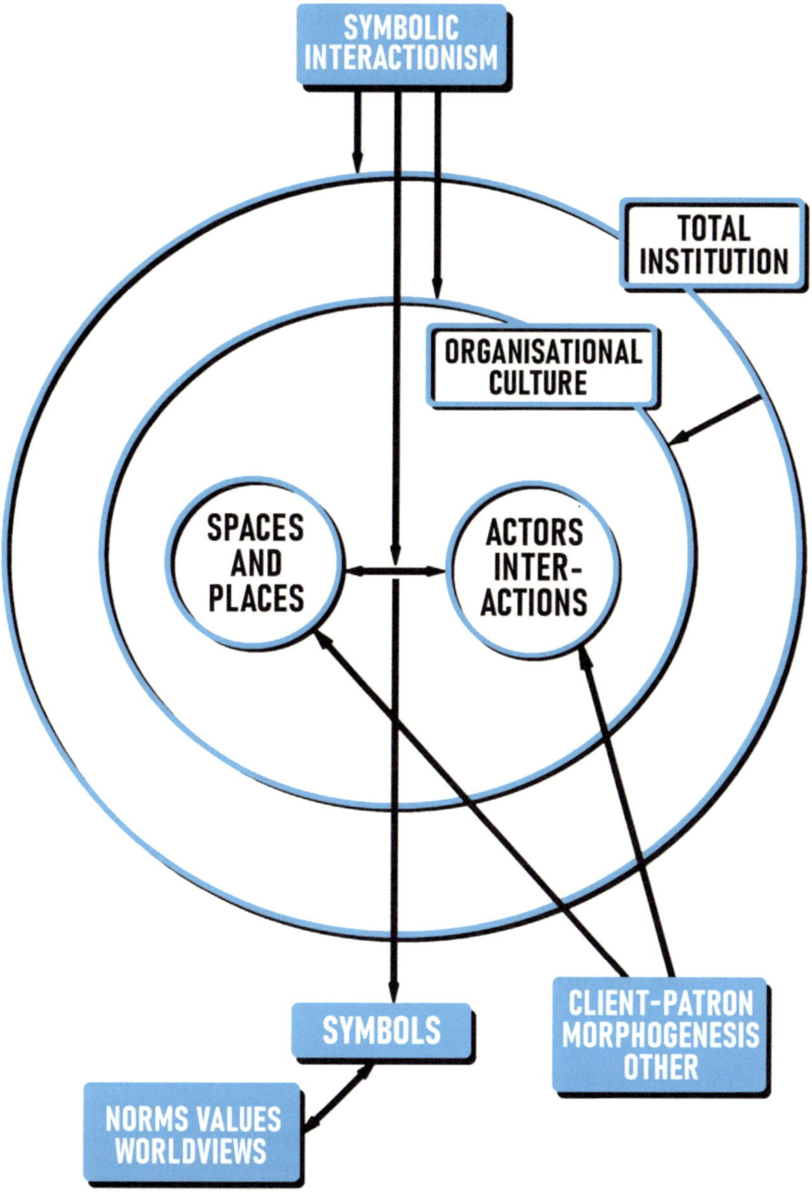

Fig. 15. The systemic nature of the theory in the project (own elaboration)

It was already in the course of our study that we knew what, for a variety of reasons, we would not take into account in our investigation, although it would potentially constitute a significantly enriching element of our knowledge, and, subsequently, its presentation. We had no influence on some issues. First, because of the specificity of the place of research, it was not recommended that more than three researchers stay on the grounds of the guarded centre at the same time. This number of individuals from outside did not significantly disturb the rhythm of the work of the staff, who were obliged to discreetly monitor the behaviour of external parties, or distort the naturalness of the interactions being the subject matter of our interests. Due to this state of things, in combination with the limited time we had to perform our multi-site research (10 months), we were unable to carry out all the tasks we had initially planned. Another factor limiting the scope of our fieldwork was the conditions specified in our permission to stay in the guarded centres. Finally, the multiplicity of tasks we ambitiously included in our research scheme made it impossible to carry our some of them for the reason of the shortage of time and people. To present the situation in more detail, we shall provide a couple of additional remarks.

The first one concerns the selection of the sample in the temporal dimension (Hammersley and Atkinson 1997: 56–61). Because of the conditions specified in our permission to perform the study, we could not conduct observations during the night (between 10:00 p.m. and 8:00 a.m.). In the course of the study, it turned out that in the centres for men, this is the time of the detainees' particular activity, which, regardless of the relevant administrative regulations, is supposedly accepted by the security staff. An insight into the above could help us understand the rhythm of the foreigners' daily activity, and deepen the triangulation studies concerning the relation of the sources discussed in Section 2.3.3.

The second remark concerns the application of comprehensive (24 h) shadowing (Czarniawska 2012: 69-90), in particular in relation to the officers fulfilling middle level managerial functions.[118] Because of the shortage of time

118 This is currently a popular research technique in the circles of the researchers dealing with the anthropology of organisations and problematics of management, as well as phenomena from the area of popular culture (e.g. music idols and their fans). This is not a new ethnographic technique – this way of acquisition of information was used in the research of functionalists and representatives of other orientations (such as the culture and personality approach), but was enriched with many methodological reflections.

and people, we did not use this technique in a systematic way, focusing on the participation in the officers' performance of their selected professional activities (such as reception-related procedures, organisation of events and inspections). However, we can see significant values of this technique both in the context of the search for sources for confrontation with declarations and descriptions collected during individual interviews with managers, and in-depth reflection concerning the building of the researcher's relations with the subjects (Mękarski 2014: 118–130).

The third remark is related to the use of visual materials as sources in our project. For legal and ethical reasons, we had to avoid both archiving and, subsequently, using all images with people. In the case of describing the synchrony of group behaviours and the specificity of interactions between the staff and the detainees, the absence of such exemplifications turns out to be particularly painful and weakens the strength of the message and the appropriateness of the adopted interpretations.

Finally, we would like to share two reflections, which can be useful for researchers planning studies in the organisational culture of detentive institutions. The first one, of a more general nature, concerns the legitimacy of the extrapolation of the obtained results. We pointed out that despite the fact that the institution of the detention of foreigners functions within the framework of the same or similar legal rules, it adopts different forms in the particular EU states at the international level, but also in the internal context of each state. Hence, its selective examination consisting in, for instance, an investigation of a single guarded centre chosen from a network will only allow to formulate a generalised report and generalisations related to the case in question. Our study documents well that a holistic examination of the phenomenon of detention should be based on a multi-site case study, and none of the particular locations can be qualified as a representative of all of them.

The second reflection is related to the selection of techniques of data recording, and, what follows, the applied analyses. In view of the profile of our interests, and partially also the shortage of time and appropriate training, we resigned from advanced analyses of the interviews from the linguistic point of view (linguistic or conversation analysis). During the ordering and analysing of the source materials, we concluded though that this direction of research may result in the acquisition of data enabling a significant broadening of the perspective of insight into the phenomenon under study.

4.2. Previous publications, directions for further work and the expected results

At the request of the Polish Academy of Sciences, the research team prepared an extensive (110 pages long) expert report concerning the guarded centres for foreigners in Poland (Niedźwiedzki, Schmidt, Stępka, and Tacik 2021). The text contains a multi-aspect, interdisciplinary analysis of the conditions and practical functioning of the GCFs, and in particular identification and analysis of: (a) tensions between the formal-legal requirements of the activity of the centres and the practices of the staff in the situation of the legal pluralism, (b) tensions between the organisational structure and furnishing of this space and forms of its appropriation by the users, (c) tensions emerging in the course of collaboration between the centres and external entities, (d) securitisation activities undertaken by the Border Guard.

In turn, a special volume of the journal *Migration Studies – Review of Polish Diaspora* (Niedźwiedzki and Schmidt 2022) enabled members of the research team to focus on their individual interests pertaining to the performed project. The volume opens with an article (*The Specific Nature of the Detention of Foreigners and its Exploration. The Polish Context*), which seeks to present the essential knowledge on the detention of foreigners in Poland and the research perspective adopted in the project. It contains characteristics of the detention of foreigners in the Polish context: directions of migration flows resulting from the location of our country, as well as the whereabouts and profiles of the detention centres. Part two familiarises the reader with the specific nature of our detention study project: its conceptual apparatus, the adopted research paradigms, the applied methodology, and the challenges related to our exploratory efforts being performed in a very specific place – the guarded centres for foreigners. The subsequent paper (*Law Application in Detention Centres for Foreigners: On the Structural Impossibility of Regulation)* approaching the topic with methods of sociology of law and legal anthropology, proposes a more general understanding of the role that the law plays in total institutions such as detention centres. It proves that the vision of the law as a tool that 'regulates' detention centres is empirically contradicted. The article *Securitization and (In)visibilization of Immigrants. An Analysis of the Polish Centres for Foreigners* aims to provide a discussion on the role of the (in)visibility and securitization of migration by looking at specific spaces and practices of the Polish Centres for Foreigners. The author confronts the traditional approach to securitization of migration, unravelling securitizing practices that operate below the threshold of hyper-visibility and traditional forms of the politics of fear. In turn, the paper *Spaces and Places of the Detention of Foreigners* considers three interrelated issues: (1) an 'inventory' of spaces and places of guarded centres for foreigners – their material substrate, (2) an attempt at the 'reading' of these spaces and places in the context of various types of regulations pertaining to their use and the daily practices in this scope, (3) perceptions of these spaces/places declared by the users and the social interactions which take place there. The subsequent article (*People in Total Institutions. The Case of Border Guard Functionaries and Employees in Guarded Centres for Foreigners*) seeks to identify, characterise and analyse the guarded detention centres in Poland as totalising institutions and the psycho-social consequences of the totalisation of the Border Guard officers and civil employees working in these centres. The said consequences result from the daily existence in the sphere affected by the totalising institution in the dimension of the legal and socio-cultural determinants of the functioning of the centres and the impact of the outside world on the BG officers and civil employees. The author of the article *'External Limbo' – 'Internal Limbo'. On the Detention of Immigrants in Polish Guarded Centres for Foreigners* analyses the mental consequences of detention faced by the immigrants detained in the Guarded Centres for Foreigners. Based on the case study of a female immigrant staying at the GCF, the considerations make it possible to diagnose the conditions prevailing in the institution and pose a question on the sense of the system of the detention of foreigners. In the paper *On the Need for the Education of Officers and Civilian Employees of Guarded Centres for Foreigners*, the author undertakes an attempt at the showing of a fragment of a very broad map of problems related to designing the knowledge, skills and abilities, as well as attitudes of the individuals directly involved in the activities of the detention centres in Poland. This is because the training system of the Border Guard is short in courses and other training forms making up an educational subsystem addressed to the officers and civil employees of the GCFs.[119]

There were five individual initiatives in the form of papers which were pending publication at the time when this book was published. The text *Detention of Foreigners as a Research Topic and Methodological Challenge* (Schmidt 2020: 91–106) contained the first information on the research project we conducted – its

119 A broader idea and attempts at the development of an IT system that would play the role of both a repository of knowledge and an educational tool addressed to all the specialisations and levels of training in the Border Guard were presented in a separate text by J. Schmidt and P. Boćko (2021: 89–118).

theoretical and methodological assumptions as well as the specificity of the detention institution. The paper was a harbinger of a broader text on the topic, which was contained in a book published six months later (Niedźwiedzki and Schmidt 2020). In turn, the article *The Perfect Space: the Perspective of the Management of Guarded Detention Centres for Foreigners in Poland* presented ideas of BG officers representing the authorities on the appearance and functioning of an ideal detention centre for foreigners. The resulting data were acquired in the course of a series of focus group interviews carried out in all the guarded centres in Poland (Schmidt 2021: 163–183). Maciej Stępka used materials from the study in his postdoctoral book (*Identifying Security Logics in the EU Policy Discourse. The 'Migration Crisis' and the EU*) (Stępka 2022) and in two papers. In both of them (*Searching for solutions to contemporary crises. The evolution of resilience in the Polish strategic discourse (2007–2020)* and *Resilience – Searching for Security in Times of Protracted Crises),* the empirical materials from the study were used to illustrate a change in the understanding of the flexibility and adjustment in the Polish strategic discourse and the importance of resilience in times of crises caused by spatial movements of people (Stępka 2021a, 2021b).

The year 2023 will witness the publication of two case studies devoted to two subcultures of the organisational culture of guarded centres, developed within the milieu of officers and civil employees being first line officers – having direct, daily, intensive contact with the foreigners: guidance counsellors and sentry guards.[120] Dariusz Niedźwiedzki is in the process of the preparation of a monograph concerning interpersonal relations in detention centres – especially between the management of various levels and the subordinates, employees of the particular sections, as well as relations with employees of external entities. The relations will be analysed in the context of the achievement of the basic, founding purpose of the guarded centres – securing the procedure of the issuing of decisions obliging foreigners to leave Poland or covering them by a form of international protection. Maciej Stępka intends to prepare for publication a methodological paper on conducting fieldwork research 'under surveillance', and in a further perspective a monograph devoted to the security and care nexus in immigrant detention.

Our project works are related to assistance and educational activities. The former were presented in the information block of the above-discussed issue

120 Jacek Schmidt, *Etnografia kultury detencyjnej. Strzeżone ośrodki dla cudzoziemców w Polsce.* [*Część 1: Wychowawcy*]; Agnieszka Chwieduk. *Etnografia kultury detencyjnej. Strzeżone ośrodki dla cudzoziemców w Polsce.* [*Część 2I: Wartownicy*].

of the journal *Migration Studies – Review of Polish Diaspora* (Niedźwiedzki and Schmidt, 2022). The empirical materials collected during the study will also be used in a design of a BA and MA course of migration studies (the former is going to be opened in the academic year of 2024–2025) at the Faculty of International and Political Studies, Jagiellonian University, coordinated by the Jagiellonian Centre for Migration Studies.

Conclusion

This book is a corrected and extended version of its counterpart issued in the Polish language. Nevertheless, its basic function continues to be that of a methodological introduction to the presentation of the empirical material acquired during research in the guarded centres in Poland. When setting out to commence writing, we were conscious what information it should contain, and what knowledge we wanted to provide to the reader. The preparation of its subsequent fragments resembled the performance of our fieldwork, during which we maintained methodological openness and flexibility, applying principles of procedure characteristic for the grounded theory. We kept asking ourselves questions concerning complementing the text, with a view to (owing to self-reflection) maintaining, for the reader's sake, a thorough transparency of the methodology of our procedures during the performance of our study. We feel that we managed to maintain such transparency.

The detailed goals we set ourselves in the draft of this book can be divided into two groups. The first one was the need to fill in a considerable information gap in the knowledge on the phenomenon of the detention of foreigners in Poland. This was not only about a routine 'collection' of data resources of different kinds, but also about their in-depth association directed at the discovery in what way they make up the dynamic picture of the detention-related reality and its reading by its participants. The second group of goals was connected with the questions we formed in the course of the project's conceptualisation. Since questions of this sort have never yet been posed, it was impossible to intend to confront the sought-for answers with the state of knowledge. Nevertheless, we set out a certain direction for the activities that were exploratory and, in view of the innovative nature of the topic of the study and the features of the research team, also multidimensional and multi-faceted. The main problem focusing our detailed questions can be defined by quoting our problem question: What are the discriminants of the organisational culture of the totalising institution in its spatial and interactive dimensions, and, consequently, what norms, values, worldviews and ideologies are components of this culture – the cultural knowledge of the social actors? Finding an answer to this question necessitates a deep immersion in the 'forest of symbols'[121] and signs of a different order. The assessment of our actions shall

121 The term was borrowed from the title of Victor Turner's famous study *The Forest of Symbols: Aspects of Ndembu Ritual* (Turner 1970).

lie entirely with the reader. In the case of the book, it is going to be fragmentary, since it can only be based on the criterion of validity and significance of the research idea and the roads leading to its implementation. A comprehensive evaluation can only appear when the acquired results are publicised.

We feel very satisfied by the very fact that the project has been carried out within its time constraints, without us having at our disposal any meaningful financial means to run it, in compliance with the concept developed in the course of painstaking team discussions. We provide this text to the reader in the hope that it will prove useful both at the level of general methodological reflection and considerations concerning the detention of foreigners, and in particular its state in Poland and the possibilities for further in-depth examination of this phenomenon.

The period of the pandemics, the migration crisis on the Polish-Belarusian border sparked off by the Belarusian authorities, and migration-related consequences of the war in Ukraine waged by Russia – the last two engaging the BG to an extraordinary level – have been limiting our contacts with the detention centres in the last couple of years. Nevertheless, in connection with plans of further study visits in the guarded centres, which are going to be connected with educational activity, we are going to undertake actions related to the presentation of some results of our work with a view to obtaining selective feedback from participants of our earlier research. This applies to group interviews/discussion panels, which were conducted using projection techniques.

Kraków-Poznań (Suchy Las), December 2022

Bibliography

Adamczyk Anita (2021). *(Nie)intencjonalna polityka migracyjna Polski*, Poznań: Uniwersytet im. Adama Mickiewicza w Poznaniu - Wydawnictwo Naukowe Wydziału Nauk Politycznych i Dziennikarstwa.

Agamben Giorgio (2008). *Homo sacer. Suwerenna władza i nagie życie*, przeł. Mateusz Salwa. Warszawa: Prószyński i S-ka.

Anderson Leon (2006). *Analitic Autoethnography*, "Journal of Contemporary Ethnography", vol. 35(4), pp. 373–395.

Angrosino Michael (2007). *Doing Ethnographic and Observational Research*. Los Angeles-London-New Delhi-Singapore: Sage.

Angutek Dorota (2013). *Kulturowe wymiary krajobrazu. Antropologiczne studium recepcji przyrody na prowincji: od teorii do empirii*. Poznań: Bogucki Wydawnictwo Naukowe.

Appadurai Arjun (1996). *Modernity at Large. Cultural Dimensions of Globalization*. Minneapolis: University of Minnesota Press.

Applebaum Anne (2003). *Gulag: A History of the Soviet*. New York: Doubleday.

Arbogast Lydie (ed.) (2016). *Migrant Detention in the European Union: A Thriving Business*. Migreurop. http://migreurop.org/IMG/pdf/migrant-detention-eu-en.pdf [1.12.2022]

Archer Margaret (1995). *Realist Social Theory: The Morphogenetic Approach*. Cambridge: Cambridge University Press .

Archer Margaret (2000). *Being Human: The Problem of Agency*. Cambridge: Cambridge University Press.

Archer Margaret (2013). Jak porządek społeczny wpływa na ludzkie sprawstwo? Refleksyjność jako mechanizm pośredniczący miedzy struktura a sprawstwem. In: Adam Mrozowiecki, Olga Nowaczyk, and Irena Szlachcicowa (eds.), *Sprawstwo. Teorie, metody, badania empiryczne w naukach społecznych*. Kraków: Zakład Wydawniczy Nomos, pp. 19–35.

Augé Marc (1995). *Non-places. Introduction to an Anthropology of Supermodernity*. London-New York: Verso.

Balzacq Thierry, Basaran Tugba, Bigo Didier, Guittet Emmanuel-Pierre and Olsson Christian (2010). *Security Practices* (In: *International Studies Encyclopedia*). Denmark: Robert A. Blackwell Publishing.

Banks Marcus (2007). *Using Visual Data in Qualitative Research*. Los Angeles-London-New Delhi-Singapore: Sage.

Baranowska, Aneta (2013). *Człowiek w instytucji totalnej*. Kraków: Zakład Wydawniczy Nomos.

Barbour Rosaline (2007). *Doing Focus Groups*. Los Angeles-London-New Delhi-Singapore: Sage.

Barker Chris (2003). *Cultural Studies. Theory and Practice*. London-Thousand Oaks-New Delhi: Sage.

Barthes Roland (2004). Wstęp do analizy strukturalnej opowiadań. In: Michał Głowiński (red.), *Narratologia*. Gdańsk: słowo/obraz terytoria, s. 13-54.

Baudrillard Jean (2005). *Symulakry i symulacja*, przeł. Sławomir Królak. Warszawa: Sic!.

Bauman Zygmunt (1989). *Modernity and the Holocaust*. Oxford: Polity Press.

Bauman Zygmunt. (1998). *Globalization: The Human Consequences*. New York: Columbia University Press.

Berger Peter L. and Thomas Luckman (1966). *The Social Construction of Reality*. New York: Penguin Books.

Białas Jacek and Klaus Witold (eds.) (2014). *Wciąż za kratami. Raport z monitoringu strzeżonych ośrodków dla cudzoziemców przeprowadzony przez Helsińską Fundację Praw Człowieka oraz Stowarzyszenie Interwencji Prawnej*. Warszawa: Helsińska Fundacja Praw Człowieka oraz Stowarzyszenie Interwenci Prawnej.

Bigo Didier, Bonditti Philippe and Olsson Christian (2013). Mapping the European Field of Security Professionals. In: Didier Bigo, Sergio Carrera, Elspeth Guild and Rob B.J. Walker (eds.), *Europe's 21st Century Challenge: Delivering Liberty*. London: Ashgate, pp. 49–65.

Blumer Herbert (1969). *Symbolic Interactionism. Perspective and Method*. Englewood Cliffs, NJ: Prentice Hall.

Bohnsack Ralf (2004). Dyskusja grupowa - teoria i praktyka rekonstrukcji kolektywnych wzorów orientacji. In: Sławomir Krzychała (ed.), *Społeczne przestrzenie doświadczenia. Metoda interpretacji dokumentarnej*. Wrocław: Wydawnictwo Naukowe Dolnośląskiej Szkoły Wyższej Edukacji TWP, pp. 36-48.

Boissevain Jerremy (1974). *Friends of Friends. Networks, Manipulators, Coalitions*. Oxford: Basil Blackwell.

Borraccetti Marco (2014). Immigration Policy and Detention as a Solution for Undocumented Immigrants Staying Illegally in the EU. In: Michela Ceccorulli and Nicola Labanca (eds.), *The EU, Migration and the Politics of Administrative Detention*. London–New York: Routledge, pp. 42-58.

Bosworth Mary (2014). *Inside Migration Detention*. Oxford: Oxford University Press.

Bourdieu Pierre (2008). *Zmysł praktyczny*, przeł. Maciej Falski. Kraków: Wydawnictwo Uniwersytetu Jagiellońskiego.

Bourdieu Pierre (2009). *Rozum praktyczny. O teorii działania*, przeł. Joanna Stryjczyk. Kraków: Wydawnictwo Uniwersytetu Jagiellońskiego.

Bourdieu Pierre and Wacquant Loïc J. D. (2001). *Zaproszenie do socjologii refleksyjnej*. przeł. Anna Sawisz. Warszawa: Oficyna Naukowa.

Brocki Marcin (2000). *Język ciała w ujęciu antropologicznym*. Wrocław: Astrum.

Brudzińska Jagna (2014). Horyzontalna a wertykalna struktura interdyscyplinarności. Spojrzenie fenomenologiczne. In: Joanna Kurczewska and Magda Lejzerowicz (eds.), *Głosy w sprawie interdyscyplinarności. Socjologowie, filozofowie i inni o pojęciach, podejściach i swych doświadczeniach*. Warszawa: Instytut Filozofii i Socjologii PAN, pp. 251–255.

Bruycker Philippe de (ed.) (2015). *Alternatives to Immigration and Asylum Detention in the UE. Time for Implementation*. http://odysseus-network.eu/wp-content/uploads/2015/02/FINAL-REPORT-Alternatives-to-detention-in-the-EU.pdf [15.10.2020]

Buchowska Stana (ed.) (2016). *Kryminologiczne i społeczno-kulturowe aspekty migracji i handlu ludźmi. Wybrane problemy*. Warszawa: Centralny Ośrodek Szkolenia SG.

Burdziej Stanisław (2011). *Niektóre problemy z tłumaczeniem „Frame Analysis" Ervinga Goffmana – perspektywa tłumacza*, „Przegląd Socjologii Jakościowej", vol. 7(2), pp. 46–53. http://www.qualitativesociologyreview.org/PL/archive_pl.php [18.03.2020].

Bursztа Wojciech (1998). *Antropologia kultury*. Poznań: Zysk i Spółka.

Calhoun Craig and Rhoten Diana (2010). Integrating the Social Sciences: Theoretical Konowledge, Methodolical Tools, and Practical Applications. In: Robert Frodeman, Julie Thomson Klein, and Carl Mitcham (eds.), *The Oxford Hanbook of Interdyscyplinarity*. Oxford: University Press, pp. 103–118.

Canelle Gaile S. and Lincoln Yvonna S. (2018). *Ethics, Research Regulations, and Critical Social Sciences*. In: Norman Denzin K. and Yvonna S. Lincoln (eds.), *The Sage Handbook of Qualitative Research*. Los Angeles-New Delhi-Singapore-Washington DC-Melbourne: Sage, Vol. I, pp. 213–263.

Carter Robert (2013). *Sprawstwo a to, co pozaludzkie*. In: Adam Mrozowiecki, Olga Nowaczyk, and Irena Szlachcicowa (eds.), *Sprawstwo. Teorie, metody, badania empiryczne w naukach społecznych*. Kraków: Zakład Wydawniczy Nomos, pp. 36–45.

Castles Stephen and Miller Mark J. (1993). *The Age of Migration: International Population Movements in the Modern World*. London: Macmillan.

Cegiełka Dawid, Chrzanowska Agnieszka, Klaus Witold, and Wencel Katarzyna (2011). *Przestrzeganie praw cudzoziemców umieszczonych w ośrodkach strzeżonych. Raport z monitoringu*, "Analysis, Reports, Expertises", nr 3, pp. 1–40; *Century*. Thousand Oaks: Sage.

Certeau Michel de (1984). The practice of everyday life. Berkeley – Los Angeles – London: University of California Press.

Charmaz Katty (2006). *Constructing Grounded Theory. A Practical Quide Through Qualitative Analysis.* London – Thousand Oaks – New Delhi: Sage Publications.

Cheek Julianne (2018). The Marketization of Research: Implications for Qualitative Inquiry. In: Norman Denzin K. and Yvonna S. Lincoln (eds.), *The Sage Handbook of Qualitative Research.* Los Angeles-New Delhi-Singapore-Washington DC-Melbourne: Sage, vol. I, pp. 559–599.

Chlebny Jacek (2011). *Postępowanie w sprawie o nadanie statusu uchodźcy.* Warszawa: Wydawnictwo C.H. Beck.

Chomczyński Piotr (2013). Instytucja totalna w obiektywie. Socjologiczna analiza architektury wybranych zakładów karnych. In: Tomasz Ferenc and Marek Domański (eds.), *Architektura przymusu. Interdyscyplinarne studium nad dyscyplinującymi funkcjami architektury*. Łódź: ASP, pp. 115–122.

Chuk Sylwia and Latusek-Jurczak Dominika (2012). Etyka w badaniach jakościowych. In: Dariusz Jemielniak (ed.), *Badania jakościowe. Podejścia i teorie.* Warszawa: Wydawnictwo Naukowe PWN, t. 1, pp. 23–40.

Chwieduk Agnieszka (2015). *Zanurzenie w etyce i kulturze. Antropologiczne projekty zaangażowane społecznie*, „Studia Migracyjne – Przegląd Polonijny", nr 2(156), pp. 165–179.

Chwieduk Agnieszka (2019). *Rumuński sposób na Europę. Antropologiczne studium społeczności lokalnej z Săpânța.* Poznań: Instytut im. Oskara Kolberga.

Chwieduk Agnieszka and Schmidt Jacek (2012). Metodologia badań. In: Michał Buchowski and Jacek Schmidt (eds.), *Migracje a heterogeniczność kulturowa. Na podstawie badań antropologicznych w Poznaniu.* Poznań: Nauka i Innowacje, pp. 23–52.

Chwieduk Agnieszka and Skórzyńska Izabela (2021). *Dydaktyka performatywna: doświadczenie, działanie, refleksja.* Poznań: Wydawnictwo Nauka i Innowacje.

Clapham Christopher (1982). Clientelism and the State. In: Ch.Clapham (ed.), *Private Patronage and Public Power. Political Clientelism in the Modem State.* New York: St.Martin's Press, pp. 15–16.

Code of Ethics: Critical Reflections on Research Ethics in Situations of Forced Migration (2018). International Association for the Study of Forced Migration ‹IASFM›.

Code of Ethics of the American Anthropological Association (1998). https://www.google.com/url?client=internal-element-cse&cx=014098710621475256389:siqvltyr90s&q=https://s3.amazonaws.com/rdcms-aaa/files/production/public/FileDownloads/pdfs/issues/policy-advocacy/upload/ethicscode.pdf&sa=U&ved=2ahUKEwiY09nL0qnsAhVjlosKHc8aD9EQFjABegQICRAB&usg=AOvVaw3aqWrXx3EAh-jDbH90tbl1 [20.20.2020]

Cooley Charles H. (1902). *Human Nature and Social Order*. New York: Trow Directory Printing and Bookbinding Company.

Cornelisse Galina (2010). *Immigration Detention and Human Rights*. Leiden–Boston: Martinus Nijhoff Publishers.

Coser Lewis A. (1974). *Greedy Institutions. Patterns of Undivided Commitment*. New York: The Free Press.

Cote-Boucher Karine, Infantino Federica and Salter Mark B. (2014). *Border Security as Practice: An Agenda for Research*, "Security Dialogue", nr 45(3), pp. 195–208.

Creswell John W. (2009). *Research Design: Qualitative, Quantitative and Mixed Methods Approach*. Los Angeles-London-New Delhi-Singapore: Sage.

Crewe Ben (2009). *The Prisoner Society: Power, Adaptation and Social Life in an English Prison*. Oxford: Oxford University Press.

Crotty Michael (1998). *The Foundations of Social Research: Meaning and Perspective in the Research Process*. London: Sage Publication.

Czarniawska Barbara (2012). Nowe techniki badań terenowych: shadowing. In: Dariusz Jemielniak (ed.), Badania jakościowe. Metody i narzędzia, T. 2, Warszawa: Wydawnictwo Naukowe PWN, pp. 69–90.

Czyżewski Marek (2010). Analiza ramowa, czyli „co tu się dzieje?". In: Erving Goffman (ed.), *Analiza ramowa*, przeł. Stanisław Burdziej, Kraków: ZW Nomos, pp. VII-XLVII.

Dąbrowski Paweł (2011). *Cudzoziemiec niepożądany w polskim prawie o cudzoziemcach*. Warszawa: Wydawnictwo Uniwersytetu Warszawskiego.

Davies Christie (1989). *Goffman's Concept of the Total Institution: Criticisms and Revisions*, "Human Studies", vol. 12, pp. 77–95.

Deleuze Gilles (2014). *Fałda: Leibniz a barok*, przeł. Mateusz Janik i Sławomir Królak. Warszawa: Wydawnictwo Naukowe PWN.

Denzin Norman K. (1978). *The Research Act. A Theoretical Introduction to Sociological Methods*. New York: Mc Graw-Hill.

Denzin Norman K. (1983). *A Note on Emotionality, Self and Interaction*, "American Journal of Sociology", vol. 89(3), pp. 402-409.

Denzin Norman K. (1997). *Interpretive Ethnography. Ethnographic Practices for the* 21st. *Century*. Thousand Oaks: Sage.

Denzin Norman K (2012). *Triangulation 2.0*, "Journal of Mixed Methods Research", vol. 3, pp. 80–88.

Denzin Norman K. (2014). *Interpretive Autoethnography*. Los Angeles: Sage.

Denzin Norman K. and Lincoln Yvonna S. (2018). Introduction: The Discipline and Practice of Qualitative Research. In: Norman K. Denzin and Yvonna S. Lincoln (eds.), *The Sage Handbook of Qualitative Research*. Los Angeles–New Delhi–Singapore–Washington, DC–Melbourne: Sage, vol. I, pp. 29–71.

Dijk Teunvan van (2001). Critical Discourse Analysis. In: Deborah Schiffrin, Deborah Tannen, Heidi E. Hamilton (eds.), *The Handbook of Discourse Analysis*, Oxford: Blackwell Publishers, pp. 354–371.

Domecka Marieta (2013). Wprowadzenie do polskiego tłumaczenia książki Margaret S. Archer 'Człowieczeństwo. Problem sprawstwa'. In: Margaret S. Archer (ed.), *Człowieczeństwo: problem sprawstwa*, przeł. Agata Dziuban, Kraków: Zakład Wydawniczy Nomos, pp XLI–LIV.

Douglas Mary (1992). *Risk and Blame*. London: Routledge.

Dul Andrzej R. (1995). Komunikacja niewerbalna w teorii i badaniach. In: Alina Kapciak, Leszek Korporowicz and Andrzej Tyszka (eds.), *Komunikacja międzykulturowa. Zbliżenia i impresje*. Warszawa: Instytut Kultury, pp. 43-68.

Eco Umberto (1997). Function and Sign. In: N. Leach (ed.), *Rethinking Architecture: A Reader in Cultural Theory*. London: Routledge, pp. 174–186.

Eisenstadt Shmuel N.(1958). *Bureaucracy and Bureaucratization*, "Current Sociology", vol. 7, pp. 99–124.

Eisenstadt Shmuel N. and Curelaru Miriam (1976). *The Form of Sociology—Paradigms and Crises*. New York: John Wiley.

Eisnestadt Shmuel N. and Luis Roniger (1984). *Patrons, Clients and Friends*. Cambridge: Cambridge University Press.

Elder-Vasss Dave (2007). Reconciling Archer and Bourdieu in an Emergentist Theory of Action, "*Sociological Theory*", vol. 25(4), pp. 325–347.

Ellis Carolyn and Bochner Arthur P. (2003). Autoethnography, Personal Narrative, Reflexivity. Researcher as Subject. In: Norman. K. Denzin and Yvonna S. Lincoln (eds.), *Collecting and Interpreting Qualitative Materials*. Thousand Oaks–London–Delhi: Sage, pp. 199-258.

Ethical Guidelines for Good Research Practice (Association of Social Anthropologists of the UK and the Commonwealth 1999).

European Asylum Support Office (2019). *Judicial analysis. Detention of applicants for international protection in the context of the Common European Asylum System.* https://euaa.europa.eu/sites/default/files/Detention-JA-EN-PDF.pdf [1.12.2022]

European Council on Refugees and Exiles (2021). *Reception, Detention and Restriction of Movement at EU External Borders.* https://ecre.org/wp-content/uploads/2021/07/ECRE-Heinrich-Boll-StiftungReception-Detention-and-Restriction-of-Movement-at-EU-External-Borders-July-2021.pdf [1.12.2022]

European Law Institute (2020). *Detention of Asylum Seekers and Irregular Migrants and the Rule of Law: Checklists and European Standards.* https://www.europeanlawinstitute.eu/fileadmin/user_upload/p_eli/Publications/Detention_and_the_Rule_of_Law.pdf [1.12.2022]

Fairclough Norman (2003). *Analysing Discourse. Textual Analysis for Social Research.* London: Routledge.

Fassin Didier (2005). *Compassion and Repression: The Moral Economy of Immigration Policies in France,* "Cultural Anthropogy", vol. 20, pp. 362–387.

Fine Gary Alan (2010). Dziesięć kłamstw etnografii – dylematy etyczne w terenie. In: Katarzyna Kaniowska i Noemi Modnicka (red.), *Etyczne problemy badań antropologicznych.* Wrocław–Łódź: Polskie Towarzystwo Ludoznawcze, s. 87–51.

Flick Uve (2007a). *Designing Qualitative Research.* Los Angeles-London-New Delhi-Singapore: Sage.

Flick Uve (2007b). *Managing Quality in Qualitative Research.* Los Angeles-London-New Delhi-Singapore: Sage.

Flynn Mathew and Flynn Michael (eds.), (2017). *Challenging Immigration Detention: Academics, Activists, and Policy-Makers.* Cheltensham: Edward Elgar.

Flyvbjerg Bent (2006). *Five Misunderstandings about Case-Study Research,* "Qualitative Inquiry", vol. 12(2), pp. 219–245.

Foucault Michel (1986). *Of Other Spaces,* "Diacritics", vol. 16, pp. 22–27.

Foucault Michel (1987). *Historia szaleństwa w dobie klasycyzmu,* przeł. Helena Kęszycka. Warszawa: Państwowy Instytut Wydawniczy.

Foucault Michel (1993). *Nadzorować i karać. Narodziny więzienia,* przeł. Tadeusz Komendant. Warszawa: Wydawnictwo Fundacji Aletheia.

Foucault Michel (2005). *Inne przestrzenie,* przeł. Agnieszka Rejniak-Majewska, „Teksty Drugie", nr 6, pp. 117–125.

Frodeman Robert, Klein Julie Thompson, and Mitcham Carl (eds.) (2010). *The Oxford Handbook of Interdyscyplinarity.* Oxford: University Press.

Geertz Clifford (1973). *The Interpretation of Cultures.* New York: Basic Books.

Geertz Clifford (1983). *Local Knowledge. Further Essays in Interpretive Anthropology.* New York: Basic Books.

Geertz Clifford (1988). *Works and Lives: The Anthropologist as Author*. Stanford: Stanford University Press.

Gellner Ernest (1977). Patrons and Clients. In: Ernest Gellner, and John Waterbury (eds.), *Patrons and Clients in Mediterranean Societies*. London: Duckworth, pp. 1–6.

Gellner David N. and Hirsch Eric (eds.) (2001). *Inside Organizations. Anthropologists at Work*. Oxford–New York: Berg.

Gibbs Graham (2007). *Analyzing Qualitative Data*. Los Angeles–London–New Delhi–Singapore: Sage.

Giddens Anthony (1991). *Modernity and Self-Identity. Self and Society in the Modern Age*. Cambridge: Polity Press.

Glaser, Barney G. (1978). *Theoretical Sensitivity*. Mill Valley, CA: The Sociology Press.

Glaser, Barney G. and Strauss Anselm L. (2006 [1967]). *The Discovery of Grounded Theory. Strategies for Qualitative Research*. New Brunswick–London: Aldine Transaction.

Global Detention Project (2018). *Immigration Detention in Poland: Systematic Family Detention and Lack of Individualized Assessment* [country report, october 2018], https://www.globaldetentionproject.org/wp-content/uploads/2018/10/Immigration-Detention-in-Poland-October-2018-WEB.pdf [20.12.2019].

Goćkowski Janusz (1999). Kręgi kompetencji merytorycznej w perspektywie antropologii wiedzy. In: Janusz Goćkowski and Przemysław Kisiel (eds.), *Kręgi kompetencji i perspektywy poznawcze*. Kraków: Wydawnictwo i drukarnia „Secesja", pp. 67–90.

Goffman Erving (1959). *The Presentation of Self in Everyday Life*. New York: Doubleday Anchor Original.

Goffman Erving (1961). *Asylums. Essays on the the Social Situations of Mental Patients and Other Immates*. New York: Anchor Press.

Goffman Erving (1967). *Interaction Ritual: Essays on Face-to-Face Behavior*. Anchor Books.

Goffman Erving (1971). *Relations in Public: Microstudies of the Public Order*. New York: Basic Books.

Goffman Erving (1986 [1974]). *Frame Analysis: An Essayon the Organization of Experience*. Boston: Northeastern University Press.

Griffin Marie L. (2001). *The Use of Force by Detention Officers*. New York: LFB Scholarly Publishing LL.

Griffiths John (1986). *What Is Legal Pluralism?*, "Journal of Legal Pluralism and Unofficial Law", vol. 24, pp. 1–55.

Gronow Antti (2008). The Over- or the Undersocialized Conception of Man? Practice Theoryand the Problem of Intersubjectivity, "*Sociology*", vol. 42(20), pp. 243–259.

Grzymała-Moszczyńska Halina and Nowicka Ewa (red.) (1998). *Goście i gospodarze. Problemy adaptacji kulturowej w obozach dla uchodźców oraz otaczających je społecznościach lokalnych*. Kraków: ZW Nomos.

Guia Maria Joao, Koulish Robert, and Mitsilegas Valsamis (eds.) (2016). *Immigration Detention, Risk and Human Rights: Studies on Immigration and Crime*. Cham: Springer.

Habermas Jürgen (1983). *Teoria i praktyka. Wybór pism*, tłum. Małgorzata Łukasiewicz, Zdzisław Krasnodębski. Warszawa: Państwowy Instytut Wydawniczy.

Hałas Elżbieta (2001). *Symbole w interakcji*. Warszawa: Oficyna Naukowa.

Hall Edward T. (1983). *The Dance of Life: The Other Dimension of Time*. Garden City, New York: Anchor Books/Doubleday.

Hall Edward T. (1989). *Beyond Culture*. New York: Anchor Books/Doubleday.

Hall Edward T. (1990). *The Hidden Dimension*. New York: Anchor Books Edition.

Hall Mildred Reed and Hall Edward T. (1995). *The Fourth Dimension in Architecture: The Impact of Building on Behavior*. Santa Fe: NM Sunstone Press.

Hammersley Martyn and Atkinson Paul (1997). *Ethnography. Principles in Practice*. London–New York: Routledge.

Hanson Allan (1989). *The Making of the Maori*, "American Anthropologist", vol. 91, pp. 890–902.

Hatch Mary Jo with Cunliffe Ann L. (2013). *Organization Theory. Modern, Symbolic and Postmodern Perspectives*. Oxford: Oxford University Press.

Heidegger Martin (1977). *Budować, mieszkać, myśleć. Eseje wybrane*, przeł. Krzysztof Michalski and Krzysztof Pomian. Warszawa: Czytelnik.

Heidegger Martin (2005). *Bycie i czas*, przeł. Bogdan Baran. Warszawa: Wydawnictwo Naukowe PWN.

Hofstede Geert, Hofstede Gert Jan, and Minkov Michael (2010). *Cultures and Organizations – Software of the Mind: Intercultural Cooperation and Its Importance for Survival*. New York–Chicago–San Francisco–Lisbon–London–Madrid–Mexico City–Milan–New Delhi–San Juan-Seou–Singapore–Sydney–Toronto: McGraw-Hill Education Ltd.

Hornowska Elżbieta, Brzezińska Anna Izabela, Kaliszewska-Czeremska Katarzyna, Appelt Karolina, Rawecka Joanna, and Bujacz Aleksandra (2012). *Paradoksalny efekt triangulacji?*, „Edukacja", vol. 4(130), pp. 72-83.

Huysmans Jef (1998). *Security! What Do You Mean?: From Concept to Thick Signifier*, "European Journal of International Relations", vol. 4(2), pp. 226–55.

Huysmans Jef (2011). *What's in an Act? On Security Speech Acts and Little Security Nothings*, "Security Dialogue", vol. 42(4–5), pp. 371–83.

Jankowska Patrycja (2017). *Detencja cudzoziemców w Polsce – granice konfliktu interesów*, "Internetowy Przegląd Prawniczy TBSP UJ", vol. 4, s. 152-162.

JansenYolande, Celikates Robin, and de Bloois Joost (eds.) (2015). *The Irregulation of Migration in Contemporary Europe. Detention, Deportation, Drowning*. London–New York: Rowman&Littlefield.

Jezierski Wojtek (2010). *Total St. Gall: Medieval Monastery as a Disciplinary Institution*. Stockholm: Stockholm University.

Kacperczyk Anna (2012). *Autoetnografia - technika, metoda, nowy paradygmat? O metodologicznym statusie autoetnografii*, „Przegląd Socjologii Jakościowej",vol. 10(3), pp. 32-74.

Kamiński Marek M. (1990). *Badacz w instytucji totalnej*. „Kultura i Społeczeństwo", vol. 1, pp. 247–250.

Kaniowska Katarzyna (2010). Etyczne problemy badań antropologicznych. In: Katarzyna Kaniowska and Noemi Modnicka (eds.), *Etyczne problemy badań antropologicznych*. Wrocław-Łódź: Polskie Towarzystwo Ludoznawcze, pp. 19-31.

Kaufman Robert R. (1974). The Patron-Client Concept and Macro-Politics: Prospects and Problems, "*Comparative Studies in Society and History*", vol. 16(4), pp. 284–308.

Kemmis Stephen and Mary Wilkinson (1998). *Participatory Action Researchand the Study of Practice*. In: Bill Atweh, Stephen Kemmis, and Patricia Weeks (eds.), *Action Research in Practice: Partnerships for Social Justice in Education*. New York: Routledge, pp. 21-36.

Kempny Marian (1994). *Antropologia bez dogmatów – teoria społeczna bez iluzji*. Warszawa: Instytut Filozofii i Socjologii PAN.

Kita Małgorzata (2012). „Razem". Konsiliencja, interdyscyplinarność, transdyscyplinarność. In: Małgorzata Kita and Magdalena Ślawska (eds.), *Transdyscyplinarność badań nad komunikacją medialną*, t. 1: *Stan wiedzy i postulaty badawcze*. Katowice: Wydawnictwo Uniwersytetu Śląskiego, pp. 11-30.

Klaus Witold and Rusiłowicz Karolina (eds.) (2012). *Migracja to nie zbrodnia. Raport z monitoringu strzeżonych ośrodków dla cudzoziemców*. Warszawa: Stowarzyszenie Interwencji Prawnej oraz Helsińska Fundacja Praw Człowieka. https://interwencjaprawna.pl/wp-content/uploads/monitoring_osrodkow_strzezonych_2012.pdf [10.10.2020].

Klein Julie Thompson (2010). A Taxonomy of Interdyscyplinarity. In: Robert Frodeman, Julie Thompson Klein and Carl Mitcham (eds.). *The Oxford Handbook of Interdyscyplinarity*. Oxford: University Press, pp. 15-30.

Klineberg Otto (1940). *Social Psychology*. New York: Henry Holt.

Kluszczyńska Marta (2017). *Ośrodek dla uchodźców jako element międzynarodowego reżimu uchodźczego – próba opisu antropologicznego*, niepublikowana praca magisterska napisana pod kierunkiem prof. UAM dra hab. Jacka Schmidta w Instytucie Etnologii i Antropologii Kulturowej UAM.

Knorr-Cetina Karin (1981). Introduction: The Micro-Sociological Challenge of Macro-Sociology: Towards a Reconstruction of Social Theory and Methodology. In: Karin Knorr-Cetina and Aaron V. Cicourel (eds.), *Advances in Social Theory and Methodology: Toward an Integration of Micro- and Macro-Sociologies*. Boston: Routledge & Kegan Paul, pp. 1–47.

Kochanowska Marta (2008). Funkcje pracowników socjalnych w polskich ośrodkach dla uchodźców. In: Izabela Czerniejewska and Izabella Main (eds.), *Uchodźcy: teoria i praktyka*. Poznań: Stowarzyszenie „Jeden Świat", pp. 127–142.

Koczanowicz Leszek (2014). Interdyscyplinarność między rabunkiem a dialogiem. In: Joanna Kurczewska and Magda Lejzerowicz (eds.), *Głosy w sprawie interdyscyplinarności. Socjologowie, filozofowie i inni o pojęciach, podejściach i swych doświadczeniach*. Warszawa: IFIS PAN, pp. 264–272.

Konecki Krzysztof (2000). *Studia z metodologii badań jakościowych. Teoria ugruntowana*. Warszawa: Wydawnictwo Naukowe PWN.

Konecki Krzysztof (2007). Procesualne ujęcie organizacji. Organizacje, struktury, procesy i tożsamości. In: Łukasz Sułkowski and Czesław Sikorski (red.), *Metody zarządzania kulturą organizacyjną*. Warszawa: Difin, pp. 7–21.

Kostera Monika (2011). Badania etnograficzne organizacji. In: Monika Kostera (ed.), *Etnografia organizacji. Badania polskich firm i instytucji*. Sopot: Gdańskie Wydawnictwo Psychologiczne, pp. 9–22.

Kostera Monika (2013). *Antropologia organizacji. Metodologia badań terenowych*. Warszawa: Wydawnictwo Naukowe PWN.

Krasnodębski Zdzisław and Nellen Klaus (eds.) (1993). *Świat przeżywany. Fenomenologia i nauki społeczne*. Warszawa: Państwowy Instytut Wydawniczy.

Krzychała Sławomir (2004). Dokumentarna interpretacja tekstu – od samobieżnego toku dyskusji do refleksywnej interpretacji dyskursu. In: Sławomir Krzychała (ed.), *Społeczne przestrzenie doświadczenia. Metoda interpretacji dokumentarnej*. Wrocław: Wydawnictwo Naukowe Dolnośląskiej Szkoły Wyższej Edukacji TWP, pp. 49–63.

Kuligowski Waldemar (2001). *Antropologia refleksyjna*. Poznań: Wydawnictwo Poznańskie.

Kunter Aylin (2012). *Analiza dyskursu*, przeł. Marta Höffner. In: Dariusz Jemieliniak (ed.), *Badania jakościowe. Metody i narzędzia*. T. 2. Warszawa: Wydawnictwo Naukowe PWN, pp. 189–201.

Kurczewska Joanna (2014). Autorytet i interdyscyplinarność. In: Joanna Kurczewska and Magda Lejzerowicz (eds.), *Głosy w sprawie interdyscyplinarności. Socjologowie, filozofowie i inni o pojęciach, podejściach i swych doświadczeniach.* Warszawa: Instytut Filozofii i Socjologii PAN, pp. 273-288.

Kurczewska Joanna and Lejzerowicz Magda (eds.) (2014). *Głosy w sprawie interdyscyplinarności. Socjologowie, filozofowie i inni o pojęciach, podejściach i swych* doświadczeniach. Warszawa: Instytut Filozofii i Socjologii PAN.

Kvale Steinar (2007). *Doing Interviews.* Los Angeles–London–New Delhi–Singapore: Sage.

Labanca Nicola and Ceccorulli Michela. (2014a). Introduction. In: Michela Ceccorulli and Nicola Labanca (eds.), *The EU, Migration and the Politics of Administrative Detention.* London-New York: Routledge, pp. 1-16.

Labanca Nicola and Ceccorulli Michela (2014b). The Geography and History of Camps. In: Michela Ceccorulli and Nicola Labanca (eds.), *The EU, Migration and the Politics of Administrative Detention.* London-New York: Routledge, pp. 81-108.

Laclau Ernesto and Mouffe Chantal (1985). *Hegemony and Socialist Strategy: Towards a Radical Democratic Politics.* London–New York: Verso.

Landé Carl H. (1983). Political Clientelism in Political Studies: Retrospect and Prospects "*International Political Science Review*", vol. 4(4), pp. 435–454.

Leavitt John (2012). Znaczenie i czucie w antropologii emocji. przeł. Agnieszka Kościańska and Michał Petryk. In: Małgorzata Rajtar and Justyna Straczuk (eds.), *Emocje w kulturze.* Warszawa: Wydawnictwo Uniwersytetu Warszawskiego, pp. 59-99.

Lefebrve Henri (1991). *The Production of Space.* Oxford: Blackwell.

Leibniz Wilhelm (1969). *Wyznanie wiary filozofa, Rozprawa metafizyczna, Monadologia, Zasady natury i łaski oraz inne pisma filozoficzne*, przeł. S. Cichowicz, J. Domański, H. Rzeczkowski, and H. Moese. Warszawa: PWN.

Lemondżawa Ekaterina (2017). *Nr 56: Pamiętaj, nazywam się Ekaterina*, przeł. Manana Gelashvili and Jagoda Dolińska. Tbilisi-Warszawa-Poznań: Bractwo Trójka.

Lincoln Yvonna S., Lynham Susaz and Guba Egon G. (2018). Paradigmatic Controversies, Contradictions, and Emerging Confluences, Revisited. In: Norman Denzin K. and Yvonna S. Lincoln (eds.), *The Sage Handbook of Qualitative Research.* Los Angeles–New Delhi–Singapore–Washington, DC–Melbourne: Sage. vol. 8, pp. 213–263.

Lipsky Michael (2010). *Street-Level Bureaucracy. Dillemas of the Individual in Public Services.* New York: Russel Sage Foundation.

Little Kenneth B. (1965). *Personal Space*, "Journal of Experimental Social Psychology", vol. 1(3), pp. 237-247.

Łodziński Sławomir and Szonert Marek (2016). Polityka migracyjna w Polsce w latach 1989–2015. In: Jacek Schmidt, and Dariusz Niedźwiedzki (eds.), *Społeczno-kulturowa identyfikacja cudzoziemców. Raporty i ekspertyzy*. Poznań: Wydawnictwo Naukowe UAM, pp. 11-66.

Łodziński Sławomir and Szonert Marek (2017). *„Niepolityczna polityka"? Kształtowanie się polityki migracyjnej w Polsce w latach 1989–2016*, „Studia Migracyjne – Przegląd Migracyjny", z. 2(164), pp. 39-66.

Łodziński Sławomir, Marek Szonert (2023). Polityka migracyjna „bez polityki". Antynomie tworzenia polityki migracyjnej w Polsce w okresie 2016-2022, *„CMR Working Papers"*, Nr 130 (188), Ośrodek Badań nad Migracjami UW, Warszawa luty 2023.

Low Setha M. and Zúñiga-Lawrence Denise (2003). Locating Culture. In: Setha M. Low and Denise Lawrence-Zúñiga (eds.), *The Anthropology of Space and Place. Locating Culture*. Malden, MA: Blackwell, pp. 1-47.

Lubaś Marcin (2003). *Rozum i etnografia. Przyczynek do krytyki antropologii postmodernistycznej*. Kraków: ZW Nomos.

Luhmann Niklas (2007). *Systemy społeczne. Zarys ogólnej teorii*. Kraków: ZW Nomos.

Lutz Catherine A. (2012). Emocje, rozum i wyobcowanie. Emocje jako kategoria badawcza, przeł. Justyna Straczuk. In: Małgorzata Rajtar and Justyna Straczuk (eds.), *Emocje w kulturze*. Warszawa: Wydawnictwo Uniwersytetu Warszawskiego, pp. 27-56.

Lutz Catherine and White Geoffrey M. (1986). *The Anthropology of Emotions*, "Annual Review of Anthropology", vol. 15, pp. 406-430.

Majcher Izabella, Flynn Michael, and Grange Mariette (2019). *Immigration Detention in the European Union. In the shadow of the "Crisis"*. Geneva: Springer.

Malinowski Bronisław (1989). *A Diary in the Strict Sense of the Term*. London: The Athlone Press.

Malinowski Bronisław (2005). *Argonauts of the Western Pacific. An Account of Native Enterprise and Adventure in the Archipealagoes of Melanesian New Guinea*. London: Routledge.

Mannheim, Karl (1940). *Man and Society in a Age of Reconstruction. Studies in Modern Social Structure*. London: Rautledge and Kegan Paul Ltd.

Marrevijk Affons van and Yanow Dvora (eds.) (2010). *Organizational Spaces. Rematerializing the Workaday World*. Cheltenham: Edward Elgar.

Mead, George H. (2015). *Mind, Self, and Society: The Definitive Edition*. Chicago: Chicago University Press.

Mękarski Michał (2014). *Shadowing jako budowanie relacji badacz-badany*, „Barbarzyńca. Pismo Antropologiczne", nr 1(20), pp. 118-130.

Merleau-Ponty Maurice (2001). *Fenomenologia percepcji*. przeł. Małgorzata Kowalska. Warszawa: Aletheia.

Merton Robert K. (1968). *Social Theory and Social Structure*. New York: The Free Press.

Migreurop (2014). *Detention of Migrants. The Favourite Means of Migration "Management"*, "Migreurop Brief" (2), pp. 1-4; http://www.migreurop.org/IMG/pdf/Note_de_MIGREUROP_detention_EN_Web.pdf [1.05.2019].

Miles Mathew B. and Huberman Michael A. (1994). *Qualitative Data Analysis*. Los Angeles-London-New Delhi-Singapore-Washington DC: Sage.

Miszewski Kamil (2007). *Kiedy badacz jest tajnym agentem. O postrzeganiu niejawnej obserwacji uczestniczącej jako etycznie problematycznej, metodach badań ilościowych, zakulisowych wymiarach życia społecznego i ich związkach ze wszystkim tym, o czym przed chwilą*. „Przegląd Socjologii Jakościowej", Tom III(2), pp. 33–62 http://www.qualitativesociologyreview.org/PL/Volume4/PSJ_3_2.pdf [1.12.2022]

Moran Joe (2010). *Interdyscyplinarity*. New York: Routledge.

Moran Dominique, Gill Nick and Conlon Deirdre (eds.) (2013). *Carcelar Spaces: Mobility and Agency in Imprisonment and Migrant Detention*. Farnham: Ashgate.

Morgan Gareth (2006). *Images of Organization*. Los Angeles–London–New Delhi: Sage.

Morgan David (2007). *Paradigsm Lost and Pragmatism Regained: Methodological Implications of Combining Qualitative and Quantitative Methodes*, "Journal of Mixed Methods Research", vol. 1(1), pp. 48-76.

Mountz Alison, Coddington Kate, Catania R. Tina and Loyd Jenna M. (2013). *Conceptualizing Detention*, "Progress in Human Geography", nr 37(4), pp. 522–541.

Mucha Janusz (1986). *Socjologia jako krytyka społeczna*. Warszawa: Wydawnictwo Naukowe PWN.

Mutch Alistair (2004). *Contraints on the Interanl Conversation: Margaret Archer and the Structural Shaping of Thought*, "Journal for the Theory of Social Behaviour", vol. 34(4), pp. 429–445.

Nethery Amy and Silverman Stephanie (eds.) (2015). *Immigration Detention: The Migration of a Policy and Its Human Impact*. London: Routledge.

Nicolescu Besarab (2006). *Methodology of Transdycyplinarity*. https://www.academia.edu/14441459/METHODOLOGY_OF_TRANSDISCIPLINARITY [20.08.2019]

Niedźwiedzki Dariusz (2010). *Migracje i tożsamość. Od teorii do analizy przypadku*. Kraków: ZW Nomos.

Niedźwiedzki Dariusz and Schmidt Jacek (2020). *Detencja cudzoziemców w Polsce. Perspektywa teoretyczno-metodologiczna*. Kraków: Nomos.

Niedźwiedzki Dariusz and Schmidt Jacek (eds.) (2022). *Detention fo Foreigners. Case of Poland*, „Studia Migracyjne – Przegląd Polonijny", vol. 4.

Niedźwiedzki Dariusz, Schmidt Jacek, Stępka Maciej, and Tacik Przemysław (2021). *Strzeżone ośrodki dla cudzoziemców jako kultura organizacyjna. Analiza prawna, politologiczna, socjologiczna i antropologiczna*. Ekspertyza przygotowana na zlecenie Komitetu Badań nad Migracjami Polskiej Akademii Nauk, p. 110. https://publikacje.pan.pl/dlibra/results?q=Strze%C5%BCone&action=SimpleSearchAction&mdirids=&type=-6&startstr=_all&p=0 DOI: 10.24425/139584

Nohl, Arnd-Michael (2004). Analiza komparatywna – w stronę fundamentalnej zasady interpretacji dokumentarnej. In: Sławomir Krzychała (ed.), *Społeczne przestrzenie doświadczenia. Metoda interpretacji dokumentarnej*. Wrocław: Wydawnictwo Naukowe Dolnośląskiej Szkoły Wyższej Edukacji TWP, pp. 64-85.

„Ośrodek dla cudzoziemców w Wędrzynie nie spełnia standardów ochrony ich praw. Wnioski po trzeciej wizytacji BRPO", https://bip.brpo.gov.pl/pl/content/rpo-wedrzyn-cudzoziemcy-osrodek-standardy [1.12.2022]

Ottavy Eva (2014). Camps in Poland and Romania: Accessiom to the EU, a Step Towards Detention of Foreigners. In: Michela Ceccorulli and Nicola Labanca (eds.), *The EU, Migration and the Politics of Administrative Detention*. London–New York: Routledge, pp. 128-144.

Patton Michael Q. (2002). *Qualitative Research and Evaluation Methodes*. Thousand Oaks, CA: Sage.

Pawlak Mikołaj and Ireneusz Sadowski (2017). *Nowy instytutcjonalizm w analizach polskiego społeczeństwa – tradycje, stań badań i perspektywy*, „Studia Polityczne", tom 45(2), pp. 27–52.

Perry Nick (1974). *The Two Cultures and the Total Institution*, "British Journal of Sociology", vol. 25, pp. 345–355.

Piattoni Simona (ed.) (2001). *Clientelism, Interests, and Democratic Representation: The European Experience in Historical and Comparative Perspective*. Cambridge: Cambridge University Press.

Pomieciński Adam and Sikora Sławomir (eds.) (2009). *Zanikające granice. Antropologizacja nauki i jej dyskursów*. Poznań: Wydawnictwo Biblioteka Telgte.

Posern-Zieliński Aleksander (1987). Subkultura. In: Zofia Staszczak (ed.), *Słownik etnologiczny. Terminy ogólne*. Warszawa-Poznań: PWN, pp. 334-336.

Posłuszny Łukasz (2017). *Instytucje totalne dzisiaj: stan badan, krytyka, rekonfiguracje*, „Studia Socjologiczne", vol. 4(227), pp. 121-145.

Potter Jonathan (1997). *Discours Analysis as a Way of Analysing Naturally-Occurring Talk*. In: David Silverman (ed.), *Qualitative Research: Theory, Method and Pracice*. London: Sage., pp. 144–160.

Przybysz-Zaremba Małgorzata (2015). Zakład karny jako przestrzeń widziana z perspektywy osadzonego - studium przypadku. In: Teresa Sadoń-Osowiecka (ed.), *Miejsce, przestrzeń, krajobraz – edukacyjne znaki*. Gdańsk: Wydawnictwo UG, pp. 286-305.

Quane Helen (2013). *Legal Pluralism and International Human Rights Law: Inherently Incompatible, Mutually Reinforcing or Something in Between?*, "Oxford Journal of Legal Studies", vol. 33(4), pp. 675–702.

Rafalik Norbert (2012). *Cudzoziemcy ubiegający się o nadanie statusu uchodźcy w Polsce - teoria a rzeczywistość (praktyka) (stan prawny na dzień 31 grudnia 2011 r.)*, "CMR Working Papers", nr 55(113). Warszawa: Uniwersytet Warszawski–Centrum Badań nad Migracjami.

Rancew-Sikora Dorota (2007). *Analiza konwersacyjna jako metoda rozmów codziennych*, Warszawa: Wydawnictwo TRIO.

Rapley Tim (2007). *Doing Conversation, Discourse and Document Analysis*. London: Sage Publication.

Repko Allen F. (2006). *Disciplinig Interdyscyplinarity: The Case for Textbooks*, "Issues in Integrative Studies", nr 24, pp. 112-142.

Repko Allen F. (2012). *Interdyscyplinary Research: Process and Theory*. London: Sage.

Rock Frances (2007). *Communicating Rights. The Language of Arrest and Detention*. New York: Palgrave Macmillan.

Rorty Richard (1990). Pragmatism and Anti-Representationalism. In: J.P. Murphy (ed.), *Pragmatism from Peirce to Davison*. Boulder, CO: Westview, pp. 1-6.

Rosner Katarzyna (2003). *Narracja, tożsamość i czas*. Kraków: Universitas.

Ryan Bernard and Mitsilegas Valsamis (eds.) (2010). *Extraterritorial Immigration Control. Legal Challenges*. Leiden-Boston: Martinus Nijhoff Publishers.

Sarana Gopala (1975). *The Methodology of Anthropological Comparisons. An Analysis of Comparative Methods in Social and Cultural Anthropology*. Tucson: University of Arizona Press.

Schmidt Jacek (2009). *Nowe tożsamości w czasach transformacji europejskich. Imigranci z Polski w Niemczech*. Poznań: Wydawnictwo NEWS-Witold Nowak.

Schmidt Jacek (2014). O użyteczności antropologii społeczno-kulturowej w obszarze studiów europejskich. In: Jacek Czaputowicz (ed.), *Studia europejskie.*

Wyzwania interdyscyplinarności. Warszawa: Wydział Dziennikarstwa i Nauk Politycznych Uniwersytetu Warszawskiego, pp. 327-334.

Schmidt Jacek (2020). *Detencja cudzoziemców jako temat badawczy i wyzwanie metodologiczne*, „Studia Migracyjne – Przegląd Polonijny", nr 2, pp. 91–106.

Schmidt Jacek (2021). *Przestrzeń idealna – perspektywa władzy. Na przykładzie strzeżonych ośrodków dla cudzoziemców w Polsce*, "Rozwój Regionalny i Polityka Regionalna", nr. 54, pp. 163–183.

Schmidt Jacek and Boćko Piotr (2021). A Heuristic System of Sociocultural Identification of Immigrants in Poland: Education – Good Practices – Safety. In: Anna Sroka, Piotr Potejko, and Rubén Dario Torres Kumbrián (eds.), *Migration and Border Security. Global Perspectives*. Berlin: Peter Lang, pp. 89–118.

Schmidt Jacek and Niedźwiedzki Dariusz (eds.) (2016a). *Społeczno-kulturowa identyfikacja cudzoziemców, Projekty szkoleniowe*. Poznań: Wydawnictwo Naukowe UAM.

Schmidt Jacek and Niedźwiedzki Dariusz (eds.) (2016b). *Społeczno-kulturowa identyfikacja cudzoziemców. Raporty i ekspertyzy*. Poznań: Wydawnictwo Naukowe.

Schütz Alfred (1953). *Common-Sense and Scientific Interpretation of Human Action*, "Philosophy and Phenomenological Research", vol. 14(1), pp. 1–38

Schütz Alfred (1964). *Collected Papers II. Studies in Social Theory*. The Hague: Martinus Nijoff.

Schütz Alfred (2008). *O wielości światów: szkice z socjologii fenomenologicznej*, przeł. Barbara Jabłońska. Kraków: ZW Nomos.

Scott James (1977). Patronage and Exploitation. In: Ernest Gellner and John Waterbury (eds.) *Patrons and Clients in Mediterranean Societies*. London: Duckworth, pp. 21–29.

Seweryn Anna (2010). Kodeks etyczny antropologa. In: Katarzyna Kaniowska and Noemi Modnicka (red.), *Etyczne problemy badań antropologicznych*. Wrocław-Łódź: Polskie Towarzystwo Ludoznawcze, pp. 33-51.

Shils Edward (1982). *The Constitution of Society*. Chcago: The University Chicago Press.

Sieniow Tomasz (2016). *Stosowanie alternatyw do detencji cudzoziemców w Polsce w latach 2014-2015. Raport z monitoringu*. Lublin: Instytut na rzecz Państwa Prawa.

Sikora Marek (2007). *Problem reprezentacji poznawczej w nowożytnej i współczesnej refleksji filozoficznej*. Poznań: Wydawnictwo Naukowe Instytutu Filozofii UAM.

Silverman David (2014). *Interpreting Qualitative Data*. Los Angeles–London–New Delhi–Singapore: Sage.

Silverman David (2018). *Doing Qualitative Research. A Practical Handbook*. Los Angeles–London–New Delhi–Singapore: Sage.

Silverman Stephanie J. and Massa Evelyne (2012). *Why Immigration Detention Is Unique*, "Population, Space and Place", vol. 18, pp. 677-686.

Snow David A. (2004). Framing Processes, Ideology, and Discursive Fields. In: David A. Snow, Sarah A. Soule and Hanspeter Kriesi (eds.), *The Blackwell Companion to Social Movements*. London: Blackwell Publishing, pp. 380–412.

Sobczak Krzysztof, 2018, *Strasburg: kara za prowokację dziennikarską dopuszczalna i proporcjonalna*, https://www.prawo.pl/prawnicy-sady/strasburg-kara-za-prowokacje-dziennikarska-dopuszczalna-i-proporcjonalna,74346.html [01.05.2019].

Soja Edward W. (1996). *Thirdspace. Journey to Los Angeles and Other Real-and-Imagined Places*. Oxford: Blackwell.

Sommer Robert (1959). *Studies in Personal Space*, "Sociometry", vol. 22(3), pp. 247-260.

Stake Robert E. (1994). Case Studies. In: Norman K. Denzin and Yvonna S. Lincoln (eds.), *Hanbook of Qualitative Research*. Thousand Oaks-London-Delhi: Sage, pp. 236-247.

Stępka Maciej (2018). *Migration and Security in the European Union. A Critical Analysis of Security Discourses and Narratives*. niepublikowana rozprawa doktorska obroniona na Wydziale Nauk Politycznych i Studiów Międzynarodowych Uniwersytetu Warszawskiego.

Stępka Maciej (2021a). *W poszukiwaniu odpowiedzi na współczesne kryzysy. Ewolucja rezyliencji w polskim dyskursie strategicznym (2007–2020)*, „Rocznik Instytutu Europy Środkowo-Wschodniej", vol. 19(2021)/1, pp. 25–42,

Stępka Maciej (2021b). *Rezyliencja jako paradygmat bezpieczeństwa w czasach przewlekłych kryzysów*, „Przegląd Politologiczny", vol. 2(2021), pp. 105–117.

Stępka Maciej (2022). *Identifying Security Logics in the EU Policy Discourse. The "Migration Crisis" and the EU*. Springer: Cham (Open Access) https://link.springer.com/book/9783030930349

Sułkowski Łukasz (2007). Recepcja nurtu interpretatywnego w naukach o zarządzaniu. In: Krzysztof T. Konecki and Piotr Chomczyński (eds.), *Zarządzanie organizacjami. Organizacja jako proces*. Łódź: Wydawnictwo Uniwersytetu Łódzkiego, pp. 22-30.

Sułkowski Łukasz and Sikorski Czesław (eds.) (2014). *Metody zarządzania kulturą organizacyjną*. Warszawa: Difin.

Sykes Gresham M. (1958). *The Society of Captives. A Study of a Maximum Security Prison*. Princeton: Princeton University Press.

Sztompka Piotr (2002). *Socjologia. Analiza społeczeństwa.* Kraków: Wydawnictwo Znak.

Tarkowski Jacek (1994). *Patroni i klienci*, seria: *Socjologia świata polityki*, t. 2:, Warszawa–Toruń: Instytut Nauk Politycznych PAN–Wydawnictwo Adam Marszałek.

Teubner Günther (1991–1992). *The Two Faces of Janus: Rethinking Legal Pluralism*, "Cardozo Law Review", vol. 13, pp. 1443–1462.

Tokarczuk Olga (2017). *Flights*. London: Fitzcarraldo Editions.

Toporow Władimir (2003). *Przestrzeń i rzecz*, przeł. Bogusław Żyłko. Kraków: Universitas.

Tuan Yi-Fu (2001). *Space na Place. The Perspective of Experience.* Minneapolis–London: University of Minnesota Press.

Turnbull Colin M. (1972). *The Mountain People*. New York: Simon & Schuster.

Turner Victor (1970). *The Forest of Symbols: Apects of Ndembu Ritual.* Ithaca and London: Cornell University Press.

Ugelvik Thomas (2014). *Power and Resistance in Prison: Doing Time, Doing Freedom*. Basingstoke: Palgrave Macmillan.

Ugelvik Thomas (2016). *Low-Trust Policing in a High-Trust Society. The Norwegian Police Immigration Detention Centre and the Search for Public Sphere Legitimacy*, „Nordisk politiforskning", t. 3(2), pp. 181–198.

Ustawa z dnia 12 grudnia 2013 r. o cudzoziemcach (2020). (Dz.U. z 2013 r., poz. 1650; t.j. Dz.U. z 2020 r., poz. 35).

Van Maanen John (1988). *Tales of the Fields: On Writing Ethnography*. Chicago: The University of Chicago Press.

Vanderlinden Jacques (1986). Le pluralisme juridique. Essai de synthèse. In: John Gilissen, and Jacques Vanderlinden (eds.), *Le pluralisme juridique*. Bruxelles: Éditions de l'Université de Bruxelles, pp. 19–56.

Waever Ole (2004). *Aberystwyth, Paris, Copenhagen New 'Schools' in Security Theory and Their Origins between Core and Periphery*. Montreal: Paper Presented at the Annual Meeting of the International Studies Assiciation, 17-20 March.

Walczak Monika (2016). *Czy możliwa jest wiedza interdyscyplinarna?*, „Zagadnienia Naukoznawstwa", vol. 1, pp. 113-126.

Weingrod Alex (1977). Patronage and Power. In: Ernest Gellner and John Waterbury (eds.), *Patrons and Clients in Mediterranean Societies*. London: Duckworth, pp. 41-51.

Welsch Wolfgang (1998). Transkulturowość. Nowa koncepcja kultury. In: Roman Kubicki (ed.), *Filozoficzne konteksty koncepcji rozumu transwersalnego. Wokół koncepcji Wolfganga Welscha.* Poznań: Humaniora, pp. 195-222.

Welsch Wolfgang (2004). *Tożsamość w epoce globalizacji – perspektywa transkulturowa*. In: Krystyna Wilkoszewska (ed.), *Estetyka transkulturowa*. Kraków: Universitas, pp. 31–43.

Willerton John P. (1992). *Patronage and Politics in the USSR*. Cambridge: Cambridge University Press.

Wilsher Daniel (2014). *Immigration Detention. Law, History, Politics*. Cambridge: University Press.

Wright Susan (1994). Culture in Anthropology and Organizational Studies. In: Susan Wright (ed.), *Anthropology of Organization*. London–New York: Routledge, pp. 1–31. .

Yin Robert K. (2014). *Case Study Research. Designs and Methods*. Los Angeles–London–New Delhi–Singapore–Washigton, D.C.: Sage.

Żakowska Magdalena (2011). *Russland- i Polendeutsche. Zaprogramowanie kulturowe niemieckich „Późnych wysiedleńców" z Rosji i Polski*. Łódź: Wydawnictwo Uniwersytetu Łódzkiego.

Ząbek Maciej and Łodziński Sławomir (2008). *Uchodźcy w Polsce. Próba spojrzenia antropologicznego*, Warszawa: Oficyna Wydawnicza ASPRA-JR.

Zybertowicz Andrzej (2001). *Konstruktywizm jako orientacja metodologiczna w badaniach społecznych*, „Kultura i Historia", vol. 1, pp. 118–135.

Notes on the authors and other members of the research team

Agnieszka Chwieduk is a French and Romanian philologist and a social anthropologist working as an Associate Professor in the Institute of Anthropology and Ethnology, Adam Mickiewicz University, Poznań, Poland. Her current scientific and research interests are in three areas: migration and locality studies, medical anthropology (the anthropology of psychiatry and experience) and techniques used in qualitative research, especially the process of participatory observation and the Emic Evaluation Approach. She has conducted field research in many regions of Europe, e.g. in Alsace, France and Maramureş, Romania, and in Poland (Poznań, Podlasie). She is the author of two monographs and 42 articles and review articles, and an editor of *Lud*, a leading Polish anthropological journal.

Selected publications: *Dydaktyka performatywna dla humanistów. Kwestia przypadków/ Performative didactics for humanists. A matter of cases* (with Izabela Skórzyńska, Wydawnictwo Nauka i Innowacje, 2021); *Rumuński sposób na Europę. Antropologiczne studium społeczności lokalnej z Săpânța / Romanian way to Europe. Anthropological study of the local community of Săpânța* (Instytut im. Oskara Kolberga, 2018); "Niejeden grób prawdę ci powie… O sprawstwie i pamięci zbiorowej na przykładzie Rumunii" / "More than one grave will tell you the truth… About perpetration and collective memory on the example of Romania" (*Sensus Historiae. Studia Interdyscyplinarne*, 2017, No. 27(2), pp. 93-114); „Specyficzny Polak w normalnej Francji. O polskiej imigracji w tekstach francuskich badaczy"/ "A specific Pole in normal France. About Polish immigration in the texts of French researchers" (*Studia Migracyjne – Przegląd Polonijny*, 2016, 42: 2(160), pp. 23-50); "Note de terrain. L'anthropologue et l'agence matrimoniale: une métamorphose" (*Ethnologie française*, 2010, 40: 2: *Pologne. Polska. Après le communisme*, pp. 267-272).

Dariusz Niedźwiedzki is a sociologist and social anthropologist, an Associate Professor at the Institute of European Studies of the Jagiellonian University in Krakow and its former director (2012–2020), head of the Jagiellonian Centre for Migration Studies (2014–2022), a member of the Committee on Migration Research of the Polish Academy of Sciences (since 2012) and a member of its Presidium (since 2019), as well as a Vice-President of the Polish Society for European Studies (since 2019). His scientific interests include research and analysis of the problems of constructing and reconstructing social identity, migration, social memory, ethnic conflicts, social and cultural changes in the integrating Europe, and the relationship between culture and politics. He is one of the authors and creators of the European studies in Poland. He has extensive research and educational experience at foreign universities including Oxford University, Université Montpellier IIII Paul Valéry, Kent University, University of Amsterdam, University of Banska Bistrica and University of Leuven.

Selected publications: *Detencja cudzoziemców w Polsce. Perspektywa teoretyczno-metodologiczna / Detention of foreigners in Poland. Theoretical and methodological perspective* (with Jacek Schmidt, Zakład Wydawniczy Nomos 2020); *On the banality of forgetting: tracing the memory of Jewish culture in Poland* (with Sławomir Kapralski and Jacek Nowak, Peter Lang 2018); "European integration from the perspective of local authorities. An empirical analysis of six municipalities", in: Z. Mach (ed.), *Local Community, Power and European Integration. Studies in European Integration, State and Society*, Vol. 3; Warsaw: Peter Lang Edition, 2017, pp. 45–62; "Chapter 7. European Identity of Polish Pendulum Migrants", in: Magda Góra, Zdzisław Mach, Katarzyna Zielińska (eds.), *Collective Identity and Democracy in the Enlarging Europe. Warsaw Studies in Culture and Society*, Vol. 1, Peter Lang, 2012, pp. 139–160; *Migracje i tożsamość. Od teorii do analizy przypadku/ Migrations and identity. From theory to case study* (Zakład Wydawniczy Nomos, 2010).

Angelika Poniatowska is a holder of an MA degree in psychology, who graduated from the Maria Curie-Skłodowska University in Lublin (2008). She acquired her first experience with detention while on internship in the prison in Biała Podlaska, where she was learning about work in penitentiary facilities and human behaviour under isolation.

From 2009 she has been a civil employee of the Border Guard in the Border Guard Outpost in Biała Podlaska. Since the beginning of her career, she has been connected with the Guarded Centre for Foreigners in Biała Podlaska, where she works on a daily basis with foreigners from around the world as a psychologist. Since 2012, she has also been the manager of the Educational Team responsible for the organisation of the free time of the detained foreigners, identification of their identity, guidance and preventive work, as well as supervision over the psychophysical condition of the foreigners.

She has been broadly trained in the area of intercultural differences, identification of foreigners from vulnerable groups, including victims of human trafficking, mental, physical (including sexual) violence, individuals with post-traumatic stress and mental disorders. She completed a course in court and out-of-court mediation, which allows her to solve the often complex and non-standard problems connected with the stay of foreigners in the guarded centre.

Jacek Schmidt holds a PhD degree and is an ethnologist/cultural anthropologist, professor in the Institute of Anthropology and Ethnology, Adam Mickiewicz University in Poznań [UAM], head of the Department of Ethnology, UAM, and a member of the Scientific Council of the Jagiellonian Centre for Migration Studies, Presidium of the Committee on Migration Research of the Polish Academy of Sciences (2012–2025), Ethnological Sciences Committee of the Polish Academy of Sciences (2012–2019), and the Group of Experts on Migrants of the Office of the Commissioner for Human Rights (2015–2020). Publications: he is the author of three books, an editor and co-editor of 13 books, ca. 100 papers and chapters in books, and 110 articles and encyclopaedia entries. Projects: he participated in 18 research, and research and development projects (13 domestic and 5 international). His areas of interest are: European migrations (with special focus on Poland and Germany), methodology of the social sciences, border studies, stereotype- and myth-creating processes, and antisemitism. Selected publications from the area of migration studies from the last decade: *Migracje a heterogeniczność kulturowa. Na podstawie badań antropologicznych w Poznaniu/ Migrations and cultural heterogeneity. Analyses based on anthropological research in Poznań* (edition with Michał Buchowski, Wydawnictwo UAM 2012); *Imigranci: między izolacją a integracją/, Immigrants: between isolation and integration* (edition with Michał Buchowski, Wydawnictwo UAM, 2012); *Społeczno-kulturowa identyfikacja cudzoziemców. Raporty i ekspertyzy/ Socio-cultural identification of foreigners. Reports and expert opinions* (edition with Dariusz Niedźwiedzki, Wydawnictwo UAM, 2016); *Społeczno-kulturowa identyfikacja cudzoziemców. Projekty szkoleniowe/ Socio-cultural identification of foreigners. Training projects* (edition with Dariusz Niedźwiedzki, Poznań: Wydawnictwo UAM, 2016); " 'Interaktywna Mapa Cudzoziemców' – nowa baza wiedzy o zjawisku imigracji w Polsce"/ "'Interactive Map of Foreigners' – a new knowledge base on the phenomenon of immigration in Poland", *Studia Migracyjne – Przegląd Polonijny*, 2017, No. 2, pp. 9–22; "Detencja cudzoziemców jako temat badawczy i wyzwanie metodologiczne"/ "Detention of foreigners as a research topic and methodological challenge", *Studia Migracyjne – Przegląd Polonijny*, 2020, No. 2 (176), pp. 91–106; "Przestrzeń idealna – perspektywa władzy. Na przykładzie strzeżonych ośrodków dla cudzoziemców w Polsce"/ "Ideal space – the perspective of power. On the example of guarded centers for foreigners in Poland", *Rozwój Regionalny* *i Polityka Regionalna*, 2021, No. 4, pp. 163–183; (with Piotr Boćko) "A Heuristic System of Sociocultural Identification of Immigrants in Poland: Education – Good Practices – Safety", in: Anna Sroka, Piotr Potejko, Rubén Dario Torres Kumbrián (eds.), *Migration and Border Security. Global Perspectives*, Berlin: Peter Lang, 2021, pp. 89–118; "Spaces and Places of Detention of Foreigners in Poland", *Migration Studies – Review of Polish Diaspora*, no 4.

Maciej Stępka holds a PhD in Security Studies (University of Warsaw), an MA in European Studies (Jagiellonian University) and MSc in Political Science (University of Amsterdam). He is an Assistant Professor in the Institute of European Studies at the Jagiellonian University in Kraków where he teaches courses on theories of security, European and international security policy, and EU institutions and politics. He was a guest researcher at academic institutions such as the University of Amsterdam, Utrecht University, Matej Bel University in Banska Bystrica, and École française d'Athènes. His research interests include critical security studies and migration studies, more particularly discourses and practices of security deployed during complex and persisting crises. He has authored articles and book chapters on the securitization of migration in the EU, and resilience, crisis and risk management in the EU.

His most recent publications include: *Identifying Security Logics in the EU Policy Discourse: The "Migration Crisis" and the EU* (Springer 2022); "W poszukiwaniu odpowiedzi na współczesne kryzysy. Ewolucja rezyliencji w polskim dyskursie strategicznym (2007–2020)"/ "Searching for solutions to contemporary crises: the evolution of resilience in the Polish strategic discourse (2007–2020)" (*Rocznik Instytutu Europy Środkowej i Wschodniej*, 2021, 19 (1), pp. 25–42, https://doi.org/10.36874/RIESW.2021.1.2); "Rezyliencja jako paradygmat bezpieczeństwa w czasach przewlekłych kryzysów"/ "Resilience as a security paradigm in times of protracted crises" (*Przegląd Politologiczny*, No. 02/2021, https://doi.org/10.14746/pp. 2021.26.2.7); "Humanitarian Securitization of the 2015 "Migration Crisis". Investigating Humanitarianism and Security in the EU Policy Frames on Operational Involvement in the Mediterranean", in: I. Sirkeci, E. de Freitas Castro, U. Sezgi Sozen (eds.) *Migration Policy in Crisis*, Transnational Press, London, 2018, pp. 9–30.

Przemysław Tacik is Assistant Professor at the Institute of European Studies of the Jagiellonian University of Kraków, Poland, and Director of the Nomos: Centre for International Research on Law, Culture and Power. A philosopher, lawyer and sociologist by education, he holds PhDs in philosophy (2014) and international law (2016). He has been a visiting scholar at several universities (i.e. Columbia University, SUNY at Buffalo, Université de Nice, Université Paris-1, Université d'Orléans, Heidelberg Universität, Max-Planck-Institut für ausländisches öffentliches Recht und Völkerrecht, Salzburg Universität, the Higher School of Economics in Moscow and Lisbon University). He received a scholarship of the French government (2018), a scholarship for the best young researchers awarded by the Polish Ministry for Science and Higher Education (2018–2020) and DAAD scholarship (2020). In his academic work, he combines both philosophical and legal perspectives, attempting to approach them from an interdisciplinary angle. His main fields of interest are: in philosophy – contemporary philosophy, Jewish philosophy and animal studies; in law – critical legal studies, international law and human rights law.

He has authored four books: *Socjologia Zygmunta Baumana (Sociology of Zygmunt Bauman*, 2012) *Przystąpienie Unii Europejskiej do Europejskiej Konwencji Praw Człowieka* (*The Accession of the European Union to the European Convention on Human Rights*, 2017), *The Freedom of Lights. Edmond Jabès and Jewish Philosophy of Modernity* (Peter Lang 2019), and *A New Philosophy of Modernity and Sovereignty: Towards Radical Historicization* (Bloomsbury 2021), as well as over 40 articles and one translation of a poetry volume (from French into Polish).

Annex

Research tools

1. Interviews

1.1. Individual interviews with the centre management

Issues related to the inventory of space and its furnishing in the material dimension as well as the formal conditions of the use of this space. Relevant questions pertain to:

1. investments and renovations, i.e. changes of the material space – when, out of whose initiative (what was the origin of the ideas concerning an improvement in aesthetics, if any), why, using what funds, and the assessment of these changes including ones related to the improvement of safety;
2. the needs in the scope of changing the material space and places, and perception of further needs in the scope of safety;
3. the origin of internal regulations concerning the use of the space of the centre – reasons, out of whose initiative, the appearance of the procedure and the evaluation of the regulations, what structure of the particular places is enforced by law? How much is enforced by regulations, and to what extent are the officers free to furnish them?
4. the needs in the scope of both internal and external formal regulations concerning the space of the centre. How does the subject assess the regulations concerning the space of the centre?

The issue of the evaluation of the detention centre as a tool of the internal migration policy. Relevant questions pertain to:

5. the effectiveness of the activity of the detention centre, including the issues of the assessment of procedures in the aspect of their application in the specific material space of the centre;
6. the appearance of various sorts of 'disturbances' in the activity of the centre: tensions and conflicts between the staff and the detainees, reasons behind them, their course and end (including ways of coping with these disturbances) and the role of the organisation of space in these events;
7. the evaluation of the purposefulness of the existence of the detention centre, including the opinion on the legal solutions concerning the activity of the

centre; how does the subject assess the legislation applying to his/her work? Is it appropriate concerning the reality? Does the subject have problems with the understanding of the regulations? Does it require changes – and what sort of changes, if any? Also opinions concerning the changing role of detention in a broader European context;

8. one's opinion on the importance of detention as an instrument of the Polish migration (and security) policy. Tensions and relations with other services/actors as a part of the fulfilment of duties/tasks related to detention: do the institutions the subject has contact with use the relevant law appropriately? How does he/she evaluate the activity of courts and cooperation with them?
9. the idea of a model detention centre – in the case of a positive opinion on the purposefulness of its existence.

The issue of the impact of the 'outside world' on the functioning of the guarded centre. This is about questions concerning:

10. the impact of the 'world of politics' (also perception of changes in this scope) on the functioning of the centre (perhaps indirectly by affecting the entire BG) and evaluation of this impact;
11. the impact of the NGOs on the functioning of the centre (perhaps indirectly by affecting the entire BG and the public opinion) and evaluation of this impact;
12. the impact of the 'external EU' (e.g. problem of the so-called migration crisis in Europe and an assessment of detention in its management) on the functioning of the centre (perhaps indirectly by affecting the entire BG and the public opinion).

1.2. Individual interviews with the middle management

Issues related to the inventory of space and its furnishing in the material dimension as well as the formal conditions of the use of this space. Relevant questions pertain to:

1. investments and renovations, i.e. changes of the material space – when, out of whose initiative (what was the origin of the ideas concerning an improvement in aesthetics, if any), why, using what funds, and assessment of these changes, including the ones related to the improvement of safety;
2. the needs in the scope of changing the material space, places, and perception of further needs in the scope of safety;

3. the origin of the internal regulations concerning the use of the space of the centre – reasons, out of whose initiative, the appearance of the procedure and the evaluation of the regulations, what structure of the places is enforced by the law? How much is enforced by regulations, and to what extent are the officers free to furnish them?
4. the needs in the scope of both internal and external formal regulations concerning the space of the centre. How does the subject assess the regulations concerning the space of the centre?

Issues concerning the evaluation of the detention centre as a tool of the internal migration policy. Relevant questions pertain to:

5. the effectiveness of the activity of the detention centre, including the issues of the assessment of procedures in the aspect of their application in the specific material space of the centre;
6. the appearance of various sorts of 'disturbances' in the activity of the centre: tensions and conflicts between the staff and the detainees, reasons behind them, their course and end (including ways of coping with these disturbances) and the role of the organisation of space in these events;
7. the idea of a model detention centre – in the case of a positive opinion on the purposefulness of its existence;
8. the impact of the 'world of politics' (also the perception of changes in this scope) on the functioning of the centre (perhaps indirectly by affecting the entire BG) and evaluation of this impact.

The issue of the interpretation of the space of the centre covers questions concerning:

9. the evaluation of space in the material categories: the size and furnishings of the premises (including the subject's office) – what would the subject change in this scope and why?
10. the use of the material furnishings of the centre – to what extent the detainees and the staff use the furnishings, are there any items of furnishing that are redundant from the point of view of their use?
11. the impact of the organisation of space and its features on the behaviour of the staff and the detainees – to what extent does the subject see a relation between the organisation (rules and regulations, material barriers in the space) and behaviour (in what way is the space of the centre used for the limitation of movement, behaviours, etc.). In this case, this is about

the subject's spontaneous turning attention to various forms of limitation of unconstrained movement around the centre and forms of behaviour – e.g. monitoring as a technology of control, and its impact on the use of the space (including the visibility of the monitoring, marking, etc.);

12. the existence of the so-called barriers in space (bars, security passages, etc.) and opinions on their functionality–dysfunctionality. This is about asking directly about the material barriers – should it happen that they are not mentioned by the subject in answer to the previous question;
13. opinion on the isolation facilities (medical isolation room and punishment cell), i.e. assessment of their functionality or dysfunctionality (does one's stay under isolation have any negative sides to it?), the use of isolation facilities as a 'security instrument', are isolation facilities used solely for their designed purposes, or are there any intentional actions of detainees ('falling ill') aimed at isolating themselves from others?;
14. safe/unsafe space, also in the context of the physical organisation of the centre (barriers, security passages, etc.), are there any places in which the subject feels more/less secure than in others, does the fact that the centre is a closed facility mean that it is safer or not necessarily? What does the provision of security mean and what does the danger result from?

The issue of formal and informal conditions of the use of the space of the centre covers questions concerning:

15. the external and the internal regulations of law and administrative provisions organising the time, scope and manner of the use of the particular places and segments of space by staff members. This is about acquiring information on the good and bad sides of such regulations (including an assessment of the level of their restrictiveness) and the desired changes in this scope, if any, as postulated by the subject. Auxiliary questions: what construction of the individual places are enforced by law? How much is enforced by regulations, and to what extent are the officers free to furnish the places? What is the subject's assessment of the regulations concerning the space of the centre?;
16. the external and the internal regulations of law and administrative provisions organising the time, scope and manner of the use of the particular places and segments of space by the detainees. This is about acquiring information on the good and bad sides of such regulations and the desired changes in this scope, if any, as postulated by the subject;
17. the performance of certain activities according to the scheme developed and adopted by the subject (including the existence of this type of security practices related to control, disciplining, enforcement or exacting of a

specific behaviour). To what degree do the regulations control the daily routines in detail? To what extent is this sort of practices familiar to other staff members?;

18. the existence of traditions and customs in the centre changing the daily routine, e.g. is the subject's birthday or name day a day like any other day? How does the centre and the work of the staff function during religious festivities, and do such differences in the life of the centre also apply to the detainees' special festive days? Is the law strictly complied with in the realities of the work in the centres? Do people 'turn a blind eye'? What is done when the law is not clear?

The issue of the inter- and intragroup relations taking place within the space of the centre covering the relations within the groups of the staff and the detainees as well as the ones between the former and the latter. This issue covers questions concerning:

19. the vertical structure of the staff of the centre, above all the relations between the subordinates and the superiors, the extent to which this order is ruled by the law and by the superiors' orders. Is it possible to discuss things with the superior (question the superior's will on the basis of the law//rules and regulations)? What is the subject's assessment of the law applying to his/her work? Is it appropriate concerning the reality? Does it require changes – and if so, what sort of changes? In his/her opinion, what provisions of law apply to his/her daily work? Does the subject have problems with the understanding of the provisions of the law?;
20. the differences in the position and status of the uniformed and civil employees of the centre. If there are any, what do they result from and how are they manifested in practice;
21. the relations between employees of different divisions of the staff, in particular between employees of the educational division and the other categories of employees;
22. the creation of private relations, i.e. making acquaintances and friends between staff members, whether the subject has such acquaintances/friends and does this affect the performance of the job in any way;
23. people who enjoy particular recognition and respect which does not result from their place in the professional hierarchy, i.e. informal leaders;
24. people who are particularly likeable, contact/interaction with whom provides satisfaction extending beyond that resulting from the performance of duties (looking for sociometric stars);

25. a generalised picture of the detainee, i.e. what the subject has in his/her mind, when thinking 'detainee';
26. communication barriers between the staff and the detainees (linguistic code, culture, hierarchy, rules and regulations, body language, emotions) and how he/she copes with them;
27. conflicts between the staff and the detainees – what they result from, how they are handled, what to do to avoid them;
28. conflicts between the detainees – are there any at all, what are the reasons behind them, what is their course, how they are solved.

1.3. Individual interviews with other officers and civil employees of detention centres

The issue of the interpretation of the space of the centre covers questions concerning:

1. evaluation of space in the material categories: the size and furnishings of the premises (including the subject's office) – what would the subject change in this scope and why;
2. the use of the material furnishings of the centre – to what extent the detainees and the staff use the furnishings, are there any items of furnishing that are redundant from the point of view of their use;
3. the impact of the organisation of space and its features on the behaviour of the staff and the detainees – to what extent does the subject see a relation between the organisation (rules and regulations, material barriers in the space) and the behaviour (in what way is the space of the centre used for the limitation of movement, behaviours, etc.). In this case, this is about the subject's spontaneous turning attention to various forms of limitation of unconstrained movement around the centre and forms of behaviour – e.g. monitoring as a technology of control, and its impact on the use of the space (including the visibility of the monitoring, marking., etc.);
4. the existence of the so-called barriers in space (bars, security passages, etc.) and opinions on their functionality–dysfunctionality. This question concerning the material barriers should be asked directly if they are not mentioned by the subject in answer to the previous questions;
5. the possibility of the organisation of space (agency) by the staff (are there any places at work they like more than others), the appropriation of space (is there any space they consider their own), the process of adaptation to space (this is about the memory of the first days of work in the centre, the emotions accompanying that stay in its space);

6. the existence of the private space understood as the internal space 'belonging' to a given small group (people working in a specific place, employees of a given division – e.g. the educational one, detainees residing in a given room, detainees belonging to a particular ethnic or religious group) and the public space (space open to all the employees and detainees): detainees and the staff. Ask how the particular places are called (slang names given by the users of the space), and possibly the stories behind the adoption of such names – description of the events. The aim of this question is to check the memory of relations;
7. opinion on the isolation facilities (medical isolation room and punishment cell), i.e. assessment of their functionality or dysfunctionality (does one's stay under isolation have any negative sides to it?), the use of isolation facilities as a 'security instrument', are isolation facilities used solely for their designed purposes, or are there any intentional actions of detainees ('falling ill') aimed at isolating themselves from others?;
8) safe/unsafe space, also in the context of the physical organisation of the centre (barriers, security passages, etc.); are there any places in which the subject feels more/less secure in than in others and does the fact that the centre is a closed facility mean that it is safer or not necessarily? What does the provision of security mean and what does the danger result from?;
9. the aesthetics of the space: is it at all perceived, is it important for the people who work and stay there, should anything be changed in this scope?

The issue of formal and informal conditions of the use of the space of the centre covers questions concerning:

10. the external and the internal regulations of law and administrative provisions organising the time, scope and manner of the use of the particular space and its segments by staff members. This is about acquiring information on the good and bad sides of such regulations (including an assessment of the level of their restrictiveness) and the desired changes in this scope, if any, as postulated by the subject. Auxiliary questions: what structure of the particular places does the law enforce? How much is enforced by regulations, and to what extent are the officers free to furnish the places? What is the subject's assessment of the regulations concerning the space of the centre?;
11. the external and the internal regulations of law and administrative provisions organising the time, scope and manner of the use of the particular places and segments of space by the detainees. This is about acquiring information on the good and bad sides of such regulations and the desired changes in this scope, if any, as postulated by the subject;

12. the performance of certain activities according to the scheme developed and adopted by the subject (including the existence of this type of security practices related to control, disciplining, enforcement or exacting of a specific behaviour). To what degree do the regulations control the daily routines in detail and are other staff members familiar with this sort of practices?;
13. the existence of traditions and customs in the centre changing the daily routine, e.g. is the subject's birthday or name day a day like any other day? How does the centre and the work of the staff function during religious festivities, and do such differences in the life of the centre also apply to the detainees' special festive days? Is the law strictly complied with in the realities of the work in the centres? Do people 'turn a blind eye'? What is done when the law is not clear?

The issue of the inter- and intragroup relations taking place within the space of the centre covering the relations within the groups of the staff and the detainees as well as the ones between the former and the latter. This issue covers questions concerning:

14. the vertical structure of the staff of the centre, above all the relations between the subordinates and the superiors, to what extent is this order ruled by law and by the superiors' orders? Is it possible to discuss things with the superior (question the superior's will on the basis of the law/rules and regulations)? What is the subject's assessment of the law applying to his/her work? Is it appropriate concerning the reality? Does it require changes – and if so, what sort of changes? In his/her opinion, what provisions of law apply to his/her daily work? Does the subject have problems with the understanding of the provisions of law?;
15. the difference in the position and status of the uniformed and civil employees of the centre. If there are any, what do they result from and how are they manifested in practice?;
16. the relations between employees of different divisions, in particular between employees of the educational division and the other categories of employees;
17. the creation of private relations, i.e. making acquaintances and friends among staff members, whether the subject has such acquaintances/friends, does this affect the performance of the job in any way;
18) people enjoying particular recognition and respect which does not result from their place in the professional hierarchy, i.e. informal leaders;

19. people who are particularly likeable, the contact/interaction with whom gives satisfaction extending beyond that resulting from the performance of duties (looking for sociometric stars);
20. generalised picture of the detainee, i.e. what the subject has in his/her mind, when thinking 'detainee';
21. the issue of the diversity of detainees in terms of their cultural and mental features, attitudes and behaviours, as well as whether and if so, how, the detainees are profiled from the point of view of security. Who and using what technology performs such actions? What categories of danger–security are created/used in the interactions between the staff and the detainees?
22. changes of attitudes and behaviours of the detainees over time, i.e. the problem of their adaptation to life in the centre, including the question of the 'multiple-detainees', i.e. contacts with the individuals who are readmitted to the centre;
23. formal and informal preparations for contact with the detainees, i.e. the issue of education, training, self-teaching, including the problem of emotional preparation, what emotions the subject feels in contact with the detainees, and whether he/she finds this work emotionally/mentally tiring;
24. interactions with the detainees in the aspect of the ideas about these interactions – to what extent the detainees' behaviours are surprising in practice (examples of such behaviours), and why according to him/her such surprises appear;
25. the detainees' search for contact with the staff – in what form and circumstances; the most typical and atypical events from this area;
26. communication barriers between the staff and the detainees (linguistic code, culture, hierarchy, rules and regulations, body language, emotions) and how he/she copes with them;
27. bonds between members of the staff and the detainees – whether and how they are established, what is their nature, and what the subject thinks about such bonds;
28. conflicts between the staff and the detainees – what they result from, how they handle them, what to do to avoid them;
29. bonds between the detainees – whether they are established and what is their nature;
30. conflicts between the detainees – are there any at all, what are the reasons behind them, what is their course, how are they solved?

1.4. Focus group interviews with employees of the BG sections/teams – guidelines

Focus group interviews are designed for the subjects' collective solving of the problem/tasks posed by the researcher. We assume at least one focus group interview in every centre.

The number of participants: 6–10. The subjects should represent all the sections/teams. Individuals from the management (danger of taking over the discussion) and people who were interviewed individually should be excluded.

Conditions: a room in which the subjects could sit in a circle, write and draw.

Duration: 1–2 hours

Topic of the focused group interview: **The ideal guarded centre for foreigners**

Auxiliary questions (obviously, they should be additionally built up with content):

1. what in your opinion should an ideal guarded centre be like?
2. how should it be constructed from the architectural point of view? What places/spaces should it have? Can you draw a sketch of such a centre? And sketches of the particular places within the centre?
3. What material furnishings should it have?
4. what principles of selection of the staff of such a centre should apply?
5. How should detainees be located? A division into centres for men, women, and families? Should the ethnic or national origin be taken into account? Should the detainee's religion be a factor here?
6. What are the most important principles of the organisation of the functioning of the centre? Please specify ten.
7. What should the most important rules of contact between the staff and the detainees be?
8. How to avoid conflicts between the staff and the detainees? How to solve them?
9. How to minimise the possibility of an outbreak of conflicts between the detainees? How to solve them?
10. Are guarded centres for foreigners necessary?

2. Other research tools

2.1. Observation notes – monitoring of the centre's closed and open spaces

We are interested in all the closed spaces (with the exception of the offices of administration located in a separate building and in the independent corridor for staff in the building proper of the centre). Such spaces also include the corridors used by the detainees, reception areas, visiting rooms, and the dining room. Open spaces include: walking areas, spaces designated for sports and recreation, and the smoking area.

The scope and form of the use of these spaces by the detainees and the staff should be recorded. More precisely:

1. who appears in these spaces (in the case of the detainees, we are interested in their age, gender, ethic origin, and whether they appear individually or in groups);
2. chronology (full dates, hours, how long for – try to carry out the observation systematically – at all hours of our work in the centre);
3. the detainees' activity: their performance of the activities consistent with the designation of a given place, other forms of activity (social life, telephone conversations, etc.); it is also important what 'props' they use while staying in a given place (e.g. using mobile phones while using a computer). What is also important is the communication attitude in interactions with other detainees and the staff (avoiding vs seeking contact, friendliness, indifference or hostility, trying to create conflicts), including the so-called communication etiquette – the language of gestures (such as shaking hands, gestures, facial expressions) and linguistic conventions (the language of communication, using first name terms, greeting formulas and other messages);
4. activity of the staff: forms of supervision, assistance-related interactions with the detainees, disciplining, including the so-called communication etiquette – the language of gestures (e.g. hand-shaking, gesticulations, facial expressions) and verbal conventions (the language of communication, using first name terms, greeting formulas and other messages).

Position of the researcher and types of sources

Monitoring shall be based on:

(a) extrospective observations - both from the point of view of the glassed guardroom, a selected place in the corridor, and through the screens of monitors recording imaging from the cameras;
(b) direct observation - presence in the place in question (not always possible, e.g. in the prayer rooms or residential rooms);
(c) the above should be accompanied by the acquisition of information on the topic in question from employees of the educational team and sentry guards. This is both about the current information (such as 'who is this person') and activities ('how often does he come here', 'what does he usually do there'). Information on this topic shall also be acquired during our

multi-thread interviews with the staff. It remains an open question whether we shall manage to talk to the detainees.

Issues related to the recording:

It is up to the researcher whether they will record their findings in the form of voice, hand-writing (in the researcher's journal), typewriting (tablet or any other device), or a combination of these techniques. It should only be remembered that the records: (a) should be clear enough to enable effective archiving, (b) should take into account other factors, if any, affecting the recorded forms of activity, such as the impact of the researcher's presence, or the impact of the staff's presence on the detainee, conditions resulting from rules and regulations for the particular space, the weather (important for open spaces), routine and occasional events taking place in the centre (e.g. educational or cultural ones, admission of new detainees, a local conflict, etc.); additionally, the fact of the conducting of the monitoring jointly with another researcher should each time be recorded, (c) working records should clearly separate the descriptive part from the comments (the researcher's interpretations of the observed phenomena and his/her side remarks).

Issues to do with the collating of raw data and their archiving

After completion of the first study visit, a template observation sheet shall be drawn up for all the researchers to fill in for their collected data. This standardisation of records will simplify the collation of the materials of the entire team and their subsequent comparative analysis, including the export to the analytical programme. The template shall include instructions concerning the recording allowing the separation of descriptions from the interpretations, linking the content and the source type, etc.

Observation notes should contain:

1. time of observation;
2. information on the type of place subjected to observation (bathroom, corridor, office of a particular section, treatment room, duty-room in the custody suite, etc.);
3. list of participants (number, general features such as the place in the employment structure, gender, etc.);
4. characteristics of the participants (objectivised description of the appearance as a part of the personal façade);
5. chronology of events, i.e. their sequence from the commencement of the social situation (how did it begin?) until its ending (how did it cease?);
6. detailed descriptions of interactions (objectivised description of the way of being, i.e. behaviour, as a part of the personal façade; no interpretation!);

7. records or descriptions of verbal interactions (enabling detailed recapitulation of the conversation);
8. own reflections, interpretations of the social situation under description.

When conducting observations and preparing reporting notes, we should apply the guidelines concerning sensitisation to proxemic and kinesic issues in the study.

2.2. Reporting note from a social situation

Social situation:

1. should be understood as an environment made available to the individuals located within one's sensory perception;
2. is tantamount to a physical environment, a piece of space the reach of which is marked by the perception of participants of the meeting;
3. the participants are not just present (as physical elements) – they are co-present, i.e. interact with each other verbally and non-verbally;
4. has its duration – it starts when the actors perceive one another and when the mutually monitored events take place, and ends, when the person(s) by the actor (researcher) leaves the environment of sensory perception;
5. people's mutual monitoring takes place according to certain rules, conventions and principles organising the direct contact of the interacting actors.

In practice, social situations are:

- researchers' informal contacts/conversations with staff members or detainees;
- observation of such contacts/conversations between staff members, detainees or representatives of both these groups;
- interactions, as a part of which we acquire existing data from staff members.

Reporting note from a social situation should contain:

1. information on the type of place in which the social situation occurred (bathroom, corridor, office of a particular section, treatment room, duty-room in the custody suite, etc.);
2. list of participants (number, general features such as the place in the employment structure, gender, etc.);
3. characteristics of the participants (objectivised description of the appearance as a part of the personal façade);
4. chronology of events, i.e. their sequence from the commencement of the social situation (how did it begin?) until its ending (how did it cease?);

5. detailed descriptions of the interaction (objectivised description of the part of the personal façade in the form of way of being, i.e. behaviour; no interpretation!);
6. records or descriptions of verbal interactions (enabling detailed recapitulation of the conversation);
7. own reflections, interpretations of the social situation under description.

When preparing reporting notes, we should apply the guidelines concerning sensitisation to proxemic and kinesic issues.

2.3. Instruction: sensitivity to proxemic and kinesic issues

The guidelines concerning the monitoring of closed and open spaces included several desiderata relating to the recording of the activity of the detainees and the staff connected with their communication (internal communication – between the detainees; external communication – between the detainees and the staff). The issues need to be further clarified, which shall result in sensitising the researcher to the scope of conducting observation and its details.

1. personal distance. Western cultures are marked by different models and standards than external cultures (Caucasian, Asian, etc.). For us (researchers and the staff), the expected – 'obvious' – interpersonal distances described in relevant literature as intimate, personal, social and public tend to be defined and practised by representatives of external cultures in a different way. This often leads to misunderstandings, sometimes even conflicts. In connection with the above, it is recommended that forms of the staff's contact with the detainees be recorded in the context of interpersonal distance and its perception manifested by the parties;
2. 'thickening' of space: in this case, we deal with different socially/culturally determined habits, and in consequence different perception of this phenomenon by the detainees and the staff – that is why such instances and the staff's reactions should be recorded each time;
3. etiquette – this is about civilities (such as forms of salutations) and familiarity expressed by gestures (in particular that of touch, e.g. patting on the back), and the expression of non-friendly behaviours;
4. visual communication (avoiding eye contact *vs* intensive gazing at the other person + interpretation of intention, e.g. hostile or challenging gaze);
5. auditory communication (loudness of behaviour and scope of its acceptance by the staff; also applies to listening to loud music);
6. olfactory communication (connected with interpersonal distance) – e.g. seeking to stir a reaction to one's breath and the actual reactions of the other party; kitchen smells from residential rooms;

7. physiology and hygiene – neat or untidy appearance (washing, shaving, general bodily appearance and clothing), olfactory messages connected with hygiene, frequency and scope of the use of the sanitary facilities, the manifested and the declared illnesses;
8. tidiness *vs* mess – applies to both public (tidying after recreation and games, washing, etc.) and residential spaces (doing the beds, airing the rooms, storing clothes and other belongings, etc.);
9. attitude to property – equipment and objects belonging to the centre (respect, devastation, improper use, adaptation for own purposes);
10. religious and ethnic messages - expressed by clothing, symbolic props, music, gestures, and manifestation of the intergroup distance or intragroup solidarity in the community of detainees (e.g. avoidance, moving around the centre in a group, appropriation of space, conflict behaviours, etc.);
11. nutrition (eating meals in the dining room or residential room, independent cooking – it is worth having a look into the lists of shopping arranged by the BG); ways of eating (e.g. using cutlery);
12. contact with the outside world – frequency of visits and profile of guests (e.g. family, individuals from abroad), the staff's attitude to guests – rigorous or liberal attitude to the rules and regulations applying to visits; interest in the cultural and recreational offer, coaching, etc. provided by external entities;
13. interest in the offer concerning the spending of one's free time prepared by the educational team (passive and active participation, popularity of the particular forms of activity).

Comments:

(a) non-verbal communication may take the form of autonomous behaviour, coexist with verbal communication as mutually complementing messages, or play the role of an automatic reaction of the body to external stimuli (e.g. frowning in displeasure when recalling unpleasant events). The above typology is also important from the perspective of the methodology of conducting problem and group interviews – hence, it will be referred to in the guidelines applying to these research techniques;

(b) in the description of all the above-specified issues, one should be sensitive to differences between the genders and the relations between men and women. On this occasion, the gender of the researcher should also be taken into account, as it may be a factor affecting the behaviour of detainees and the course of communication in the situation when he/she interacts with the subjects;

(c) in the case of centres for families, it is necessary to be sensitive to the behaviour of children, forms of care over them and upbringing measures on the part of their parents and the staff, the staff's expectations towards the parents and children and the parent's expectations towards the staff and their interest in the educational offer (including ways of informing about the offer);

(d) in the case of all the above issues, researchers should remain sensitive to interethnic differences and relations, as well as the staff's attitudes towards representatives of different cultures;

(e) we are exceptionally interested in the varied styles of the detainees' daily life and the staff's attitude to these behaviours (including the issue of undesirable behaviours) and classifying detainees as potentially dangerous (more broadly speaking: a category of detainees as a risk group);

(f) since interpretation of many behaviours in question can be difficult, it is necessary to focus on their detailed description;

(g) it is necessary to endeavour to register the interpretation of communication events by the detainees, which will allow a more in-depth examination of the sense of acts of internal and external communication.

2.4. Instruction: inventory of the space of the centre

Our object of interest covers all closed spaces (with the exception of offices of the administration located in a separate building). Such spaces also include the corridors used by the detainees and the staff, reception areas, visiting rooms, and the dining room. Open spaces include: walking areas, spaces designated for sports and recreation, and the smoking area. The inventory shall also cover the organisation of the space of the centre as a whole – the layout of the particular closed and open spaces (taking into account a description of their functionality). Moreover, the inventory must take into account a description of the 'external' view – the body of the centre and its characteristic features (bars, barbed wire, gates, etc.), and its location (autonomous or located as a part of a complex of other BG facilities; the nearest neighbourhood, e.g. an open centre for foreigners, housing estates, natural conditions). Our interests also cover the history of the facility including its modernisation and adaptations.
Details:

1. the inventory should cover all the places and open spaces, taking into account their size, furnishings, and decoration;
2. the viewing of the internal and external spaces must be carried out both from the micro and the macro perspective – as autonomous units and in the context of the entire space of the centre respectively.

Types of sources:

(a) observation resulting in iconographic material (photographs and site plans) and descriptions combined with comments;
(b) existing sources (architectural plans, chronicles, reports, inventory of the assets, catalogues of resources of the educational division and records of frequency of their use, the available software and conditions ruling access to the internet [e.g. the issue of the social media, instant messaging, sending videos and photos], monitoring of the detainees' online activity, information whether the above issues also apply to the devices belonging to the detainees [tablets and smartphones], monitoring of the detainees' activity in the centre);
(c) information from the staff concerning the issues specified under (a) and (b).

Issues related to recording:

(a) a register of photographs should be created – each file with an image should have a working numerical title with the author's initials (e.g. 1-JS, 2-JS, 1-DN, 2-DN, 1-MS, 2-MS, etc.). Each author shall create a file with a two-column table in which he/she will record titles of the files with the photographs and their short descriptions;
(b) a register of existing sources shall be created – every researcher acquiring materials should record the fact in his/her tabular record file (simultaneously introducing a short description);
(c) when recording information from the staff, aim at making a note of its connection with the materials specified under (a) and (b).

Place for comments:

3. Principles of transcribing and archiving the material

- use font Times New Roman, size: 12-point, spacing between lines: 1.5;
- italicise all quoted statements;
- write all comments in ordinary font in square brackets; each time start in a new line;
- the comments may pertain to various issues – they may: - refer directly to the content of the interlocutor's statement quoted above; - indicate some other sources corresponding with the statement; - inform about the omitted threads and reasons behind this state of things; - be a preliminary, working form of recapitulation; - inform about changes in the social situations of the study

(e.g. the appearance of third parties); - indicate the need to introduce some changes (corrections or complementation in the research tool);

- transcription should contain the content of the posed questions (in bold), be recorded in a chronological order (reflecting the course of the conversation) and must cover the entire conversation – including the threads which are not related to the content of the posed questions and research guidelines. This means that at this stage of archiving we do not quote the numbers of the guidelines or arrange the statements in accordance with the template of the research tool;
- if the conversation was conducted with two or more individuals simultaneously, we give them codes R1, R2, R3 and use the codes each time before the relevant quotations of their statements;
- at the beginning of the transcribed text, provide information on the individual's particulars (position, whether an officer or a civil employee, the unit in which they work, their seniority and previous employment, gender). This text should be entitled the INDIVIDUAL'S PARTICULARS;
- under the individual's particulars, provide information on the arrangement of the interview (superior's suggestion, researcher's choice, someone's order, accident), prevailing conditions (place, broadly understood comfort of the conversation, presence of the third parties, simultaneous performance of professional duties, etc.), the interlocutor's attitude to the researcher and the topic of the interview, his/her so-called façade (openness, being martinet-like, striving for political correctness, etc.), duration, and full date. This block of information should be entitled SOCIAL SITUATION. It may also contain significant information other than that quoted above;
- in the case of interviews which for a variety of reasons were not recorded on a Dictaphone, the record in the form of the researcher's report should be ordered in accordance with the research guidelines; if the report contains content which does not relate to them, it should be provided with information on the reported content;
- another category of materials to be elaborated is the researcher's inventory and observation notes. In this case, provide information on the object of inventory/observation and its time and place in the title.

Studies in European Integration, State and Society

Edited by Zdzisław Mach

Vol. 1 Józef Niżnik: Democracy versus Solidarity in the EU Discourse. 2012.

Vol. 2 Grzegorz Żuk: Europe in Polish Public Discourse. 2013.

Vol. 3 Zdzisław Mach (ed.): Local Community, Power and European Integration. 2017.

Vol. 4 Janusz Józef Węc: Germany's Position on the System Reform of the European Union in 2002–2016. 2018.

Vol. 5 Krzysztof Kowalski / Łucja Piekarska-Duraj / Barbara Törnquist-Plewa (eds.): Narrating Otherness in Poland and Sweden. European Heritage as a Discourse of Inclusion and Exclusion. 2019.

Vol. 6 Marek Aleksander Cichocki / Tomasz Grzegorz Grosse (eds.): The Many Faces of Crisis. An Analysis of Crisis Management from an Economic and Political Perspective. 2019.

Vol. 7 Marek Aleksander Cichocki (ed.): Contemporary States and the Crisis of the Western Order. 2019.

Vol. 8 Marta Kołodziejczyk: The Use of Technology for the Regulation of the European Union Immigration and Asylum Policy. 2020.

Vol. 9 Paweł Kubicki / Bożena Gierat-Bieroń / Joanna Orzechowska-Wacławska: The European Capital of Culture 2016 Effect. How the ECOC Competition Changed Polish Cities. 2020.

Vol. 10 Łucja Piekarska-Duraj: The Invisible Hand of Europe. The Museum as a Civilizing Tool. 2020.

Vol. 11 Milan Bufon / Tove H. Malloy / Colin H. Williams (eds.): Societies and Spaces in Contact. Between Convergence and Divergence. 2021.

Vol. 12 Elżbieta M. Mach / Grzegorz Pożarlik / Joanna Sondel-Cedarmas (eds.): Post-totalitarian Societes in Transformation. From Systemic Change into European Integration. 2022.

Edited by Zdzisław Mach and Bożena Gierat-Bieroń

Vol. 13 Emilia Moddelmog-Anweiler / Zdzisław Mach (eds.): Religion in the Public Sphere in Central and Eastern Europe. 2022.

Vol. 14 Janusz Józef Węc: The System Reform of the Economic and Monetary Union (2010-2022). Dynamics-Successes-Failures 2023.

Vol. 15 Kinga Anna Gajda: Heritage in Central and Eastern Europe. 2023.

Vol. 16 Dariusz Niedźwiedzki / Jacek Schmidt: Introduction to Immigrant Detention in Poland. Theory and Methodology. 2023.

www.peterlang.com